S

Schriftenreihe des Instituts für
Management und Tourismus

Herausgegeben von Christian Eilzer,
Bernd Eisenstein und Wolfgang Georg Arlt

PETER LANG

Alisha Ali / John S. Hull (eds.)

Multi-Stakeholder Perspectives of the Tourism Experience

Responses from the International Competence Network of Tourism Research and Education (ICNT)

Bibliografische Information der Deutschen Nationalbibliothek
Die Deutsche Nationalbibliothek verzeichnet diese Publikation
in der Deutschen Nationalbibliografie; detaillierte bibliografische
Daten sind im Internet über http://dnb.d-nb.de abrufbar.

Gedruckt auf alterungsbeständigem, säurefreiem Papier.
Druck und Bindung: CPI books GmbH, Leck

ISSN 2194-0002
ISBN 978-3-631-74686-8 (Print)
E-ISBN 978-3-631-75537-2 (E-PDF)
E-ISBN 978-3-631-75538-9 (EPUB)
E-ISBN 978-3-631-75539-6 (MOBI)
DOI 10.3726/b14468

Contents

Contents

Editorial Introduction

The phenomenal growth of the tourism industry is coupled with the necessity to create worthwhile stakeholder experiences. The advances in the experience and sharing economies, continually changing consumer behaviour, with millennials at the forefront, and the proliferation of Information and Communication Technologies (ICTs) have shifted the operations landscape of the traditional tourism industry. Those businesses which can identify, innovate and (re-)create meaningful experiences for stakeholders will be the ones to succeed. The stimulus to produce this text stems from forward-thinking debates at the annual International Competence Network of Tourism Research and Education (ICNT) conference on the contemporary issues impacting the future of the tourism industry. This text provides a reflection for the reader to contemplate the various players involved in delivering and shaping the tourism experience. This eclectic collection of chapters stimulates the reader to not only view experiences from a tourist point of view but also to appreciate the role of additional stakeholders representing breweries, universities, hotel restaurants, travel intermediaries, resorts and Destination Marketing Organisations (DMOs).

The first chapter presented is on Brewing Tourism in Baja. It provides an insight into the growing demand for artisanal beer and clearly demonstrates that tourists are experience-seekers; in this case it is beer. The powerful message revealed in this chapter is that the growth of beer tourism has led to the rejuvenation of the Baja area which was once recognised for having an illicit reputation. Using a case study, Chapter 2 offers insight into how a 'sense of place' approach can be used in a resort environment not only to retain employees for the long-term but also as members of the community. Understanding how this mechanism works can be used by other hospitality employers to create a better staff experience to alleviate attrition. Attracting and retaining talent is a critical issue for the hospitality industry. Chapter 3 provides us with a different interpretation of the consumer experience. The tourism industry is impacted by shocks to the system. One of these recent shocks has been the migrant crisis in Europe. This chapter explores the view of Finnish travellers to one of their popular summer spots, the Greek Islands, amid the influx of migrants to these islands. The findings of this chapter demonstrated the resilience of the Finnish tourists as they still found the islands to be an attractive holiday spot. Additionally the altruistic behaviours of the tourists were demonstrated.

The constructive approach to tourism research is investigated in Chapter 4. This focuses on how to enhance applied research and make this practical for students and businesses. The constructive approach concentrates on practical problem solving which leads to innovation. Some fruitful examples have been provided in this chapter which demonstrate how such an approach can be utilised to bridge the gap between business and academia whilst creating a worthwhile learning experience for students.

Chapter 5 brings to the fore the profile of the pelagic birdwatcher. Birdwatching has become a widespread activity; however, very little is known about pelagic birdwatchers. Through an Importance-Performance Analysis, a profile of these birdwatchers was determined. This knowledge is necessary in helping destinations and tour operators design experiences for this niche group of birdwatchers. We enter into the world of hotel restaurants in Chapter 6. Most hotels will have a restaurant, however very little has been researched on the contribution such restaurants have in the gastronomic offer of a destination. This chapter discusses the important part played by such restaurants in translating the cuisine of a local area to guests. In some instances, it might be a guest's first contact with local food at a hotel's restaurant. This chapter elucidates the factors important for creating the tourist experience when dining at these restaurants and the contribution to the local gastronomy.

Chapter 7 draws our attention to the digital landscape and the changing face of travel intermediation. ICTs have drastically reshaped the buying and selling of travel experiences which has altered the way intermediaries operate. The key message brought out in this chapter is that travel intermediaries always have to keep innovating to keep up-to-date with the changes in technology or consumer behaviour. They have to be at the forefront of creating experiences. Failure to do so will cause them to be left behind. Chapter 8 provides a detailed account of student satisfaction with the services they receive prior to enrolment and if this has an impact on their enrolling in a course. Understanding this student experience is critically important in a time when Universities are being asked to account for their value, and student recruitment is key. The approaches identified by Rettig and Horster can be adopted by other institutions to improve the recruitment experience and assist in retaining students.

The article by Pernecky and Poulston in Chapter 9 pays attention to a new subculture called the Cultural Creatives and their accommodation preferences when they travel for business or leisure. Given the specific characteristics associated with this group, this research further determined if their values had an impact on the accommodation types selected. The finding also sheds light on how their accommodation preferences were aligned to sustainable leadership practices. This knowledge is highly valuable for accommodation providers when designing their offer for this group of customers. Chapter 10 introduces us to a global destination brand study. Tourists today have a greater selection of destinations to choose from and this presents challenges for DMOs. DMOs need to have a clear understanding how their destination is positioned in the mind of customers in order to create likeability and appeal. Using a case study approach, this chapter investigates the brand value of international tourism destinations from an international perspective. Deep insights are provided for DMOs in benchmarking their destination. Given that the theme of this text is on multi-stakeholder perspectives, it is fitting that the final chapter of this instalment focuses on the concept of experience in tourism research. The concept of tourism experience is widely documented research however this chapter provides a succinct review of the literature on tourism to provide a more robust understanding of the term 'experience'. This chapter also identified gaps in the literature and avenues for progressing research in this domain.

This cutting-edge volume provides a wealth of knowledge into different insights into tourism user experiences. It will be of value for anyone concerned about innovating the tourism experience. We hope this text has provides useful insights in understanding a number of critical aspects of developing a future-proof tourism industry.

Alisha Ali and John Hull

María Isabel Ramos Abascal

Brewing Tourism in Baja

1 Beer Tourism as a Strategy for Regional Development

Baja, known as the state of Baja California, is located at the north of Mexico and is a region that has proven itself in the last few years as a tourist attraction for travellers motivated by food and drink. This state is home to the Ruta del Vino (Wine Trail), one of the most mature products for gastronomic tourism in Mexico with some of the best vineyards in the country located here. Recently, there has been a growing interest in the production and consumption of artisanal beer, which complements both the tourist activity and the economy of this destination. Therefore, a correct assessment of gastronomic tourism of Baja may contribute to the sustainable development of this region.

The Ruta del Vino has become a magnet of pleasure for the public, where in addition to tastings, one finds creative travels through vineyards and wine cellars, and restaurants which offer meals prepared with high-quality local ingredients. In the same way, the destination has an excellent hospitality infrastructure with more than 100 available rooms and some spas (although visitors now require a larger number of these establishments). More than half of Baja's tourists have resolved the scarcity of hotel rooms by using other, collaborative forms of economy such as AirBnB, or by staying with friends or family members. This has increased the traveller's level of satisfaction and has significantly increased the number of visitors (SecturBC, 2016, p. 39). Those who don't have the good overnight accommodation mainly stay overnight in Tijuana or Ensenada.

A little more than 10 years ago Baja experienced a growing interest in beer. This was motivated by visitor demand and an assertive response by the wine producers. There are numerous producers of artisanal beer, which generated an increase in the number of people travelling to this area looking for the special food and beverage flavours that are produced there. These interests complement in an important way the wine and gastronomy tourist product. Even some wine cellars have joined the microbrewery movement in order to compensate for the seasonal nature of wine tourism and to balance their income over the entire year. That is, the old tradition of brewing in the region has made a comeback and has become a matching offer that permits the visitor to enjoy year-round gastronomic activities.

Understanding this phenomenon, interpreting its causes and previewing its effects enable the destination and the participating players to orient the development of artisan beer production in order to assure its sustainability in three dimensions: ecological, human, and economic.

2 Beer as a Reason to Travel

It is becoming increasingly evident, due to examples from around the world, which artisan beer is developing as a considerable attraction on offer to tourists (Rogerson, 2016). Beer is the most democratic festive drink and a large part of the adult population in the world enjoys a good mug of quality beer from time to time. It is one of those drinks that can be drunk among friends without any sort of pretext. This alcoholic beverage has a millennial-old tradition with the greatest consumption in the world. Mexico is today the principal exporter of beer, with more than 27 million hectoliters per year (V.V.A.A., 2016).

Beer is generally made from only four ingredients: water, malt, yeast, and hops; nevertheless, there seems to be infinite varieties of different styles and flavours, as there are in any bio-cultural process. Culture and nature meet in different forms to obtain the characteristic flavours of each region, strengthening pride of ownership and the identity of the social groups which make them, supporting strong elements of the gastronomic culture of each region.

These different and distinctive flavours and the different ways of drinking have made beer the star of numerous festivals around the world. One of the most outstanding is Oktoberfest in Munich, Germany, which brings together every year (according to data from the festival: www.oktoberfest.de) drinking enthusiasts who travel to that city to celebrate beer and what it represents. This great beer festival has inspired others. As examples, in Mexico as in other countries there are simultaneous versions of Oktoberfest, like Oktoberfest in Creel or Oktoberfest in Ensenada (in Baja), and more endemic versions such as the International Festival of Tacos and Beer, in the city of Puebla. Around the world there are other beer festivals, promoted by European descendants. These have become a powerful gastronomic reason to travel. In addition to its consumption, beer also promotes other activities so that visitors can go from place to place, such as visits to industrial beer producers, workshops about artisanal beer, barley fields, the places where hops are grown so they can participate in the delicate work of harvesting, or even for the entertainment as the one that Heineken offers—the Heineken Experience, in Amsterdam—where one must buy tickets in advance due to the huge demand for this eight-hour interactive tour. These are just a few of the activities in which travellers can develop the beer theme.

Paul Ruschmann, known as the beer traveller for his prolific output of articles about beer tourism, suggests to the readers of his website (beerfestivals.org, 2016), the majority of whom live in the United States, that of the 60 beer festivals that are worth visiting, the Great Welsh Beer and Cider Festival in Cardiff, Wales, the Texas Craft Brewers Festival in Austin, and the popular San Diego Festival of Beer right on the California/Baja California border are the most outstanding. Another great festival is Cask Ale Week, that, according to its organisers, is for 'celebrating Britain's national drink' during a week at the beginning of autumn when pubs and breweries offer events, tastings, and entertainment—all about beer.

The resurgence of interest in brewing has become linked to certain cultural aspects that have the intention of embracing the past and the goal of inspiring a vision of the future, such as the training and educational experiences that are provided in abbeys and monasteries of the Trappists in Belgium. Some producers and consumers visit the monks as a homage and appreciation of their ancestral methods of making beer (De Myttenaere, 2014).

There are also collaborative events, in which visitors can take an active part in the process of obtaining the ingredients for preparing beer, such as at the Pick and Brew, which the Casa del Lúpulo (Hops House) presents in Baja California. Pick and Brew is a program at the end of August during which volunteer enthusiasts, interested in beer culture, are instructed in how to pick the virgin female hops flowers in order to obtain one of the four essential ingredients for beer making.

Festivals in which beer is the main attraction are presented on a large and small scale around the world, with the tendency to increase their frequency and affluence. Spain, Italy, South Africa, and Australia stand out for the quality of their beer festivals combining the production of wines with this renewed interest in artisan beer rather than industrially produced beer. Microbreweries complement the gastronomic offerings in destinations, both in their cost (which is usually higher than industrially made beer), raising the average expenditure of the tourist, and in their distinctive character which favours building unique gastronomic experiences.

3 Artisan Beer in Mexico

We refer to artisanal beer as a motivator for travel because, as opposed to industrially made beer, it cannot easily be taken to other destinations, it is not part of a distribution chain, its small production lots usually escape being part of the standardisation of industrial beers, and on occasion its movement requires special attention to temperature. For all these reasons, one is infrequently able to drink artisanal beer outside the place where it is produced. Buying and consuming these beers directly at the microbrewery where it is produced has advantages which motivate and enrich a trip, especially when it is possible to talk face-to-face with the master brewer while one is enjoying a drink, and food service usually provides ideal options for beer pairings. Enjoying a beer becomes a connection of experiences, with a charge of sensory importance: flavours, fragrances, sounds, and other complicated sensations strengthen the impact of the practice and stimulate memories. At the same time, they narrow the gap between the host and the guest.

But, what is an artisanal beer? The definition can vary depending on the country, but in general it should meet certain norms. The most general are that the brewery should be small, independent, and traditional. The term 'artisanal' in the brewery refers to that which is produced with skill, not necessarily with one's hands, since microbreweries frequently make beer using machinery like large breweries—with the difference that the process is normally watched over and attended personally by the Master Brewer. Little or nothing is left automatic, permitting small variations between each production lot.

Artisanal beer also must comply with the Reinheitsgebot, or German Beer Purity Law as decreed approximately 500 years ago (1516) by William IV, Duke of Bavaria. At that time, the production of beer was limited to three ingredients: water, barley, and hops. Yeasts are not considered under this law because Louis Pasteur did not identify them until 1880. Prior to that time, the transformation of sugars into alcohol was considered to be a mystic event—and beer was thought to be a spontaneous gift of God to humankind.

In Mexico, there is no official norm that determines what is and is not artisanal beer. The Mexican Association of Brewers leans toward the definition of the Association of Artisanal Beer, which allows up to 25% stock participation by any brewer's group that is dominant in the market. The annual production must be fewer than 5 million hectoliters, in addition to limiting, of course, the production to the aforementioned four ingredients.

On the other hand, the Asociación Cervecera de la República Mexicana (Brewers' Association of the Mexican Republic) establishes its limit a maximum production of 650,000 hectolitres and the requisite of not belonging to any large brewers' group (Zapfe, 2016), but it coincides with the amount that must be produced using traditional methods.

The non-existence of an official norm or a common agreement among the master brewers in Mexico, and due to the poor availability of malt and hops in the country are the reasons why we see in the offerings of small producers in which barley or another cereal that can be malted, such as rice, wheat, oats or corn; in the same way, we find formulas with modified flavours such as cacao, vanilla, chile, coconut, and an infinity of ingredients, natural or not, which achieve an even greater amplification in the extensive family of ales and lagers.

Microbreweries depend on import permits for malt and hops to be able to produce. We must underline that even though those two basic ingredients for the production of beer are produced within the borders of Mexico, their harvests are still insufficient to keep up with the supply necessary to fill the growing demand of Mexican brewers.

Today, artisanal beer in Mexico represents 1% of the national production. Due to this, accusations of practices of oligopoly have come up due to the dominance of the market by two powerful groups: Anheuser-Busch InBev and Heineken (which were at one time the property of the Mexican Grupo Modelo) and FEMSA-Cuauhtémoc-Moctezuma. Small producers depend on the availability of supplies for their subsistence; this has driven many to decide to consent to participate in shares in these huge groups. The end result is that participation facilitates something that gives results. In this way, the difficulties in the chain of supply and the logistics of importation are overcome to guarantee the malt and hops necessary for production, conservation, and standardisation of the product in terms of quality and quantity, but this exchange takes away the autonomy in making decisions. The participation also strengthens the distribution of the product, given that these two huge groups suggest exclusivity to their buyers in exchange for various benefits.

Another difficulty that confronts artisanal brewers is the inequity of taxation. The taxes that the micro-producers should pay are far higher than those paid by the huge brewery groups. This means that the price of artisanal beer goes up by as much as 400%. This special tax on production and service (IEPS) is levied on all beers at 26.5% over the sales price, to which is added the value-added tax (IVA). The difference is because artisanal beer is placed under the rule of ad valorem, which forces a product to pay more taxes according to the value it has (Villamil, 2016). Additionally and different from industrial beers, the majority of malts and hops is imported, which raises taxes because of customs duties. For now, the different independent brewers' associations continue to solicit, without success, the Chamber of Delegates for reconsideration of taxation imposed on artisanal beer. Should that goal be achieved, it could reduce the retail price by as much as 25%.

Artisanal Beer in Baja

The northern part of the state of Baja California has a long-standing beer tradition for two reasons: the first for its geographic location, which facilitates access to hops and malt available in the United States. This access to the border means that these supplies can be shipped in small lots in luggage, avoiding customs duties. In addition, brewers have the possibility of acquiring second-hand equipment, diminishing importation and transportation costs, given Baja's short distance from the city of San Diego, where there is also great activity revolving around artisanal beer. Another factor is the preference in the community for this drink, given that the average temperatures are higher than in the rest of the country almost all year long.

Whether this was the cause or consequence, there has been a migration of master brewers from Europe to this region since the first breweries opened at the beginning of the 20th century. This migration can also be noticed in the musical tastes of the population, in the 'corridos del norte' and the 'música de banda', as played by Los Tucanes of Tijuana or Los Huracanes del Norte. The cross-cultural roots of the genre are confirmed by the music, which may follow different rhythms, including European polka (Czech Republic) or Waltz (Vienna). Depending on the local tradition (dell'Agnese, 2015, p. 174), the style of dance and even of the instruments such as the accordion disclose a link with Central Europe of the past.

Perhaps the best-represented beer of the region is the Tecate Brewery, which since 1944 has been produced in the city of the same name (Reyna & Krammer, 2012). The beer is a pilsner, the style originally developed in Pilsen, Czech Republic (Alworth, 2015), a clear, light lager, which established the standard, becoming one of the styles most accepted by the consumer market. The music and the drink which are enjoyed in this region allude to cultural aspects of old Czechoslovakia.

It is exactly in the region of Baja where the largest concentrations in the country of producers of artisanal beer are located. There are nearly 100 workshops. Local history of craft beer produced in an organised way dates back to only a little more than 20 years, influenced in a relevant way by the beer movement in southern California in the United States. The movement grew rapidly in Baja because of the availability of equipment and supplies and its close proximity to the city of San Diego; which is distinguished for being outstanding in the international artisanal beer movement. To have an idea of how quickly the microbreweries in America have multiplied, in 1965 the United States registered only one establishment with the pertinent characteristics (Hindy, 2014, p. 5); nowadays there are thousands.

A recent reform to the Reglamento de Expendio de Bebidas Alcohólicas in the state of Baja California has permitted convenience stores to sell wine and beer to take out, which has also increased the average expenditure of tourists and day-trippers.

4 Behaviour of Food and Drink Tourism in Baja California

As mentioned earlier, in Baja California three different factors have come together regarding food and drink; those factors have promoted the makeup of viable gastronomic tourism. The principal attraction in the area is the Ruta de Vino (Wine Trail), which is located 100 kilometers from the border with the state of California, United States, and is quite close to the Pacific coast. The vineyards and the olive orchards are an essential part of the gastronomic landscape of Valle de Guadalupe, and the available culinary packages have been greatly enriched by restaurants which stand out on international lists; two of these are Corazón de Tierra and Laja, which distinguish their gastronomic offerings by using local ingredients and bringing together their dishes as part of the culinary identity of the region. Establishments within the vineyards complement the offerings of food trucks and food carts serving fish and seafood. It is possible to enjoy fresh local flavours at very accessible prices.

In spite of the multiple activities that the Ruta del Vino offers, overnight stays by travellers are not significant. This is due principally because in Valle de Guadalupe there are only a few more than 100 commercial rooms available, making it necessary to reserve months ahead of time. The growing demand of tourists for a place to spend the night has forced some warehouses and private homes to offer accommodations through AirBnB or similar offers, in addition to the outstanding number of tourists who stay in the homes of friends or family members. This is about 69% of total tourists (SecturBC, 2016).

In a review of tourist online inquiries, the constant factor that takes tourism and other visitors to the region is gastronomy. One in four mentions that food and drink were the factors that inspired their trips. Meanwhile, 60% mention food and drink as a secondary factor. That is, 85% of the persons interviewed mentioned gastronomic interests. Among the outstanding activities related to gastronomy we see: visit the Ruta del Vino, wine tastings, participate in harvest events, taste local food, and take at least a two-hour food-related class. The tourist office is beginning to consider the possibility of including another question in the survey with regard to knowledge or consumption of beer as a gastronomic activity in the destination (Casas, 2016).

Gastronomic tourism is followed in popularity as a motive for travel by medical tourism. Therefore, dental offices are seen one after another along the Mexican border. Shopping tourism is yet another factor for travel; the state welcomes tourists seeking entertainment. Finally, the segment that has almost doubled in size during the current year is wedding or other social event tourism, along with visits to Pueblos Mágicos ('Magic Towns').

Tourist satisfaction is the principal tool of the destination, now that 56% choose to travel to Baja California based on the recommendation of a friend or family member. The closeness of the state of California and the possibility of arriving by automobile slightly favour the presence of foreign tourists and day-trippers over national tourism. The great majority of frequent visitors are adults under the age of 35; the stand-out fact is that one of every three is traveling alone. Another important segment of tourism are cruise passengers who usually leave the cruise ship to go to breweries and wine bars, especially those who normally stay near the ship, close to the coast. For them, Ensenada offers a wide range of options for visitors. Others decide to join a tour or rent an automobile to explore the Ruta del Vino.

As a real solution for paying attention to tourist requests, there are examples of illicit businesses being converted into beer tasting salons. One case in particular is that of a table dance hall in the city of Tijuana, which since the end of 2015 has functioned as a tasting room called Norte Brewing Company. In the space and in the logo of the establishment one can still see the pole for the pole dance. This is just one case; but there are other similar cases of illicit businesses which are now legal entities. In addition, beer has rejuvenated abandoned malls, such as the Plaza del Zapato (shoe mall) which still has that name but today is transformed into a cluster of breweries where it is possible to find a large number of artisanal beers. The building is rescued and this has also created employment in Tijuana. In addition to invigorating the mall's economy, this conversion contributes to the creation of new, formal jobs in the growing tourist industry for those interested in nightlife and in diversity of flavours.

The difference between Mexico and the United States with respect to the minimum drinking age is also a factor in causing young people from the USA, who are usually residents of southern California between 18 and 21 years old, to cross the border with the goal of buying and consuming alcoholic beverages, given that in Mexico the legal age for buying and consuming alcohol is 18 and that in the USA is 21. Whether or not this sort of trip includes an overnight stay will determine if these young people will be tourists or merely day-trippers.

5 Challenges to Overcome

Even though Baja is better consolidated every day as an attractive destination for travellers interested in food and drink, both international and national competition are constant. Baja as a destination and in particular the Ruta del Vino require continuous redesign. The return rate of tourists and day-trippers is very high, and the expectation is that they will continue to find satisfactory experiences during every new visit. If we consider the growth of tourism all over the world, Baja needs to place special attention in the aspects that visitors have pointed out as deficient in the surveys we have performed. Although nearly all tourists are interested in tasting local foods, there are two points that take away from the experience: the relationship of price to quality and slow service. That is, they consider the gastronomic experience to be expensive and although they acknowledge that service is pleasant and courteous, it is not as efficient as they hoped it would be.

General cleanliness in the city is another factor that travellers point out. In addition, the lack of spas seems to be a component of any tourist package that puts the destination at a disadvantage. This is due to Baja's close proximity compared to California and Arizona, in the United States, and Los Cabos, in Baja California Sur. It is not a coincidence and is in fact an undeniable advantage that this brewery grouping is so close to San Diego as San Diego has one of the largest and most active clusters of microbreweries in the world. This proximity insists that Mexican brewers do not allow quality and service to lessen. Assiduous tourists always contrast standards of service.

The promotion that is given to microbreweries, as much as to the independents as to those that are created in vineyards and wine cellars and tasting rooms, bars, and beer sellers in the northern region of Baja, can bring great benefits of sustainable development to the destination. One of the most important of these is the possibility of strengthening sustainable development to create jobs, creating legal beer selling businesses where there were once illicit businesses and where crimes were even committed such as human trafficking. As a positive consequence of converting these illicit businesses, there would be an increase of tax payments and the possibility of employee protection in conformity with the law. Without a doubt, making beer in this region of Mexico is linked to its population in the past, given that breweries were one of the economic precursors of the region when the number of inhabitants was very few. Today just as in the past, beer attracts new residents and gives them a modus vivendi, rescuing a European heritage that at times becomes diluted in the multicultural nature of the region but which shines anew in festivities where music, dance, and drink remind us of central and eastern Europe, and where the polka is the step which persists in the presence of a beer culture which made Mexico its home.

In questions of ecology, the boom in Baja's cuisine has favoured the cultivation of foods and the raising of animals, the arid land of the semi-desert in conjunction with sea breezes has allowed the transformation of the landscape of Valle de Guadalupe into innumerable rows of grape and olive fronds. Now there are pilot projects for the cultivation of hops and barley.

Beer is the ideal complement to the seasonality which is imposed on gastronomic tourism, promoting and incorporating the most people into its economic activities that are derived from this business, bettering living conditions all year long in a significant manner and not simply season by season which created a seasonal population with very little putting down of roots. As we have seen, the principal gastronomic attraction in Baja is found in the Ruta del Vino in Valle de Guadalupe, even though the hundred or so commercial rooms in the destination are now insufficient to house the growing number of visitors. We have seen society's participation in preparing rooms and offering them for rent through mechanisms of collaborative business, which is a growing tendency.

Gastronomic tourism in general and beer tourism in particular, although not statistically significant, appears to be a growing international tendency. In addition, quality gastronomic tourism is one of the aspects of travel that tourists truly appreciate and which is an important component of the tourist experience in this destination (Hall & Gössling, 2016). The different associations of artisanal brewers need to continue to fight to obtain equality of conditions in tax charges, now that the development and number of microbreweries of both small and medium size represent the possibility of self-employment and the development of gastronomic tourist attractions in different destinations.

Interest in beer is shared by a large number of people all over the world, some as consumers and others as producers, given that they are found everywhere. Social networks have been converted into an indispensable tool to bring us together for the exchange of opinions and knowledge. It is exactly through these media that activities with respect to beer should be diffused and promoted as being attractive enough to justify travel.

Tourism motivated by beer is an attraction that can create businesses that present gastronomic interest and that can be included in the design of tourist products (Pechlaner, Raich, & Fischer, 2009). Given that water is the principal ingredient of beer, in olden times breweries chose to establish themselves near natural sources of water which presented them with the best qualities: water free of chlorine, soft water for light beers and hard water for dark beers, both with controlled acidity. Because of this, springs and rivers of meltwater provide the ideal place to establish a brewery; today, water can be treated with the goal of creating the optimal qualities for whatever kind of beer one wants to make, while the remaining ingredients can be obtained even in faraway places (Ramos, 2016). With correct techniques and the supervision of a Master Brewer, this gastronomic attraction can be added to any destination.

References

Alworth, J. (2015). *The Beer Bible*. New York: Workman Publishing Co.

Casas, A. (2016). Interview with the chief of the Planning Department and Statistics of the Secretary of Tourism of Baja California/Interviewer: Ma. Isabel Ramos, Tijuana, Baja California.

Beer Festivals. Retrieved 26 September 2016 from http://www.beerfestival.org.

Das Oktoberfest in Zahlen. Retrieved 23 September 2016 from http://www.okto berfest.de/de/02/content/zahlen/.

De Myttenaere, B. (2014). Territorial representation, touristic attractiveness, and promotion of Trappist Monks beer in Belgium. *Journal of Hospitality and Tourism*, 12(2), 54.

Dell'Agnese, E. (2015). Welcome to Tijuana: Popular music on the US–Mexico Border. *Geopolitics*, 20(1), 171–192. doi: 10.1080/14650045.2014.979914.

Hall, M., & Gössling, S. (2016). *Food tourism and regional development, networks, products and trajectories*. London: Routledge.

Hindy, S. (2014). *The craft beer revolution*. New York: Palgrave Macmillan.

Ramos, M. I. (2016). *La cerveza una bebida natural, en A.A.V.V. El libro de la cerveza mexicana*. México: Museo Citadino. S.A de C.V.

Reyna, M. del C., & Krammer, J. P. (2012). *Apuntes para la historia de la cerveza en México*. México: Instituto Nacional de Antropología e Historia.

Rogerson, C. M. (2016). Craft beer, tourism and local development in South Africa. In C. M. Hall & S. Góssling (Eds.), *Food tourism and regional development: networks, products and trajectories*. London: Routledge.

SecturBC. Secretaría de Turismo de Baja California. (2016). Investigación, análisis y proyección de visitas que viajan a Baja California por distintos motivos y estadías. 3er. reporte. Septiembre de 2016. México: Staconsultores.

Pechlaner, H., Raich, F., & Fischer, E. (2009). The role of tourism organizations in location management: The case of beer tourism in Bavaria. *Tourism Review*, 64(2), 28–40.

V.V.A.A. (2016). *El libro de la cerveza mexicana*. México: Museo Citadino. S.A de C.V.

Villamil, V. (2016). Buscan bajar impuestos a cervezas artesanales. El Financiero, Economía 17/10/2016.

Zapfe, H. (2016). *Guía cervecera, ABC de la cerveza, historia y evolución en México*. México: El Gourmet.

Sarbjit S. Gill, F. Anne Terwiel, John S. Hull

Developing Sense of Place as a Staff Retention Strategy: The Case of Sun Peaks Resort

1 Introduction

At a time when the growth of the tourism industry in British Columbia (BC) is set to outpace the growth of the labour market, it is vital that tourism employers consider succession planning and staff retention strategies as critical to their ongoing success. By 2020 it is predicted that over 100,000 tourism jobs may go unfilled as a result of the creation of 44,000 new jobs and the loss of the 57,000 employees predicted to leave the tourism workforce (Go2hr, 2012). During this time, tourism employers risk both being understaffed and losing knowledgeable staff to other resorts or other industries (Vaugeois, Maher, Heeney, Rowsell, Bence, & McCartney, 2013). The tourism industry of BC has an annual turnover rate of 30.7% compared to an annual turnover rate of 8.6% for other BC industries (Vaugeois et al., 2013). This difference is magnified in rural and resort communities such as Sun Peaks Mountain Resort Municipality ([SPMRM], Sun Peaks), our case study community. The loss of these employees is costly. It is generally estimated that the cost of recruiting a new employee—inclusive of both the direct and indirect costs—is 1.5 times the departing employees' income (Chikwe, 2009; Deery & Shaw, 1999). Therefore, from the vantage point of an impending labour shortage, the high turnover rate, and employee replacement costs, an investigation into employee retention strategies at snow sports resorts is warranted.

Literature pertaining to the retention of resort employees has mainly focused on workplace factors (Dickson & Huyton, 2008). At Sun Peaks, employees live, work and play in a unique setting; a small isolated mountain community with many natural and built amenities. Understanding the comprehensive experience of resort employees, both inside and outside of the workplace, can help to illuminate factors influencing resort lifestyle and employment considerations. The human geography concept of 'sense of place,' simply explained as the feelings and attachment one has toward a place (Agnew, 1987), can contribute to our understanding of the full employee experience at a snow sports resort.

The purpose of this research is to understand why and how 'sense of place' can be applied to better appreciate the comprehensive experience of resort employees.

To that end, we have piloted an original mixed methods study at Sun Peaks in order to measure and describe the employee experience.

2 Case Study Location: Sun Peaks Mountain Resort Municipality, British Columbia

Sun Peaks is a mountain resort community located 410 kilometres northeast of Vancouver, BC, which is primarily known for snow sports (Sun Peaks Resort, 1996). It has both winter and summer recreational facilities (SPRC, 2014a). In the winter, Sun Peaks Resort boasts 4,270 acres of skiable terrain spread over three mountains, and many kilometres of groomed and backcountry Nordic trails. Come summertime, one can enjoy 16 hiking trails, 35 biking trails, and a golf course (SPRC, 2014a). The resort sees over 500,000 visits annually (Scherf, 2011), and today, is home to a mountain community of about 700 full-time residents, an additional 600 to 700 winter residents, plus 500 seasonal employees (Sun Peaks Resort Media Centre, 2017). Sun Peaks Resort LLP (SPR LLP) is the biggest employer and SPMRM governs the community, overseeing essential local services and community development. Sun Peaks remains a small, single-industry town—isolated and dependent entirely on tourism to drive the economy (SPMRM, 2012). That poses some unique challenges.

The resort is a four-season resort destination, though winter and summer dominate, with spring and fall operating as shoulder seasons. Aiming to reap year-round economic benefits and build a distinct mountain community, the municipality envisions 1,500 permanent residents by 2033 with strong availability of year-round jobs, making it easier for amenity migrants to put down their roots (SPMRM, 2013). SPMRM has identified resort employees as a likely source of permanent community members (SPMRM, 2012), underscoring the importance of these employees to resort operations and community growth. However, the current realities are as follows: 75% of Sun Peaks' economic activity still takes place in wintertime, between mid-December and April, and this seasonal disparity results in limited permanent year-round employment opportunities, making it difficult to retain employees in the local workforce and as the permanent residents of Sun Peaks (SPMRM, 2012).

SPR LLP and SPMRM are actively taking steps to tackle these issues. SPMRM takes advantage of Resort Municipality Initiative (RMI) grants, designed for resort improvements to attract more tourists and encourage longer stays, to diversify their summer product portfolio (Interior Daily News, 2014). Both SPR LLP and SPMRM supported the grassroots development of the Discovery Centre for Balanced Education, which has now become two schools, a School District 73 elementary school called Sun Peaks Elementary, and the privately run Sun Peaks Secondary Academy. The value of a fully functioning school as an attractor of year-round residents was recognized early by both organisations.

Of course, issues persist as the resort and the resort community develops and transitions. Inconsistent shuttle service between Kamloops and Sun Peaks, and the lack of a gas station, are just two of the cited issues new settlers face (SPMRM, 2012). This research study will shed light on more of these communal factors and how they play a part in resort employees' experiences and influence their employment and lifestyle decisions.

3 Employment Dynamics at Snow Sports Resorts

Many authors have identified service excellence as a key competitive advantage that is essential for creating customer loyalty (BC Jobs Plan, 2014; Dickson & Huyton, 2008; Ismert & Petrick, 2004; Thomas, 2002), and that makes employees a crucial stakeholder at any destination (Dickson & Huyton, 2008; Flagestad & Hope, 2001; Murphy, 2008; Vaugeois et al., 2013). Employees are the face of the resort (Murphy, 2008), and the service they provide helps to form the consumer experience, influencing visitors' intentions to return, recommend, and spend more money (BC Jobs Plan, 2014). However, establishing service excellence and consistency in service is a challenge in the isolated resort communities, given the resort employment dynamics and high turnover.

3.1 The Resort Employee Makeup

To operate profitably year around, resorts must systematically handle staffing levels depending upon peak, shoulder, and low seasons (Adler & Adler, 2003). This variation results in an interesting mix of employees at resorts, typically made up of migrants, locals, seasonal workers, and amenity migrants, each with their own motivations, desires and preferences.

Migrants: Migrant labour, made up of both in-migrant (domestic) and international labour, is becoming increasingly important to resorts' financial stability (Duncan, Scott, & Baum, 2013). These labourers are more concerned with lifestyle and camaraderie than with wages (Lundberg, Gudmundson, & Andersson, 2009) and often fill the less desirable positions (Benach, Muntaner, Delclos, Menéndez, & Ronquillo, 2011; Murphy, 2008). They have varied motivations to take up employment at snow sports resorts: developing sports skills; engaging in work while travelling to finance their lengthy trip; obtaining a working holiday visa to both work and enjoy the place; and/or leisure consumption (Higham & Hinch, 2009).

Although valuable due to their low demands, these migrant employees are vulnerable to exploitation (Benach et al., 2011), are at higher risk of stress as they undergo a series of changes and adjustments at a new place (Bhugra, 2004; Higham & Hinch, 2009), rarely become permanent migrants, and they are far less likely to develop attachment with the place (Higham & Hinch, 2009). This results in a consistently high turnover, loss of knowledge, and recruitment costs for the employer (Murphy, 2008).

Locals: Local employees are more concerned with wages than camaraderie (Lundberg et al., 2009). Local employees are also much more likely to return season after season (Alverén, Andersson, Eriksson, Sandoff, & Wikhamn, 2012) and build stronger ties with the place (Adler & Adler, 2003). A research study conducted by Ismert & Petrick (2004) found that three factors influenced the job satisfaction of returning employees: money, management attitude, and benefits.

Seasonal Workers: Much of the research on seasonal employees at snow sports resorts has focused on the factors influencing their job satisfaction, which has been deemed as a key indicator for their intention to return (Mozafari, Asli, & Bejestani, 2012). Alverén et al. (2012) found that four factors influenced the job satisfaction of seasonal employees: camaraderie, feedback, management attitude, and responsibility.

Amenity Migrants: An emerging trend amongst resort employees is the recruitment of amenity migrants. These individuals are attracted to communities that provide high-quality amenities to satisfy their lifestyle motivations (Vaugeois et al., 2013). Prominent migration paths include a move to mountain tourism communities (Gripton, 2009) for the natural beauty, different pace of life, recreational opportunity and other desirable amenities. Demographically, these migrants are almost at the age of retirement or have been retired, and may possess high disposable income (Nepal & Jamal, 2011).

Managing these heterogeneous employees is a major challenge for resort managers. Resort employees themselves, living, working and playing in the same small community, face an array of challenges concomitant with resort employment.

3.2 The Challenges with Resort Employment

Vaugeois et al. (2013) lists the following as the most common challenges faced by all tourism employees: unfavourable pay; unfavourable/stressful work conditions; long hours; part-time, temporary, and/or seasonal jobs; lack of benefits; limited opportunities for promotion or pay increases; emotionally and physically demanding work; and monotony in job tasks. For snow sport resort employment, the following challenges are added: seasonality, emotional labour, lack of privacy, housing, commute, and added stress (Adler & Adler, 2003; Dickson & Huyton, 2008; Gill & Williams, 2011; Higham & Hinch, 2009; Law et al., 1995; Mill, 2008; Murphy, 2008; Nepal & Jamal, 2011; Vaugeois et al., 2013).

These challenges undoubtedly influence employment decisions and have led to the establishment of a 'culture of turnover' in resort communities (Vaugeois et al., 2013).

3.3 The Culture of Turnover at Resorts

The turnover culture usually develops when turnover is accepted as a norm by employees, management, and owners at the workplace (Chikwe, 2009; Deery & Shaw, 1999). Turnover can be both beneficial and detrimental to a resort's operations, as highlighted in Table 1, but it is widely agreed that the turnover is expensive (Murphy, 2008).

Table 1: Benefits and Detriments of Turnover at Resorts[1]

Benefits of turnover	Detriments of turnover
• Accommodate seasonal demand fluctuations by hiring employees for a specific period • Terminate employment of those unfit for work conditions at resorts • Increased morale amongst the staff if there is a change of a task and/or supervisor	• Loss of key employees and management to the competitors or other areas of the tourism industry • Loss of knowledge • Loss of valuable time spent on recruitment • Direct costs involved with leaving, advertising, recruiting, training, and management and clerical time • Indirect costs involved with lack of productivity, low morale, loss of reputation and goodwill, and overtime

As indicated previously, employee turnover costs, which include both direct and indirect costs, are generally estimated to be 1.5 times the departing employee's income (Chikwe, 2009; Deery & Shaw, 1999). Importantly, turnover affects consistency in the level of service delivered to the guests. Therefore, from the financial and 'service excellence as a competitive advantage' perspectives, it makes sense for resorts to take initiatives to minimise turnover.

---

1   Source: Chikwe, 2009; Deery & Shaw, 1999; Murphy, 2008; Vaugeois et al., 2013.

3.4 Combatting Resort Employee Turnover

Several strategies have been suggested to combat resort employee turnover: better recruitment and selection strategies, higher wages, more training and development opportunities (Chikwe, 2009; Vaugeois et al., 2013), career advancement opportunities, multi-skilling of employees, creating a positive/welcoming environment for employees, partnering with organisations on opposite seasonal cycles, and non-monetary benefits (Vaugeois et al., 2013). Murphy (2008) further adds that to establish service excellence at the resort, the staff need to be treated similarly to guests; resort management should extend the same culture of care to resort staff as they expect resort staff to provide to the guests. Improving communication, increasing employee responsibility, and showing appreciation will aid in stress alleviation of employees and demonstrate care.

Vaugeois et al. (2013) listed the ways a variety of resort employers are creating positive work environments: recognising work as a means to an end; flexible schedules; non-monetary perks such as ski/recreation passes; monetary perks such as bonus pay and paying slightly higher than industry average; and job sharing. Other strategies to combat turnover and retain employees include: refined management philosophy and practices; developing a customer service orientation; and building relationships with employees to encourage them to return for a second season. While research is available on the work environments of resort employees, very limited research is available on how the additional elements of the resort setting play a role in employee experience (Dickson & Huyton, 2008). Understanding the place that the resort setting occupies in the overall employee experience in isolated resort communities is critical. The 'sense of place' construct may be a strong concept in addressing this gap in the literature.

4 Sense of Place

'Sense of place' is a concept within the discipline of human geography, generally defined as the personal and emotional attachment one has to a place (Agnew, 1987). The political geographer Agnew (1987) lists three antecedents that make a place 'a place': location, locale, and sense of place. The 'location' represents a set of geographic coordinates or the bounds of the place; the setting where the place is located (Cresswell, 2004). Sun Peaks Resort, our case study, claims the coordinates 50.878122, −119.910271 on the map (Google Maps, 2014).

The second antecedent 'locale' represents the 'material visual form' of the place where one encounters, interacts, experiences, produces and consumes the meaning of the place (Cresswell, 2004). A locale can be a cafe, a post-office, a workplace, or a ski hill—anywhere where one can interact with the elements of the place including its peoples. Based on Dickson & Huyton's (2008) work on snow sports resorts and Sun Peaks Resort's website (SPRC, 2014b), the following locale factors were identified at Sun Peaks:

accommodation; leisure activities; natural environment; social venues; support services (*such as clinic, church, child care, school, and more*); the village (*shopping needs, groceries, restaurants, and more*), workplace(s), and people in Sun Peaks (*visitors, employees, residents, management*).

The final antecedent 'sense of place' is made up of feelings and the emotional attachment one forms after interacting with the 'locale' of the 'location' (Cresswell, 2004). With each new interaction, 'sense of place' is actively constructed and reconstructed (Tuan, 1977), resulting in a highly individualistic 'sense of place' shaped by the people, environment and personal experiences in that place (Higham & Hinch, 2009). It is noted that while how one consumes the meaning of place can be mediated, such as through the people met, the marketing & signage encountered, the way buildings and facilities are constructed, and in many other forms, the meaning one produces after interacting with the locale is highly subjective and personal (Higham & Hinch, 2009). To repeat, the consumption of place can be mediated but the meaning one produces always remains personal. Based on the literature, a simple framework can explain the continuous consumption and production of a personal 'sense of place':

Locale Elements + Personal Encounter(s) = Sense of Place

A Construct–Understanding Employees' Sense of Place at a Snow Sports Resort

Working with the framework Locale Elements + Personal Encounter(s) = Sense of Place, the factors listed above as elements of locale can be added, as in Table 2.

When an employee encounters a locale factor in Sun Peaks, the 'sense of place' is produced and then reproduced with each new encounter (Agnew, 1987). Cross (2001) aids in the comprehension of this individualistic sense of place developing within resort employees, based on a variety of locale factors. Seeking a common definition of 'sense of place' across disciplines, Cross (2001) broke down the 'sense of place' into two components: 'relationships to place' and 'community attachment'.

Cross mentions one can form 6 types of relationships to place, and multiple relationships at the same time. Table 3 details these relationships and the process by which they are formed. However, Cross (2001) highlights that one can only have a singular 'sense of place'.

Table 2: Developing a Framework to Understand Employees' 'Sense of Place' at a Snow Sports Resort[2]

Snow Sports Resort Locale Elements	Personal Encounter(s)	Sense of Place
• Accommodation • Leisure activities • Natural Environment • Social venues • Support Services (such as health clinic, church, child care, school, etc.) • Village (for shopping, restaurants, more.) • Workplace(s) • Employees • Management • Residents • Visitors	• Encounters of an employee with the resort locale elements	• The feelings an employee has towards the place and its elements can be understood based upon Cross' 'sense of place' construct (Cross, 2001)

Table 3: Reproduction of Cross' Sense of Place Construct Component – Relationships to Place[3]

Relationship	Type of Bond	Process
Biographical	Historical and familial	Being born in and living in a place, develops over time
Spiritual	Emotional, intangible	Feeling a sense of belonging, simply felt rather than created
Ideological	Moral and ethical	Living according moral guidelines for human responsibility to a place, guidelines may be religious or secular
Narrative	Mythical	Learning about place through stories, including: creation myths, family histories, political accounts and fictional accounts
Commodified	Cognitive (based on choice and desirability)	Choosing a place based a list of desirable traits and lifestyle preferences, comparison of actual places with ideal
Dependent	Material	Constrained by lack of choice, dependency on another person or economic opportunity

2   Source: Chikwe, 2009; Deery & Shaw, 1999; Murphy, 2008; Vaugeois et al., 2013.
3   Source: Cross, 2001.

The 'sense of place' is a combination of varied factors that marry together to produce a 'sense of place'. The attachment one forms with the place, satisfaction level(s), consideration of the place as a home, strength of local identity, and future desires are all factors that influence how one perceives the place and sees themselves a part of it. The depth of one's attachment is an indication of their 'sense of place' illustrating how and if they're rooted in the community (Table 4).

Table 4: Reproduction of Cross' Sense of Place Construct Component – Sense of Place Typology[4]

Sense of Place	Satisfaction	Home as Insidedness	Local Identity	Type of Attachment	Future Desires
Rootedness Cohesive	High	Here (physical, spiritual, emotional)	Strong	Biographical spiritual ideological	Continued residence and/or employment
Rootedness Divided	Variable	Here and there (physical, spiritual, emotional)	Split	Biographical spiritual dependent	Variable
Place Alienation	Low	There (physical, spiritual, emotional)	Weak	Dependent	Desire to leave place/employment, but unable
Relativity	Variable	Anywhere	Moderate	Commodified (biographical) (dependent)	To live in ideal place and/or hold ideal employment, wherever that may be
Uncommited Placelessness	(Moderate)	Anywhere/no-where	Weak	None	No specific expectations of place and/or of employment

The development of a framework to understand how snow sports employees consume and produce place meaning, based on varied locale factors, will allow the identification of specific factors that may positively or negatively influence the employee experience. The sense of place construct allows researchers to categorise and classify the experiences of resort employees, understand the relationships and

---

4   Source: Cross, 2001.

depth of attachments they form to Sun Peaks, and provide insight into the collective 'sense of place' constructed and experienced by employees.

5 Methodology

This pilot study utilised an original, mixed methods survey instrument, distributed to employees via survey link embedded in a postseason email from their employer. Participating employers included the largest employer, SPR LLP, and a number of independent resort businesses. The anonymous survey collected quantitative data to assess demographics and psychographics, to build a profile of Sun Peaks employees, and the qualitative data aided in understanding employees' 'sense of place' of Sun Peaks, observed via their stated behaviours and attitudes, knowledge and perceptions of Sun Peaks and their employment and resident experience. This data was filtered through Cross' (2001) 'sense of place' construct to develop an understanding of employees' sense of place. The data was collected over a 28 day-period via Vovici, an online survey tool, ending in late June 2014. The data was analysed via SPSS and NVivo software.

6 Results

A total of 89 responses were received, 75 of which were deemed fit for analysis, as resort volunteers and business owners were eliminated from the data pool. About 49.3% of the respondents were seasonal employees and 50.7% were permanent employees.

6.1 Profile of Sun Peaks Employees

Demographics: 46.7% of respondents were male and 53.3% were female. The majority of the respondents are under the age of 30 (61.3%), well-educated, and single (52%). Among them, 76% were in-migrants from within Canada, 54.7% of which were Canadian citizens, with 76% hailing from 100 km outside Sun Peaks. A quarter of Sun Peaks' workforce was made up of international workers.

Behaviours: When working in Sun Peaks, most reside within the resort municipality (73.3%) in a private rental (42.7%). On average, an employee has participated in 8 different leisure activities with skiing, hiking, snowboarding, ice-skating, and biking proving the most popular with over 50% employee participation. On average, community/support services are scarcely utilized. A total of 65.3% of the employees had used the medical clinic, 26.7% had used the ski/snowboard programs provided to employees free of charge, and 18.7% haven't used any community/support services at all. Other community/support services saw fewer than 17.3% employee use.

Employment dynamics: A total of 84% of respondents were dependent on a single employer for income when working in Sun Peaks. While 56.0% had only worked with their most recent employer for 1–2 seasons/years and 53.3% had been worked in Sun Peaks for 3 seasons/years or more. Nearly all the respondents held full-time employment (90.7%), regardless of seasonal or permanent employment. Most were in a non-management/general employee role (66.7%) where they interacted with visitors regularly (89.3%). Among them, 62.7% of respondents felt valued by their employer and 86.7% believed they received the necessary training to perform their job well. The three things they enjoyed the most about their job were: interacting with varied people (41.3%), their job duties (28.0%), and camaraderie with colleagues (24.0%). The three things they least enjoyed about their job were: job duties (14.7%), negative interaction with superiors at work (13.3%) and organisational structure and direction (13.3%).

6.2 Psychographics

Perceived quality of the locale factors: In terms of the quality of the locale: the quality of nature at Sun Peaks; leisure activities; the village, and interaction with fellow employees, visitors and residents; all received a positive rating of above 80%. The locale factors that received a rating lower than 80% were: quality of workplace(s); quality of social venues; quality of staff accommodation; quality of community/support services; and quality of interaction with the management.

Prominent motivating factors to pursue employment and remain employed in Sun Peaks: The most prominent factors that led respondents to pursue employment in Sun Peaks were: to live and/or work amongst like-minded people; the mountain culture lifestyle; and mountains & nature (the physical scenery). The key factors that would keep respondents in Sun Peaks for a long time were: mountains & nature (the physical scenery); to live and/or work amongst like-minded people—mountain culture lifestyle; and a strong sense of belongingness and emotional attachment to the place.

Sun Peaks as a place to live and/or work: When asked how they found Sun Peaks as a place to live and/or work, mountain culture lifestyle (42.7%), mountain community (33.3%), and leisure activities (18.7%) were the top three items eliciting positive responses from respondents.

Sun Peaks as a place to call home: Upon being asked if there is an opportunity to build a life in Sun Peaks, the top three items identified were employment/career opportunities (26.7%), mountain community (24%), and Sun Peaks Elementary

School (13.3%). Employment/career opportunities showed up as both positive and negative metrics, while the other two were factors were only discussed positively.

Reasons one would discontinue their employment in Sun Peaks: Upon being asked the key reasons for ever discontinuing their employment in Sun Peaks, personal reasons (32%), financial reasons (26.7%), employment/career opportunities (better or lack thereof) (24%), and superiors at work (24%) were the four most cited.

Intention to continue their employment: Upon being asked if they would continue their employment in Sun Peaks, 67.1% are continuing indefinitely, 9.6% said maybe they would continue and the remaining 23.3% are not returning.

Suggestions on improving employee experience: The top four recommendations by the respondents were as follows: enhancing/providing more benefits & incentives (25.3%), better/more staff appreciation opportunities (21.3%), improving community/support services (18.7%), and providing better remuneration (18.7%).

6.3 Sun Peaks Employees' Relationships to Place

As indicated in Table 5, this research showed that respondents primarily moved to and continued to be tethered to Sun Peaks as a result of the commodified (94.7%) and ideological relationships (76.0%) they form with the place. Commodified relationships imply that employees choose Sun Peaks for the amenities and lifestyle it provides, and the ideological relationships shed light on the importance of mountain culture and like-minded community found at Sun Peaks for these employees. The dependent relationships ranked third.

Table 5: Comparison of Employees' Relationships with Sun Peaks Prior to their Employment and how they Developed Afterward

Relationship	Before Employment at Sun Peaks (Q29)	After employment at Sun Peaks (Q32)	Difference
Commodified	82.7%	94.7%	12.0%
Ideological	72.0%	76.0%	4.0%
Dependent	58.7%	68.0%	9.3%
Spiritual	38.7%	57.3%	18.6%
Biographical	36.0%	45.3%	9.3%
Narrative	10.7%	13.3%	2.6%
Total n	**n=224**	**n=266**	**15.8%**

6.4 Sun Peaks Employees' Sense of Place

The data (Table 6) highlights that Sun Peaks employees are either rooted in the community or have a relative community attachment only. They either integrate into the community and get rooted predominantly via the measure of cohesiveness, with ambivalent and divided rootedness also occurring. Some have a transactional sense of place with Sun Peaks as it fits the mould of their ideal place and/ or employment opportunity at the moment. No cases of 'place alienation' and 'placelessness' were found.

Table 6: Sun Peaks Employees' Sense of Place

Sense of Place	Frequency	Percent
Rootedness - Cohesive	24	32.0%
Relativity	24	32.0%
Rootedness - Ambivalent	15	20.0%
Rootedness - Divided	10	13.3%
Missing	2	2.7%
Place Alienation	-	-
Placelessness	-	-
Total	**73**	**100.0%**

As a result of this analysis, a key item of note is the discovery of a new sense of place 'Rootedness – Ambivalent', which fills the gap between Rootedness Cohesive and Rootedness Divided sense of places. The revised sense of place typology is as follows (Table 7), building on Cross' (2001) framework, and was used in categorizing employees' sense of place.

Table 7: Sense of Place Typology Revisited

Sense of Place	Satisfaction	Home as Insidedness	Local Identity	Type of Attachment	Future Desires
Rootedness Cohesive	High	Here (physical, spiritual, emotional)	Strong	Biographical Spiritual Ideological	Continued residence and/or employment
Rootedness Ambivalent	Variable	Here - includes surrounding communities (physical, spiritual, emotional)	Moderate to strong	Biographical Dependent Spiritual Commodified Ideological	Continued residence and/or employment

Sense of Place	Satisfaction	Home as Insidedness	Local Identity	Type of Attachment	Future Desires
Rootedness Divided	Variable	Here and there (physical, spiritual, emotional)	Split	Biographical Spiritual Dependent	Variable
Place Alienation	Low	There (physical, spiritual, emotional)	Weak	Dependent	Desire to leave place/ employment, but unable
Relativity	Variable	Anywhere	Moderate	Commodified (Biographical) (Dependent)	To live in ideal place and/or hold ideal employment, wherever that may be
Uncommited Placelessness	(Moderate)	Anywhere/ nowhere	Weak	None	No specific expectations of place and/or of employment

7 Analysis and Discussion

This original research piloted a device to measure employees' sense of place at Sun Peaks, and uncover factors impacting the employee experience in positive and negative ways.

7.1 Employees' Sense of the Place at Sun Peaks

The employees are forming commodified and ideological relationships to Sun Peaks. Almost all respondents were attracted to Sun Peaks because of the mountain lifestyle, the amenities, the sub-culture, and the like-minded community it offers. The employees have expressed that these are important attractors to live, work and play in Sun Peaks, and they continue to be important in keeping them in place. However, as the researchers dug further and cross-tabulated the place relationships data with the intention to continue employment, it was discovered that the dependent relationships, the third-most common relationship (68.0%), are creating the strongest ties to Sun Peaks, as indicated in Table 8. Dependent relationships require commitment—to a job, a mortgage, a loved one, another element—and that keeps one grounded in the place long-term (Cross, 2001).

Table 8: Sun Peaks Employees' Relationships to Place

Relationships to Place	% of Employees Retained with this Relationship to Place	Will you continue your employment?	Total n in this relationship to place
Dependent	78.0%	39	50
Spiritual	69.8%	30	43
Ideological	66.7%	38	57
Commodified	64.3%	45	70
Narrative	60.0%	6	10
Biographical	52.9%	18	34
Total n		176	264

Those forming dependent relationships to Sun Peaks were the most likely to continue employment (78%), with ideological and commodified relationships ranking third and fourth in their strength to influence employment decisions. This validates Cross' (2001) assertion that commodified and ideological relationships are mostly superficial. They can easily be formed to another place with similar amenities, and similar mountain culture and communities. The dependent relationships tether one strongly to the community.

Analysis of employees' 'community attachment' aspect revealed the sense of place to be similar to the 'relationships to place'. The employees are either rooted in Sun Peaks community, or possess relative community attachment based purely on transactional note of their ideal amenities/job needs being met. While about a third of respondents were highly satisfied in Sun Peaks and had a strong local identity, many possessed a variable level of satisfaction with the place and variable levels of local identity, potentially not strong enough to make them stick with the community through difficult periods. Of note was the fact that researchers did not find any evidence of 'place alienation' in Sun Peaks. Individuals with place alienation have a negative assessment of the place, yet they reside in the community due to dependency reasons (Cross, 2001).

Overall, examining the 'sense of place' at Sun Peaks revealed which relationships employees were forming with the place and which relationships were important to keep them in place long term. The examination of 'sense of place' also revealed that Sun Peaks needs to create more or deeper dependency factors to tether employees to the place and root them in the community long-term. Without strong dependency tethers, the turnover is likely to continue.

7.2 Key Factors Influencing Employees' Sense of Place

When asked to rate the locale factors on a 5-point scale from 'Very Poor' to 'Very Good', the mean results ranked 'quality of nature at Sun Peaks' the highest and 'quality of support services' the lowest (Table 9). It should be noted that, on this 5-point Likert scale, all of the means were above 3.

Table 9: Respondents' Perception of Locale Factors (n=72)

Locale Factors	Mean
Quality of nature at Sun Peaks	4.64
Interaction with fellow employees	4.33
Quality of leisure activities	4.09
Interaction with visitors	4.08
Interaction with residents	4.07
Quality of the village	4.07
Quality of your accommodation	4.01
Quality of your workplace(s)	3.91
Interaction with the management	3.87
Quality of the social venues	3.71
Quality of support services	3.33

To uncover the bigger factors influencing employee experience, frequencies of the key items from all open-ended questions were categorized into: those positive factors that actively bind one to the place through positive encounters, and those factors that leave a negative impression on employees, thus deterring their attachment to the place. The findings are highlighted in Table 10.

Table 10: Positive and Negative Factors Influencing Employee Experience and Sense of Place in Sun Peaks

Positive Factors (n=273)	Frequency	Negative Factors (n=203)	Frequency
The Mountain Community	46	Financial reasons (remuneration, affordability, etc.)	36
Mountain Culture Lifestyle	46	Negative interaction with superiors at work	36
Leisure activities	31	Personal Reasons	31

Positive Factors (n=273)	Frequency	Negative Factors (n=203)	Frequency
Interaction with visitors and residents	31	Lack of employment/career opportunities, or better opportunities elsewhere	26
Camaraderie with colleagues	29	Poor organizational structure and direction	16
Enjoyable job duties	28	Community/Support services	12
Natural environment of Sun Peaks	21	Visa Restrictions	12
Outdoor work setting	12	Displeasing job duties	11
Employment/Career Opportunities	10	Negative interaction with guests	9
Sun Peaks Elementary School	10	Seasonality	9
Growth and development at the resort	9	Already integrated in another community	5
Total	273		203

Based on the table above, the employees overall had a positive assessment of Sun Peaks and that positivity rested heavily with Sun Peaks' natural environment; lifestyle offerings such as activities and school; and the distinctive mountain community. In contrast, the things that contribute to a negative employee experience in Sun Peaks mainly rest in the workplace. Financial reasons such as remuneration and affordability; negative interaction with superiors at work; lack of employment/ career opportunities or better opportunities elsewhere; and poor organisational structure and direction all cause an employee to question their employment in Sun Peaks. The main deal breaker outside of the workplace is the lack of appropriate community/support services, with respondents suggesting improvements to public transportation and staff accommodation, an affordable grocery store, a gas station, better medical facilities, and affordable housing. It should be noted that, since this study was completed, a new health facility and has been constructed and two new staff accommodation complexes have been added.

7.3 Key Factors & Variables Shaping Employment Dynamics in Sun Peaks

It is evident that some key factors & variables were influencing the intention to continue employment in Sun Peaks much more than the others. The researchers tested each demographic, employment, psychographic, and behavioural variable against the intent to continue employment and found the following to be shaping the employment dynamics in Sun Peaks:

1. Employees over the age of 30 are the most likely to continue employment.
2. Those in a committed relationship (married or living-common law), separated or divorced are the most likely to continue their employment.
3. The longer one resides in Sun Peaks, the more likely they are to hold long-term employment.
4. The turnover is predominantly occurring in seasonal staff. Those in stable, permanent positions are the most likely to continue employment.
5. The more valued an employee feels by their employer, the most likely they will continue their employment.
6. The more dependent one is on a place, the more likely they will continue their employment.
7. The more rooted they are in the community, the more likely they will continue their employment.

8 Conclusions

8.1 Recommendations

The overall employee experience at Sun Peaks is positive, as measured in this pilot survey. With a stronger understanding of the factors attracting employees and keeping them in place, employers and the municipality at Sun Peaks can work together to address issues hindering employee attachment and retention. Some key recommendations flow from survey results.

1. The mountain lifestyle needs to be affordable for employees.
   Mountain lifestyle is one of the biggest attractors to move to Sun Peaks, but financial metrics, such as remuneration, lack of affordability, and expensive services, coupled with a lack of employment/career opportunities, may be keeping employees from building a life at the mountain. This issue may be addressed via creative remuneration and benefits packages, or the creation of a housing authority that manages a stock of housing for the benefit of resort employees, such as is done in Whistler, BC (Whistler Housing, 2017). Employee suggestions: better remuneration package, better benefits package, affordable housing options, and career opportunities.
2. Opportunities to form dependent relationships need to be created to root one strongly in the community.

Those with a dependent relationship to Sun Peaks, i.e. have commitments to either their loved ones, to a mortgage, to work, to career, etc. are the most likely to continue their employment and be more rooted in community. A few ways to create more opportunities to form dependent relationships are as follows:

- Improve and diversify the social scene so employees have a chance to mingle with like-minded individuals in different settings.
- Inquire into innovative housing solutions, such as cooperative housing, that would match employee remuneration. Currently, most are unable to afford housing.
- Implement career progression programs, and promote them to the employees so that they have something to work towards long-term.

3. Seasonality needs to be addressed and hiring practices need to be revised.
One of the key findings of this study was that employee attrition is majorly occurring amongst seasonal employees. Another interesting finding was that the seasonal employees under 30 tend to make their stay at Sun Peaks a short-term one, but seasonal employees over the age of 30 tend to remain longer. Therefore, it may help improve the employee retention rate if seasonal job opportunities are keenly advertised to those over 30 years of age from the surrounding communities, as the local employees are also much likely to return season after season and bear stronger ties with the place.

However, to ultimately improve employee retention is to fully transition to a four-season resort. As indicated by the findings, almost all in stable, permanent positions are continuing their employment, whereas only 40.5% of the seasonal employees expressed an intent to return for the 2014–2015 season.

4. Employees need to feel valued in the workplace to ensure retention.
Inside the workplace, the interaction between management and employees, and the organizational structure need to be improved to make employees feel valued and appreciated. As evident by the negative factors in this study, those issues exist, and as discovered upon analysing key variables and factors, the employees who feel more valued are the most likely to continue their employment. The following challenges with superiors at work are posing hindrance as uncovered in the quantitative analysis: poor communication, lack of support, un-appreciation, attitude, mistreatment, and patronisation.

A recommendation from the researchers would be for the management to do an employee check-in at the start, mid-season, and at the end of the season each year to understand their needs and wants, and to express support and care. Anonymous employee feedback can also be gathered year/season-round via Google Form survey and read weekly by the department manager/

management to uncover issues in real-time, and address them to show a culture of care and make employees feel valued, appreciated, and listened to.

5. Community/support services need to be improved to increase the quality of life and standard of living in Sun Peaks.

In terms of improving things in the municipality, there is one major issue. Community/support services need to be improved to provide a richer experience for employees. An affordable grocery store; improvements to medical facilities, public transportation, and staff accommodation; and addition of a gas station and more daily services were the suggested improvements that can be made to better the quality of life and standard of living in Sun Peaks.

Currently, the employees must make a trip to Kamloops, BC (40 km away) to buy groceries at an affordable rate. For those without a car, it is a frustrating experience. Moreover, the employees lacking access to a private vehicle have requested better public transportation services to travel in and out of the village, to the surrounding communities, and the city of Kamloops. Furthermore, installing a wireless internet service prior to employees' arrival and having a common room at all accommodations would enrich employee experience. Lastly, a bank and a gas station can reduce the extra costs of living in Sun Peaks and better medical facilities would prove beneficial according to the employees.

A key recommendation by the researchers would be to establish a rideshare program. The rideshare program can minimize the transportation costs, especially for going shopping and banking in Kamloops and minimize isolation and foster camaraderie and a sense of community.

In summary, these recommendations can lead to a more positive employee experience at Sun Peaks, thus a positive sense of place and potentially a longer stay, ultimately improving the employee retention rate and fostering a strong sense of community and pride in Sun Peaks, BC. A permanent system, if possible, should be in place to encourage regular and honest feedback from the employees. Their challenges, both inside the workplace and outside, should be understood and addressed by the employers and the resort municipality to improve the retention rate and build the mountain community. On the flip side, uncovering the positives are heavily beneficial in understanding resorts' strengths and those can be used in recruitment advertising to attract the right fits for the resort employment in Sun Peaks.

8.2 Conclusions

This research was conducted to explore the issues of employee attrition and retention at the case study snow sports resort by examining employees' sense of place, which took their comprehensive experience into account both inside and outside the workplace. The uncovered findings pinpointed to specific factors actively contributing to either a positive or a negative employee experience, and what can be improved to tether employees to the resort community retaining them long-term not only as employees but also community members.

The findings from this research study can be utilized by employers and resort municipality in Sun Peaks to improve the employee experience by understanding the characteristics of varied employees at the resort, the positive and negative factors influencing employee attrition and retention, and taking initiatives to address the big issues hindering employee attachment to the place. This also makes sense from a strategic perspective as the community of Sun Peaks has a vested interest in gaining competitive advantage through service excellence at the resort (SPRMC, 2017), and minimizing turnover makes sense both from a financial perspective and would aid in creation of that competitive advantage (Vaugeois et al., 2013). These findings can also help prepare the community of Sun Peaks for the upcoming labour shortage in 2020 (Go2hr, 2013) and help shape the strategy for the development of the mountain community (SPMRM, 2013).

For other mountain resort communities, this study can serve as a case example, and the framework utilized in this research can be adapted, modified and used to understand employees' sense of place at their resort, uncovering the specific factors at play influencing employees to move, remain and leave their destination. The benefits are immense.

Acknowledgements

The authors would like to thank the Sun Peaks Mountain Resort Municipality, Tourism Sun Peaks and Sun Peaks Resort LLP for their support in conducting this research.

References

Adler, P., & Adler, P. (2003). Seasonality and flexible labor in resorts: Organizations, employees, and local labor markets. *Sociological Spectrum*, 23(1), 59–89. doi: 10.1080/02732170390131939.

Agnew, J. A. (1987). *Place and politics: The geographical mediation of state and society*. London: Allen and Unwin.

Alverén, E., Andersson, T. D., Eriksson, K., Sandoff, M., & Wikhamn, W. (2012). Seasonal employees' intention to return and do more than expected. *The Service Industries Journal*, 32(12), 1957–1972. doi: 10.1080/02642069.2011.574280.

BC Jobs Plan. (2014). 3 year progress update. Retrieved from http://engage.gov. bc.ca/bcjobsplan/files/2014/09/BCJP_3YEARUPDATE_rev.pdf.

Benach, J., Muntaner, C., Delclos, C., Menéndez, M., & Ronquillo, C. (2011). Migration and 'low-skilled' workers in destination countries. *PLoS Medicine*, 8(6), e1001043. doi: 10.1371/journal.pmed.1001043.

Bhugra, D. (2004). *Migration and mental health*. Oxford, UK: Munksgaard International Publishers. doi: 10.1046/j.0001-690X.2003.00246.x.

Chikwe, A. C. (2009). The impact of employee turnover: The case of leisure, tourism and hospitality industry. *Consortium Journal of Hospitality & Tourism Management*, 14(1), 43–56.

Cresswell, T. (2004). *Place: A short introduction*. Malden, MA: Wiley–Blackwell.

Cresswell, T. (2009). *Place: International encyclopedia of human geography*. Thrift, N. & Kitchen, R. (Eds.). Oxford: Elsevier, Vol. 8, pp. 169–177.

Cross, J. E. (2001, November). In George Sibley (Chair). What is sense of place? Prepared for the 12th headwaters conference, Gunnison, CO. Retrieved from http://www.western.edu/academics/headwaters/headwatersconference/ archives/cross_headwatersXII.pdf.

Deery, M., & Shaw, R. (1999). An investigation of the relationship between employee turnover and organizational culture. *Journal of Hospitality & Tourism Research*, 23(4), 387–400. doi: 10.1177/109634809902300404.

Dickson, T. J., & Huyton, J. (2008). Customer service, employee welfare and snowsports tourism in Australia. *International Journal of Contemporary Hospitality Management*, 20(2), 199–214. doi: 10.1108/09596110810852177.

Duncan, T., Scott, D., & Baum, T. (2013). The mobilities of hospitality work: An exploration of issues and debates. *Annals of Tourism Research*, 41, 1–19. doi: 10.1016/j.annals.2012.10.004.

Flagestad, A., & Hope, C. A. (2001). Strategic success in winter sports destinations: A sustainable value creation perspective. *Tourism Management*, 22(5), 445–461. doi: 10.1016/S0261-5177(01)00010-3.

Gill, A., & Williams, P. (2011). Rethinking resort growth: Understanding evolving governance strategies in whistler, British Columbia. *Journal of Sustainable Tourism*, 19(4–5), 629–648. doi: 10.1080/09669582.2011.558626.

Go2hr. (2012). 2012 BC tourism labour market strategy. Retrieved from http:// www.bcjobsplan.ca/wpcontent/uploads/TLMS.Summary.pdf.

Go2hr. (2013, September 5). BC's tourism industry poised for job growth with more than 100,000 new job openings. Retrieved from https://www.go2hr.ca/news/bc-tourism-industry-poised-job-growth-more-100000-new-job-openings.

Google Maps. (2014). Sun Peaks, BC [Map]. Retrieved from https://www.google.ca/maps/place/Sun+Peaks,+BC+V0E/@50.8857844,-119.9183388,13z/data=!4m2!3m1!1s0x537fb26bf56c7faf:0x7176e908bc20277b.

Gripton, S. V. (2009). The effects of amenity migration on the resort municipality of whistler and its surrounding environs. *Environments*, 37(1), 59.

Higham, J. E. S., & Hinch, T. (2009). *Sport and tourism: Globalization, mobility and identity*. Amsterdam: Butterworth-Heinemann/Elsevier.

Interior Daily News. (2014, January 13). Attracting more visitors to sun peaks. Retrieved from http://interiordailynews.com/attracting-visitors-sun-peaks/.

Ismert, M., & Petrick, J. F. (2004). Indicators and standards of quality related to seasonal employment in the ski industry. *Journal of Travel Research*, 43(1), 46–56. doi: 10.1177/0047287504265512.

Law, J., Pearce, P., & Woods, B. (1995). Stress and coping in tourist attraction employees. *Tourism Management*, 16(4), 277–284. doi: 10.1016/0261-5177(95)00017-I.

Lundberg, C., Gudmundson, A., & Andersson, T. D. (2009). Herzberg's two-factor theory of work motivation tested empirically on seasonal workers in hospitality and tourism. *Tourism Management*, 30(6), 890–899. doi: 10.1016/j.tourman.2008.12.003.

Mill, R. C. (2008). *Resorts: Management and operation.* (2nd ed.). Hoboken, NJ: John Wiley & Sons, Inc.

Mozafari, M. M., Asli, M. N., & Bejestani, N. G. (2012). The relationship between seasonal employees' job satisfaction and organizational citizenship behavior. *African Journal of Business Management*, 6(20), 6234–6242. doi: 10.5897/AJBM11.2886.

Murphy, P. (2008). *The business of resort management.* (1st ed.). Oxford, England: Elsevier.

Nepal, S., & Jamal, T. (2011). Resort-induced changes in small mountain communities in British Columbia, Canada. *Mountain Research and Development*, 31(2), 89–101. doi: 10.1659/MRD-JOURNAL-D-10-00095.1.

Scherf, K. (2011). *Sun peaks resort: An evolution of dreams.* Sun Peaks, BC: Sun Peaks Resort.

Sun Peaks Mountain Resort Municipality [SPMRM]. (2012). Sustainability development action planning for Sun Peaks Mountain Resort Municipality – Final Report. Sun Peaks, BC: Savage & Assoc. & Westcoast CED.

Sun Peaks Mountain Resort Municipality [SPMRM]. (2013). Sun peaks social sustainability plan. Sun Peaks, BC: Centre for Sustainability Whistler.

Sun Peaks Resort. (1996). *Sun peaks resort at Tod Mountain*. Sun Peaks, BC: Sun Peaks Resort.

Sun Peaks Resort Corporation [SPRC]. (Accessed 2014a, Jan 10). Mountain stats. Retrieved from http://www.sunpeaksresort.com/winter/mountain-stats.

Sun Peaks Resort Corporation [SPRC]. (Accessed 2014b, Jan 10). Golf course information. Retrieved from http://www.sunpeaksresort.com/summer/golf/information.

Sun Peaks Resort Media Centre [SPRMC]. (2017). Recent census shows Sun Peaks as British Columbia's fastest growing incorporated municipality [Press release]. Retrieved from https://www.sunpeaksresort.com/media/new-releases/recent-census-shows-sun-peaks-as-british-columbias-fastest-growing-incorporated.

Thomas, D. F. (2002). The impact of customer service on a resort community. *Journal of Vacation Marketing, 8*(4), 380–390. doi: 10.1177/135676670200800408.

Tuan, Y. (1977). *Space and place: The perspective of experience.* Minneapolis, MN: University of Minnesota Press.

Vaugeois, N., Maher, P., Heeney, E., Rowsell, B., Bence, S., & McCartney, M. (2013, June 21). BC resort community labour market strategic analysis – Final report. Retrieved from https://www.go2hr.ca/sites/default/files/legacy/reports/go2-BC-Resort-Community-Labour-Market-Strategic-Analysis.pdf.

Whistler Housing Authority. (2017). About Whistler Housing Authority. Retrieved from https://whistlerhousing.ca/.

Eva Holmberg, Kaija Lindroth, Mona Vaahtera

Finnish Travellers' Views on the Refugee Crisis in Greece

1 Introduction

Factors such as a more crowded world, urbanisation, greater dependence on technology (Ritchie, 2004), globalisation and hybermobility (Hall, 2010) all contribute to a growing number of crises and disasters. Crises and their impacts on the tourism industry have been extensively discussed in academic research. From 2014, Europe has been highly exposed to a different type of crisis, the 'so-called' refugee crisis in the Mediterranean.

The refugee crisis is a result of an upsurge of asylees, refugees, and economic migrants from the Middle East, South Asia and Africa. The underlying reasons go back to various conflicts and natural disasters in those areas which are some of the poorest parts of the world. Many of the millions of people fleeing from their homes aim to reach Europe with the hope for safety and a better life. One of the main routes for these immigrants in 2014–2015 was the sea route from Turkey to the Greek islands.

The Greek archipelago has always been one of the main destinations for Finns during summer time. The focus of this paper is on finding out how the Finns travelling to the Greek islands reacted to the immigrant situation that exploded during 2015 and 2016. This study covers the situation until May 2016. On 7 March 2016, Turkey and EU signed an agreement stating that all refugees entering EU from Turkey will be sent back to Turkey. The intention of this arrangement was to dramatically reduce the number of refugees trying to enter Europe through Greece (European Commission News, 2016).

2 Crises and Travel Behaviour

The concept of crisis used in different contexts lacks a clear definition, resulting in some confusion of whether a crisis is the same as for instance a disaster, a turning point or a catastrophe (Ritchie, 2009; Pforr & Hosie, 2008). A general definition of a crisis is offered by Laws & Prideaux (2005) stating that a crisis is an unexpected problem seriously disrupting the functioning of an organisation, sector or nation. Various definitions of what a tourism crisis is also exist (Ritchie, 2009; Ritchie, Crotts, Zehrer, & Volsky, 2013; Tse, 2006). Tourism crises usually share the same characteristics with any other crisis. The World Tourism Organisation (1998) defines a tourism crisis as:

> Any unexpected event that affects traveller confidence in a destination and interferes with its ability to continue operating normally

Disaster is a concept often used about the notion of crisis. Sometimes these concepts are used synonymously but many experts (Faulkner, 2001; Ritchie et al., 2013) highlight that a crisis describes a situation where a system is affected by an event which to some extent is self-inflicted, whereas a disaster is something catastrophic of which the system has little control. Thus, a crisis occurs due to lack of management, whereas disasters happen without human involvement (Ritchie et al., 2013; Ritchie, 2004; Faulkner, 2001).

Crises can happen at different levels and their cause can be internal or external to the system, such as an organisation or a destination (Pforr & Hosie, 2008). The scale of the crisis usually varies from minor to major depending on the number of people impacted, costs and duration and they can be classified into different levels such as local, national, regional and international (Henderson, 2007).

Crises in tourism can be divided into the following categories (Pennington-Gray & Pizam, 2011): natural (e.g. tsunamis, earthquakes), health-related crisis (e.g. Sars, bird flu), technological (e.g. airplane crashes, oil spills) and conflict-related (e.g. riots, wars). Moreover, economic crises and their impacts on tourism have been in focus in several studies (e.g. Alegre, Mateo, & Pou, 2013; Okumus, Altnay, & Arasli, 2005). Tourism research has, though, given very little attention to crises having a huge impact on human beings, i.e. the humanitarian crises.

A humanitarian crisis is understood to be a situation where there is an exceptional and generalised threat to human life, health or subsistence. These crises usually appear within the context of an existing situation due to a lack of protection where a series of pre-existent factors (poverty, inequality, and lack of access to basic services) exacerbated by a natural disaster or armed conflict multiply the destructive effects (Francesch et al., 2010).

Why do people travel even if the number of crises seems to increase and the risks for crime, accidents and natural disasters often appear to be bigger overseas than at home? Motivations for travelling can be divided into push and pull factors (Cohen, Prayag, & Moital, 2014). Typical push factors, which are the motivations for travelling, are to escape, to relax, to experience a new culture, for social status and nostalgia (Prayag & Hosany, 2014; Swarbrooke & Horner, 2016). These motives are strongly linked to hedonic consumption (Shaw & Williams, 2004) as consumers tend to look for experiences which maximise their pleasure (Batat & Frochot, 2014). On the other hand, due to the growing interest for ethical consumption a growing number of people are interested in doing good during their leisure time and holidays, which can be seen for instance in the increasing demand for volunteer trips to developing countries (Guttentag, 2012). In the literature related to volunteer tourism, the concept of altruism has been discussed for describing tourists who are focusing on satisfying the needs of others (Butler & Tomasez, 2011).

Pull factors, the factors making a destination attractive, are for instance sun, beaches, cultural heritage and sport possibilities (Prayag & Hosany, 2014). If something negative occurs, such as a terrorist attack, it is likely to influence the attractiveness of the destination until the incident is forgotten (Avrham, 2015). A crisis is thus likely to influence the pull effect. To what extent this will happen is dependent on how potential tourists perceive the risk of something possibly happening to them (Lepp & Gibson, 2003; Wolff & Larsen, 2014; Pennington-Gray et al., 2014). Crises, and the risks related to them, are highly influenced by the media coverage. The influence of the media is likely to have a huge impact on destination image formation (Castelltort & Mäder, 2010).

3 The Refugee Crisis in Greece

Over 19 million people are facing the fact that they need to leave their homes due to war, persecution, oppression and hunger. Tens of thousands more join them every day. A large number attempt to head for Europe (Taub, 2015) and this issue has been constantly highlighted in all European media channels during the past years. Migration as such is not a new phenomenon. People have always been on the move, but today's situation can be called the world's biggest wave of mass-migration since the Second World War (Kingsley, 2015). It has even been called the 'Human tsunami' (Pasquet, 2016).

Why is this situation so critical now? What are the reasons for the problem escalating so acutely? According to Taub (2015) there are two main reasons. The first is the ongoing armed conflicts in the Middle East, sub-Saharan Africa, and elsewhere. This has impacted countries like Syria, Iraq, Afghanistan, Somalia, Eritrea, Libya and Yemen. The biggest crisis has hit Syria, forcing over four million people (1/5th of the population) to flee since the war started in 2011. The second reason seems to be the increasing nationalistic and anti-refugee politics in Western Europe and other prosperous countries. The equation becomes difficult when there are more people than ever needing help, and less willingness from those who could help to do so. At the same time, the refugee camps set up in the neighbouring countries for the fleeing people have not proven a solution, and people have realised that to have a future they need to move on and head for safer and more prosperous areas, i.e. Europe.

The current crisis is impacting all of Europe but Greece is especially affected due to its proximity to the countries experiencing armed conflicts in Afghanistan, Iraq and Syria. The number of people having to flee their homes is shocking as some 11 million out of a population of 18 million are estimated to be on the run. Some 6 million have moved inside Syria and almost 5 million are abroad (Mercycorps, 2016). Table 1 accounts for the refugees of the Syrian Civil War only by the beginning of 2016.

Table 1: Refugees of the Syrian Civil war in Different Countries at the end of 2015[1]

Country	Number of registered refugees by end of 2015 (estimate)
Turkey	2.8 million
Lebanon	1.5 million
Jordan	1.3 million
Germany	0.5 million
Greece	0.5 million

By May 2016, the number of refugees entering Greece exploded to nearly 500,000 and some 55,000 more were expected in May 2016. The route to Greece and Cyprus goes via Turkey, but refugees are also smuggled in from Libya and Alger to Europe. The Dublin Regulation (European Commission Migration and Home Affairs, 2017) requires refugees to stay in the first European country they enter. In many cases this means that they are stuck in Greece or Italy. Stathis Kyriossis, from Doctors without Borders, describes the situation in Greece as follows:

> I have worked in many refugee camps before, in Yemen, Malawi, and Angola but here on the island of Kos, this is the first time in my life that I have seen people so totally abandoned (Taub, 2015).

In the same article by Taub (2015), The Human Rights Watch also supports this bleak view by reporting that Greek reception centres lack food and health care, are overcrowded and unsanitary with inhumane treatment. The main Swedish language newspaper in Finland *Hufvudstadsbladet* highlighted the situation in its issue of 15 April 2016 by comparing the numbers of refugees using sea routes to Europe for ten days only, 1–11 April, to those during the entire year 2015.

---

1   Source: Modified from Wikipedia 2016.

Table 2: Refugee Routes over the Mediterranean[2]

	Refugees arriving over the Mediterranean in 2015	Refugees arriving over the Mediterranean on 1–11 April 2016
Alger to Spain	3 845 /72 casualties	648/ 5 casualties
Libya to Italy	153 842/ 2892 casualties	19 930/345 casualties
Turkey to Greece	853 650/ casualties 806	153 156/375 casualties
Turkey to Cyprus	269/0	27/0

The numbers in Table 2 clearly show that the route via Libya is the most danger-ous, and the one to Greece the most popular until May 2016. The burden on Greece has been huge and the European Union has been trying to find a solution to reduce the number of refugees and migrants to Greece by agreeing on a deal with Turkey. It was decided that for every illegal person sent back to Turkey the European Union will receive one person from the Turkish refugee camps. The pact was sealed on 6 March 2016, and the number of arrivals in Greece has been decreasing since this.

Despite the deal between the European Union and Turkey, boat loads of refu-gees are still arriving at Greek islands, for example Chios and Lesbos, during Spring 2016. Greek officials have been asking for help to guarantee a swift pro-cessing of the documents of these possible asylum seekers. Finland is one of the countries that agreed to help Greece by sending policemen and immigration experts to Greece in addition to material assistance (Hufvudstadsbladet, 2016).

4 Tourism in Greece

As a destination, Greece, and especially its archipelago has been popular among tourists for a long time, so also among Finnish travellers as seen in Figure 1. As a country, Greece is the 6th most popular destination for Finns and the number of trips even increased slightly despite the refugee crisis from 203,000 trips in 2014 to 237,000 in 2015 (Statistics Finland, 2016).

Greece has faced an economic crisis for several years. Tourism is one of the few industries in Greece which is doing well, and the main cash earner in the country. Tourism accounts for 17–20% of the gross domestic product (GDP), and employs one in five people, according to the Association of Greek Tourism Enterprises (SETE). The massive refugee crises cast a shadow on the booming industry in 2015, and especially the Greek islands have felt the impact of the

---

2   Source: Karlsson, 2016.

human catastrophe with roots far outside the borders of Greece. It is only natural that locals and officials are worried about the impacts of the refugee crisis on their main industry (Nenov, 2015). Due to their geographical location, some of the Greek islands such as Lesvos and Kos have been more affected than others by the refugee crisis (Leadbeater, 2016). It is difficult for the refugees to independently move on from the islands to mainland Greece.

Figure 1: Map of Greece[3]

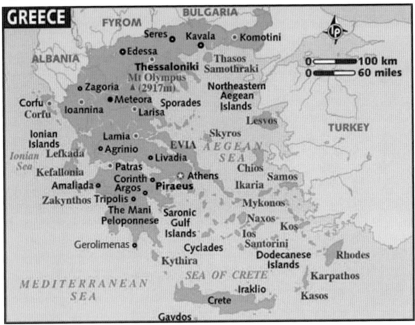

As a result of this crisis, the Greek tourism industry faced a massive decrease in bookings, and many cruises were cancelled. Some airlines even had to change their routes to avoid the affected destinations. The islands faced different situations. Lesbos, the third largest of the Greek islands, suffered the most with bookings decreasing by 90% compared to the previous season, whereas bookings at Kos plummeted by 40%. Lesbos with its 80,000–90,000 year-round inhabitants became the centre of the crisis with some 25,000 refugees in 2015. In February

---

3   Source: LonelyPlanet, 2017.

2016, the arrival numbers were 30,000. The island was unable to handle the situation alone (Tourism Review, 2016).

Some hotels on Lesbos had cancellations, and had to close their doors earlier than normal in 2015. There was also worry about 2016 as repeat customers had indicated that they will wait for things to ease up before returning. The reactions of both the locals and tourists who are on the island have been two-fold; some are complaining whilst some are helping the refugees (Hattam, 2015) The quotes below depict the viewpoints of tourists and locals (Hattam, 2015, p. 3):

> It is very sad. It goes through my heart for those people and the children who are hungry. On the other hand, it's my vacation and that's not nice to see (Tourist)
> There are hundreds of people arriving. Soon it won't be manageable (Local)
> The summer will pass and the damage to the country will be huge (Local)
> Most tourists see them with compassion, with a desire to help if they can (Local)

This situation also has an upside. Normally Lesbos has one main tourist season. However, in 2015 some of the hoteliers and travel agencies experienced a second season, thanks to the crisis. Hotels stayed open after the holiday season to accommodate non-governmental organisations (NGOs), volunteers and journalists, and travel agencies were selling ferry tickets to refugees who wanted to continue their journey to Athens (Hattam, 2015).

As the EU and the Greek government were slow in reacting, many local Greeks engaged themselves in doing what they could to help migrants. Many of them are descendants of migrants themselves, up to 60%, mainly from Turkey, and they understand the misery of the refugees. Locals, tourists, and expats joined forces to feed the new arrivals. However, driving them to the capital from where they could continue their journey is against the law, and they could be prosecuted for doing this. One of the locals told the media the following:

> I've stopped remembering names. I've stopped asking stories. It's just too hard, says an Australian residing on Lesbos who has set up a preliminary campsite behind her restaurant (Kingsley, 2015).

However, the supporters of the Greece's far-right party see the situation differently; they would like to close the borders as shown by the following statement:

> We will do everything we can to protect the Greek homeland against immigrants (Kingsley, 2015).

At the world's largest tourism fair, ITB Berlin 2016, the Greek Tourism Minister Elena Kountoura was optimistic about tourism to Greece. She indicated that

> We believe that 2016 will be even better than last year because if there were some problems last year on some islands, there is now a return to stability (Pasquet, 2016).

Also, according to protothema.gr, Greece's No. 1 news site and best-selling Sunday newspaper, tourism will experience a 6% growth in 2016. The head of tourist association SETE was quoted saying to *Reuters* that direct tourism earnings were likely to grow by 5.6% to 15 billion Euros in 2016 (Nenov, 2015). In *the Guardian* (Amin, 2016) Taleb Rifai, Secretary General of the UN's World Tourism Organisation stated

> The stories showing villagers hosting refugees, providing food and shelter to refugees, are very good opportunities to attract tourists.

Even if the crisis continues, Greece is counting on 27 million tourists in 2016, a record number. Greeks believe this is possible because Greece has a strong tourism brand. One of the reasons for Greece being such a popular destination is the genuine hospitality of the locals. During the ongoing crisis, this characteristic of the Greeks has been in great demand. When the official parties of the problem, the European Union and the Greek government failed to act, the locals acted pragmatically and in a solution-oriented way by organising accommodation, catering, and clothes supplies. The English-language newspaper *Athens Daily* is reported stating

> There is a silver lining for the tourism sector: some believe Greece's reputation for offering warm hospitality will be bolstered by the crisis (Amin, 2016).

Kingsley (2015) tells many stories about locals who have taken the initiative to show their famous hospitality, among them Andreotis, a retired policeman, himself a descendant of migrants. He went to town centre with a megaphone and called for donations. Kingsley (2015) states

> within 10 minutes there were four cars of supplies.

5 Methods

This study was conducted as a case study to gain a deeper understanding of how Finnish travellers perceived the Greek archipelago as a destination during the worst phase of the refugee crisis in 2015 and the beginning of 2016. A Case study is a research approach stressing the need for deep and detailed knowledge about certain phenomenon and especially suitable when the main research questions starts with 'how' and 'why' (Ojasalo, Moilanen, & Ritalahti, 2014; Yin, 2009). To acquire this deep knowledge, this study relies on three different data collection methods: a survey, five in-depth interviews conducted in Spring 2016 and a content analysis of the main Finnish discussion forum, Suomi24.

6 Results

The outcome of all the three different research methods points in the same direction: the pull factors of the all-time favourite destination of Finns seem to outweigh the incidents of the refugee crisis. The Finnish travellers were not really worried about the situation, did not always connect it with their holiday destinations and mainly showed interest in guaranteeing their own well-being so they could enjoy the sun, typical holiday activities and the local culinary delights. In the following section, the main results from the different studies will be presented in more detail.

6.1 Survey

The survey was conducted in the Spring of 2016 and focused on the refugee crisis especially in the Greek archipelago. The sample was rather low, only 109 respondents, but it can give some insights into what Finnish travellers especially those under 35 were thinking about the Greek archipelago as a destination at a time when Finnish media was reporting daily about the situation. Of the respondents, 73% were females, 27% males, and 78% were under 35 years old. Of the sample, 95% travel abroad at least once a year, and almost 45% three times or more. Most of the respondents were following the refugee situation in Greek archipelago by reading the newspapers and from TV, but around 10% answered that they were not following the crisis at all (Vaahtera, 2016).

Figure 2: Word Cloud of Associations of Greek Archipelago

arkkitehtuuri ateena aurinko aurinkoa aurinkoinen edullinen ensimmäiset halpa
hiekkarannat hienot hinnat hintataso historia hyvää ihanat ihmiset ihmisiä ilmasto
kauniit kaunis keväisin kirkas kohde kohtuuttoman koralli kreeta kreikan
kreikkalainen kriisi kulttuuri kuuma lapsiperheet lomailla lomakohde luonto lämmin
lämpö maisemat maisemia matkustaa monipuolinen muinaiset mutta oliivit paikka
pakettimatkat pakolaiset paljon palvelu pienet purjehdusmahdollisuudet rannat ranta
rantaloma rauhallinen rentoutuminen rodos ruoka ruokaa ruokakulttuuri saaret silti
sininen taloja talot todella turisteja turistien turistikohde turistirysä turistit
turkoosi turkoosit turvallinen upeat upeita valkoiset valkoisia vettä ystävälliset

Most respondents (75%) were prepared to travel to Greek islands during the summer season of 2016, whereas 25% said no, most of these being persons who belong to the group of respondents travelling abroad less regularly. The answers to the open-ended question 'describe Greek archipelago as a destination' are summarised in the word cloud in Figure 2. The most mentioned words were food (ruoka), sun (aurinko), landscapes (maisemat) and warm (lämmin).

Table 3: Perceptions of Greek Archipelago

	Completely disagree	Disagree	Agree	Strongly agree	Can't say
Afraid that refugees would rob me	32%	32%	25%	4%	7%
Afraid that refugees would spread epidemics	56%	19%	9%	5%	11%
Booking by a tour operator due to safety reasons	43%	25%	20%	5%	7%
Would buy food and drinks for the refugees at the destination	39%	16%	18%	5%	22%
Would buy food and drinks for the refugees already in Finland	44%	24%	16%	5%	12%
Would choose an island with no refugees	9%	22%	45%	18%	6%
Greek archipelago is less attractive as destination due to all people drowned	61%	20%	6%	2%	11%
Greek archipelago is as attractive as destination as before	5%	14%	39%	38%	5%

Table 3 shows that some of the respondents had very little concerns when it came to travelling to Greek archipelago during the time the refugee crisis were at its worst. More than 60% said that they have no worries about refugees robbing them or about refugees spreading pandemics. Since most did not see any risks with the refugees being around they would book their trip without relying on the safety established tour operators could offer. The people participating in the survey showed very little interest in altruism, almost 70% said that they would not buy products for the refugees in Finland whereas 55% stated that they would not buy anything for the refugees at the destination. The pull of Greek archipelago was, though, affected by the crisis, for instance more than 60% would choose an island in Greece where the refugee crisis would not be seen. Moreover, even if there was a lot of discussion in media about the refugees drowning in the Mediterranean during Spring 2016, the participants did not relate this as something negatively influencing the attractiveness of Greek archipelago as a destination. Therefore, the Greek archipelago was still highly appreciated as a destination, almost 80% of the respondents in the survey perceived the Greek archipelago as attractive as before even at the time when the refugee crisis was discussed daily in media.

6.2 Interviews

To better understand how the refugee crisis was perceived by travellers living in Finland, interviews were carried out in May and June 2016. These informants were found through a Facebook posting at Haaga-Helia Porvoo Campus. This message looked for people who had either been on holiday in Greece after the break-through of the crisis, or who were planning to go soon. A total of four individuals responded (see Table 4), and the selection of informants was extended by also interviewing a former student working within tourism industry in Greece. The interviews conducted were aimed at free discussions. Since all respondents had different backgrounds, motives, and intentions, no interview guide was prepared in advance.

Table 4: Personal Interviews in May and June 2016

	Nationality	Status	Greek location	Role
Respondent 1	Greek-Finnish	Student	Rhodos 2015 Athens, Piraeus, July–August 2016	Local
Respondent 2	Finnish	Student	Kos, April 2016	Tourist
Respondent 3	Finnish- in Greece	Sales Executive	Kos, May 2016	Work
Respondent 4	Finnish	Lecturer	Lesbos, Tilos, etc. 2015, 2016	Tourist
Respondent 5	Russian	Student	Thessaloniki, June 2016	Work

The first theme discussed during the interviews was the impact of refugee crisis on the overall travel behaviour of Finns. The respondents agreed upon the Greek archipelago being as popular as before despite the crisis. This is supported by the following statements:

I have not heard of Finns who would have cancelled their trips (Respondent 1)

To some, however, the refugee crisis was having an impact on their travel behaviour. Respondent 3 stressed that sales for the summer season were slow in Winter 2015, and it seemed like there were still people who did not understand that there were no longer any refugees on Kos. When it came to the respondents' own decision making and travel behavior it seems like some were not even aware of the refugee crisis as:

> The decision to travel to Kos was taken in January, following a recommendation of friends… I had no idea of refugees (Respondent 2)

The respondents had different opinions of the issue on whether tourists still had a need to get information about the situation. For instance, respondents 1 and 3, both having experiences from working in the hospitality sector in the Greek archipelago, highlighted the following:

> In 2015 a lot of our customers contacted us to inquire whether it was safe to travel here (Respondent 3)

> I have not been consulted as whether to go or not (Respondent 1)

The respondents also stressed that as a tourist you cannot always be afraid since many of those living in the tourist destinations get their daily bread from tourism. On the other hand, some of the respondents met with inquiries from friends and relatives who were wondering whether a holiday in the Greek archipelago really could be enjoyable:

> When friends heard where we are going they started to question our choice of destination, and were wondering why we wanted to go there (Respondent 2)

Why should tourists visit a place like the Greek archipelago if the news about the area is mostly negative? The respondents agreed that tourists should go there anyway, if not for other reasons but for supporting the locals in an area suffering from an economic downturn.

> To Finnish tourists: don't worry about the situation…don't change your plans…they are all people (Respondent 1)

> I don't think one can be afraid and avoid these places as that would leave locals without their daily bread (Respondent 2)

When it comes to the actual experiences at the destination, the situation in the Greek archipelago was very different in summer 2015 compared to spring 2016 when the agreement with Turkey had been signed. The big number of refugees entering the archipelago from Turkey during summer 2015 was visible for tourists and people working in the hospitality industry. As stated for a respondent living in Kos and the respondent visiting Lesbos:

> Personally, I have not been affected but last year I saw refugees by the police station and on the road (Respondent 3)

> Last summer on Lesbos I saw a lot of refugees, and heard from locals that some 600 arrived every day (Respondent 4)

One respondent got very close to the refugee crisis when they visited the village Tilos from where the Turkish shore can be seen. The respondent described the experience in the following way:

> We saw a boat approaching but it did not take the refugees all the way to the shore but they had to jump off the boat…even pregnant women. Locals arrested the captain and alarmed the police. It did not seem frightening. Locals were extremely helpful. They brought clothes and food, and also the local vicar was running around to help them. (Respondent 4)

For some of the tourists the overall economic crisis in 2015 and the lack of cash in ATMs was a bigger concern than the refugees as depicted below.

> Our customers at hotel did not talk about it (refugees) but they talked about the economic situation: ATMs not working, lack of cash (Respondent 1)

In Spring 2016, the experiences of those who visited the area were positive. There seemed to be a strong belief that everything would be fine during the main summer season:

> Everything seemed normal, the season was just starting when we visited and locals seemed confident that tourists would show up, when we arrived most refugees were gone (Respondent 2)

On the other hand, some refugees were still around since they were unable to book a ferry to mainland Greece. One respondent said for instance:

> We were not scared but a little troubled…My boyfriend was more concerned than me looking around and commenting on people we saw, wondering whether they were refugees…He stressed about the situation a little (Respondent 2)

Safety concerns were not influencing the respondents' life in the destination. Some respondents claimed that the relatives back home were more worried than themselves for instance:

> My mother was worried and my friends first refused to join the trip but had later to give in (Respondent 4)

> At home elderly people who watch the news were concerned about our safety (Respondent 2)

The respondents had diverse thoughts about their own willingness to help. Some of the respondents said that they would consider helping the refugees by doing catering, but others did not see volunteering as anything for them. The respondents' divergent views are:

I feel for the refugees as their situation is helpless and I could consider working as a volunteer, like helping with food and accommodation (Respondent 4)

We talked about the situation between us but did not consider helping or doing anything about it (Respondent 2)

6.3 Online Content Analysis

An online content analysis was conducted in June 2016 focusing mainly of the main discussion forum on the Internet, Suomi24.fi. The analysed discussions were all related to one of the main topics for discussions, 'tourism' http://keskustelu.suomi24.fi/matkailu where it is possible to discuss tourism from different angles such as the holiday of your dreams, flying, and destinations. The discussion related to destinations and the subcategory Europe and thereafter Greece was chosen for this study. Only posts comprising a comment given between 1 June 2015 and 3 June 2016 were analysed.

Altogether, the discussion forum Greece as a destination comprised 458 different posts during the time period. After going through the posts, the following main themes were discussed, hotels, where to find services and activities (where to watch ice-hockey, best bars), transport, refugees, recommendations (e.g. Parga vs Samos) and miscellaneous (e.g. weather, price level, looking for someone to travel with).

Table 5 summarises the number of posts in the different categories. As can be seen Finnish people active in this forum were mostly interested in getting information about hotels at the time when they are planning to book or have already booked their holiday. A typical post was 'tell me about your experiences from the hotel Mediterranean in Rhodes' (Suomi24, 2016a).

Table 5: Summary of Posts related to Greece as a Destination on www.suomi24.fi

Discussion themes	Number of discussions	Share of discussions
Hotels	178	39%
Miscellaneous (weather, activities, etc.)	131	29%
Recommendations	69	15%
Services	38	8%
Transport	26	6%
Refugees	16	3%
Total	458	100%

Only 3% of the discussions were related to the refugee crisis in Greece. Typical discussions related to the crisis started like this:

> Has the coziness of Crete been influenced by the crisis, can the tourists enjoy their holidays as before? (Suomi24, 2016b)

> Do you avoid Kos as a destination right now? (Suomi24, 2016c)

All in all, the same themes arose in all data, the survey, the interviews and the content analysis, and Figure 3 summarises these findings. It can be stated that the Greek archipelago, despite the discussions about the refugee crisis in both digital and traditional media, still was perceived as a fairly attractive and safe destination. The only exceptions seemed to be some islands in the Eastern part of the archipelago.

Figure 3: Summary of Findings

7 Discussion

The results of this study demonstrated that the pull factors of the Greek archipelago in the minds of Finnish travellers were not largely influenced by the worst phase of the refugee crisis during 2015 and beginning of 2016. It is a fact, though, that the only tour operator in Finland, Aurinkomatkat (Suntours) having Lesbos on its list for summer season 2016 did not manage to sell trips there resulting in a complete withdrawal of the island during that season (Aren, 2016). Thus, it is obvious that many tourists followed the news and were concerned about not being able to spend a normal holiday at the island that was among those suffering most from the crisis. Instead, these holidaymakers choose other Greek destinations such as Korfu and Parga.

Even if not specifically studied here it seems obvious that the main push factors for a holiday in the Greek archipelago were to escape, relax, and enjoy the sun and the beaches. Thus, the hedonic experiences were in focus when the holiday in the Greek archipelago was considered, even if the activities of locals helping refugees were highlighted in media. Finnish travellers seem, based on this study, not to be very altruistic during their holidays, even if there are people at the destination suffering from thirst, hunger and lack of shelter. Bremner (2016) highlights in her blog the dichotomy of a location that is sold as one's dream holiday but at the same time is a place for dark human tragedy. Is it acceptable that tourists from the rich countries in the EU just choose to close their eyes, or should they be raised to understand and support people suffering during a crisis such as the one in Greece before Turkey agreed upon closing the border?

Whereas Bali bombings reduced the number of tourists visiting the destination by 40% (Hajibaba, Gretzel, Leish, & Dolnicar, 2015), the attractiveness of many Greek islands did not decrease even though the word 'crisis' was portrayed by the media on a weekly basis at a minimum. The perception of risk seems to be the key here. Some crises are perceived as more dangerous for the traveller, and a humanitarian crisis like the refugee crisis did not, according to this study, influence the safety situation in the region. Even if Hajibaba et al. (2015) highlight that some tourists are more risk-resistant than others, normal people travelling on charter holidays did not connect the refugees to risk for robbery or pandemics.

8 Conclusion

The aim of this study was to study the perception of Finnish holidaymakers towards the Greek islands, one of Finns all-time favourite destinations, during the refugee crisis of 2015–2016. The first part of the study, the survey, shows clearly that those participating were not afraid of the refugees as such, but they would still choose a destination in the area where no refugees would be around. Moreover, very few had been thinking about the possibility that they could support the refugees by giving them something to eat or drink, or provide them with clothes. In all, the destination was perceived as attractive as it has always been.

Based on the content analysis it seems like most Finnish travellers, even during the most severe time with hundreds of refugees coming to the different Greek islands daily and media following the situation intensively, did not really connect the crisis to their holiday destination. These travellers were more concerned by practical issues such as the location of the chosen hotel, and how to get from one location to another during the holiday.

Summarising the findings from the interviews it can be stated that the refugee crisis was both acknowledged and closely experienced by the respondents. Still, it had rather limited impact on their holiday decision making and life at the destination. Safety issues were of limited concern. Some of the respondents would consider helping the refugees by proving food, but no-one had taken any action to really help the refugees on spot.

The outcome of all the three methods used points in the same direction, Finnish holidaymakers did not see the refugee crisis in Greece as their crisis. They were mostly concerned about their own travels and making the most of them without external disturbances. They did not really make a connection between what happened on the Greek islands, and the places they saw in their travel brochures. The news served daily by the media did not really worry them either, at least not enough to make them take any action for the victims of the crisis.

However, it may be wrong to blame individual citizens for the inability to react when also organisations geared towards acting in crisis situations failed to do so such as the European Union, and the National Governments. The only ones who really took concrete measures were the local Greeks whose everyday lives were suddenly shaken by boatloads of refugees.

It is very human for holidaymakers from a Nordic country like Finland to hunger for food, sun, beautiful landscape, warm weather, and the hospitality of destinations like the Greek islands, and have those as the focus of the long-awaited holiday. It seems to take more than a refugee crisis to alter that.

References

Alegre, J., Mateo, S., & Pou, L. (2013). Tourism participation and expenditure by Spanish households: The effects of the economic crisis and unemployment. *Tourism Management*, 40, 37–49.

Amin, L. (2016). Lesbos: A Greek island in limbo over tourism, refugees – and itsfuture. *The Guardian*, 24 March 2016.

Aren, C. (2016). Situation in Greece from the perspective of Suntours. Interview by Eva Holmberg, 2016-04-03.

Avrham, E. (2015). Destination image repair during crisis: Attracting tourism during the Arab Spring uprisings. *Tourism Management*, 42, 224–232.

Batat, W., & Frochot, I. (2014). Towards an experiential approach in tourism studies. In S. McCabe (Ed.), *The Routledge handbook of tourism marketing* (pp. 101–129). London, England: Routledge.

Bremner, C. (2016). European travel in turmoil: Time to face up to the humanitarian crisis. Retrieved January 22, 2017 from http://blog.euromonitor.com/2016/04/european-travel-in-turmoil-time-to-face-up-to-the-humanitarian-crisis.html.

64 Eva Holmberg, Kaija Lindroth, Mona Vaahtera

Butler, B., & Tomasez, S. (2011). Volunteer tourism: Altruism, empathy or self enhancement? Retrieved January 17, 2017 from https://pure.strath.ac.uk/portal/files/25584646/Problems_in_tourism_Volunteer_Touris m_Altruism_Empathy_or_self_enhancement.pdf.

Castelltort, M., & Mäder, G. (2010). Press media coverage effects on destinations – A Monetary-Public Value (MPV) analysis. *Tourism Management*, 31, 724–738.

Cohen, S. A., Prayag, G., & Moital, M. (2014). Consumer Behaviour in Tourism. *Current Issues in Tourism*, 17(10), 872–909.

European Commission Migration and Home Affairs. (2017). Country responsible for asylum application. Retrieved January 11, 2017 from https://ec.europa.eu/home-affairs/what-we-do/policies/asylum/examination-of-applicants_en.

European Commission News. (2016). EU and Turkey agree on European response to refugee crisis. Retrieved January 25, 2017 from http://ec.europa.eu/news/2016/03/20160319_en.htm.

Faulkner, B. (2001). Towards a framework for tourism disaster management. *Tourism Management*, 22, 135–147.

Francesch, M. C., Armengol V. F., Amado, P. G., Chevalier M. P., Aspa, J. M. R., García, J. U., Arestizábal, P. M., Arino A. V., & Arino, M. V. (2010). Alert 2010! Report on conflicts, human rights and peace building. Retrieved January 17, 2017 from http://escolapau.uab.cat/img/programas/alerta/alerta/alerta10i.pdf.

Guttentag, D. (2012). Volunteer tourism – as good as it seems. In T. V. Sing (Ed.), *Critical debates in tourism* (pp. 181–188). Bristol, England: Channel View.

Hajibaba, H., Gretzel, U., Leish, F., & Dolnicar, S. (2015). Crisis-resistant tourists. *Annals of Tourism Research*, 52, 46–60.

Hall, M. (2010). Crisis events in tourism: Subjects of crisis in tourism. *Current Issues in Tourism*, 13, 401–417.

Hattam, J. (2015). Greek islands known for tourism continue to feel impact of refugee crisis. *Skift*. 16 November 2015. Retrieved May 28, 2016 from https://skift.com/2015/11/16/greek-islands-known-for-tourism-continue-to-feel-impact-of-refugee-crisis/.

Henderson, J. C. (2007). *Tourism crises: causes, consequences and management*. Oxford, England: Elsevier.

Hufvudstadsbladet. (2016). *Många tar fortfarande båten till Grekland*. 22 March, p. 11.

Karlsson, S. (2016). Den farliga Libyenrutten lockar allt fler igen. April 2016. *Hufvudstadsbladet*. Helsinki, Finland, pp. 12–13.

Kingsley, P. (2015). Greek island refugee crisis: Local people and tourists rally round migrants. *The Guardian*, 9 July.

Laws, E., & Prideaux, B. (2005). Crisis management: A suggested typology. *Journal of Travel and Tourism Marketing*, 19(2/3), 1–8.

Leadbeater, C. (2016). Which Greek islands are affected by the refugee crisis? Retrieved January 17, 2017 from http://www.telegraph.co.uk/travel/destinations/europe/greece/articles/greek-islands-affected-by-refugee-crisis/.

Lepp, A., & Gibson, H. (2003). Tourist roles, perceived risk and international tourism. *Annals of Tourism Research*, 30(3), 606–624.

LonelyPlanet. (2017). Map of Greece. Retrieved January 30, 2017 from http://www.lonelyplanet.com/maps/europe/greece/.

Mercycorps. (2016). Quick facts: What you need to know about the Syria crisis. Retrieved May 21, 2016 from http://www.mercycorps.org/tags/syriacrisis.

Nenov, S. (2015). Greek tourism growth hinges on bailout review, refugee crisis: Tourism association. *Reuters* 17 August 2015. Retrieved May 28, 2016 from http://www.reuters.com/article/us-eurozone-greece-tourism.

Okumus, F., Altnay, A., & Arasli, A. (2005). The impact of Turkey's economic crisis of February 2001 on the tourism industry in Northern Cyprus. *Tourism Management*, 26(1), 95–104.

Ojasalo, K., Moilanen, T., & Ritalahti, J. (2014). *Kehittämistyönmenetelmät-Uudenlaista osaamista liiketoimintaan*. Helsinki, Finland: Sanoma Pro.

Pasquet, Y. (2016). Greece tourism insists on sunny outlook amid refugee crisis. *Yahoo*, 11 March 2016. Retrieved May 28, 2016 from https://www.yahoo.com/news/greece-tourism-insists-sunny-outlook-amid-refugee-crisis-065019344.html?ref=gs.

Pennington-Gray, L., & Pizam, A. (2011). Destination Crisis Management. In Y. Wang & A. Pizam (Eds). *Tourism destination marketing and management: collaborative strategies* (pp. 314–322). Wallingford: CABI.

Pennington-Gray, L., Schroeder, A., Wu, B., Donohoe, H., & Cahyanto, I. (2014). Travelers' perceptions of crisis preparedness certification in the United States. *Journal of Travel Research*, 53(3), 353–365.

Pforr, C., & Hosie, P. J. (2008). Crisis management in tourism. *Journal of Travel & Tourism Marketing*, 23, 249–264.

Prayag, G., & Hosany, S. (2014). When Middle East meets West: Understanding the motives and perceptions of young tourists from United Arab Emirates. *Tourism Management*, 20, 35–45.

Protothema. (2016). Refugee crisis threatens Greek tourism. Retrieved May 28, 2016 from http://en.protothema.gr/refugee-crisis-threatens-greek-tourism/.

Ritchie, B. W. (2004). Chaos, crises and disasters: A strategic approach to crisis management in the tourism industry. *Tourism Management*, 5, 669–683.

Ritchie, B. W. (2009). *Crisis and disaster management for tourism*. Bristol, England: Channel View Publications.

Ritchie, B. W., Crotts, J. C., Zehrer, A., & Volvsky, G. T. (2013). Understanding the effects of tourism crisis. *Journal of Travel Research*, 51(19), 12–25.

Shaw, G. & Williams, A. (2004). *Tourism and tourism spaces*. London, England: Sage.

Statistics Finland. (2016). Suomalaisten matkailu. Retrieved February 6, 2017, from http://tilastokeskus.fi/til/smat/index.html.

Suomi 24.fi. (2016a). Hotelli Mediterranean? Retrieved January 30, 2017 from http://keskustelu.suomi24.fi/t/13577042/hotelli-mediterranean.

Suomi 24.fi. (2016b). Kreetan pakolaiset, onko viihtyvyys kärsinyt? Retrieved January 30, 2017 from http://keskustelu.suomi24.fi/t/13980285/kreetan-pakolaiset-onko-viihtyvyys-karsinyt.

Suomi 24.fi. (2016c). Kokemuksia Kos saaresta tällä viikolla? Retrieved January 30, 2017 from http://keskustelu.suomi24.fi/t/13634329/kokemuksia-kos-saaresta-talla-viikolla.

Swarbrooke, J., & Horner, S. (2016). *Consumer behaviour in tourism*. Oxford, England: Elsevier.

Taub, A. (2015). Europe's refugee crisis explained. Retrieved May 28, 2016, from http://www.vox.com/2015/9/5/9265501/refugee-crisis-europe-syria.

Tse, T. S. M. (2006). Crises management. In D. Buhalis & C. Costa (Eds.) *Tourism management dynamics – trends, management and tools* (pp. 28–38), Amsterdam, the Netherlands: Elsevier.

Tourism Review. (2016). Tourism in Greece suffers due to refugee crisis. Retrieved May 28, 2016 from http://www.tourism-review.com/tourism-in-greece-hit-by-refugee-crisis-news4919.

Vaahtera, M. (2016). Pakolaiskriisin vaikutus suomalaisten innostukseen matkustaa Kreikan saaristoon. Retrieved July 10, 2017 from http://www.theseus.fi/handle/10024/111679.

Wikipedia. (2016). Refugees of Syrian Civil War. Retrieved May 28, 2016 from https://en.wikipedia.org/wiki/Refugees_of_the_Syrian_Civil_War.

Wolff, K., & Larsen, S. (2014). Can terrorism make us feel safe? Risk perception and worries before and after the July 22nd attacks. *Annals of Tourism Research*, 44, 200–209.

World Tourism Organisation. (1998). *Handbook on natural disaster reduction in tourist areas*. Madrid, Spain: UNWTO.

Yahoo. (2015). Greeks worry about impact of refugee crisis on tourism. Retrieved May 28, 2016 from https://www.yahoo.com/news/greeks-worry-impact-refu gee-crisis-tourism-111556670.html?ref=gs.

Yin, R. K. (2009). *Case study research – design and practices*. Thousand Oaks, CA, USA: Sage.

Eva Holmberg, Jarmo Ritalahti

The Constructive Approach in Tourism Research

1 Introduction

The traditional starting point of scientific research, philosophy of sciences, and dividing research methods into quantitative and qualitative is not always sufficient for research conducted at Universities of Applied Sciences. In applied research and development projects, the starting point is to reflect upon the end product and/or the expected results together with the commissioner of the project. When a preliminary understanding of what needs to be done exists, a suitable research approach can be chosen. The main approaches identified for development projects are case study research, action research, and constructive research (Ojasalo, Moilanen, & Ritalahti, 2014). This chapter focuses on how constructive research can be used in projects commissioned by stakeholders of the tourism and hospitality industry. The projects presented at the end of this chapter exemplify constructive research conducted in tourism programmes at the Finnish University of Applied Sciences.

2 Practices for Research Aiming at Development

Scientific research has long roots at universities around Europe. At universities, research conducted in social sciences have been strongly influenced firstly by positivistic thinking but later also hermeneutics and interpretive methods (Silvermann, 2013). Positivism is generally the starting point for quantitative research. Quantitative research is deterministic, starting from producing hypothesis, discussing how they will be verified, testing and finally validating or modifying the hypotheses based on the results of the research, whereas in interpretative research the social world is understood by listening to people. Thus, discussions and interviews are key activities in the latter research strategy (Goodson & Phillimore, 2004).

In research aimed at practical development, systematic data collection is taking place in order to improve existing practices or create new ways of working. In this context, the benefits of conducting research are related to the possibility of developing a more extensive understanding of the current situation. Thereby, the researcher(s) are able to argue for suggested improvements based on results presented to the commissioning organisation (Suvanto, 2014; Ojasalo et al., 2014). It is therefore crucial that all development work proceeds in a systematic, analytical and critical way (Ojasalo et al., 2014). A simplified process is shown in Figure 1.

Figure 1: A Process for Development Work[1]

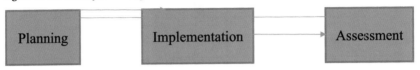

The starting point in all development work is identifying the project and the preliminary objectives of the work. Thus, instead of starting from the philosophy of science as in scientific research, in practical research, it is the end product and project objectives that influence how the development work is implemented. The next step in the development process is to study the project environment closer and to take a look at literature related to the aims of the project. After this, the aims of the project are further specified, and then the theoretical framework and the research approach is chosen. The final steps are to implement, disseminate and assess the project. Ojasalo et al. (2014) identify three main research approaches for project implementation: action research (see, for example, Tripp, 2005; Kananen, 2013), case study research (see, for example, Yin, 2013; Kananen, 2013), and constructive research. Constructive research is the most uncommon and unknown approach.

3 Constructive Research

Constructive research is a research approach where the focus is on real-life problem solving and innovations. The outcome of a project implemented with this approach, the construct, is supposed to be something new and useful for the commissioning organisation (Luukka, 2006). Compared to the more descriptive case study research (e.g. Yin, 2013) and action-oriented action research (e.g. Tripp, 2005), a research and development project done with a constructive approach is more directed towards real-life solutions (Figure 2). Constructive research was first introduced by the three Finnish researchers Kasanen, Lukka, & Siitonen (1993) in an article presenting the approach as a method for doing research for developing new systems for management accounting. These researchers argued that instead of analysing descriptive statistics, there is a need for research aiming at developing something usable like models and plans for companies.

---

1   Source: Ojasalo et al., 2014, p. 23.

An example of a constructive research project is the development of Haaga-Helia University of Applied Sciences, Porvoo Campus. The aim of the curriculum and development project was to enhance learning in and for the future, fulfil the expectations from the stakeholders on the new campus, and encourage academic staff to participate in the development of something new. The goal of the project was to produce new educational models in higher education (Ritalahti, 2015). Ojasalo et al. (2014) highlight education material, budget systems and new books as other possible products in a constructive research and development project.

Figure 2: Approaches in Research and Development Work[2]

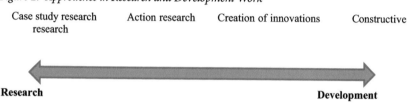

As stated earlier, the objective of constructive research is to produce novel solutions to practically and theoretically relevant real-life commissions. A constructive research project shares some features with innovation work and service design, but the final product is not necessarily an innovation or service development (Ojasalo et al., 2014). Luukka (2006) discusses the main elements of the constructive research that are presented in Figure 3. The starting point is always a practical problem. The aim is to come up with an innovation (construct) that would solve the problem. The construct is developed through knowledge sharing between different stakeholders of the project and then tested in practice by the researcher. Finally, it is important that the development project has some theoretical contribution as well.

As in all other research approaches, it is recommended that a project based on constructive research follows a standardised process. The typical process of scientific constructive research according to Luukka (2006) is

1. Finding a practical problem to solve which also is theoretically important
2. Finding out whether a long-term project with the target organisation is possible
3. Learning more about the practical and theoretical context of the project
4. Innovation of a model for solving the problem that also has a theoretical contribution

2   Source: Ojasalo et al., 2014, p. 36.

5. Implementation of the model and testing of its functionality
6. Discussion of where the model could work
7. Identifying and discussing the theoretical contribution.

Figure 3: Main Elements of Constructive Research[3]

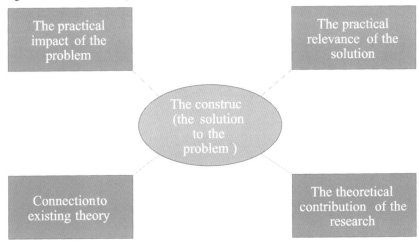

In an applied context, where the focus is on practical problem solving, it can be argued that the theoretical contribution is less important. Crucial is instead the new solution developed that offers a novel solution and new knowledge for the commissioning organisation. In the best cases, a novel solution can be used also in other contexts than in the one it was originally developed for. What is important during the research process is that data of end-users is collected and analysed along the development process. Moreover, the communication between the commissioner of the project and the researcher is very important during the entire process (Ojasalo et al., 2014). Finally, to fulfil all the features of constructive research, the developed construct should be taken into use by the commissioning organisation when the project is finished.

4 Data Collection in Constructive Research

The strategies for data collection in the constructive research are of different kinds, because the aim is to create something new, with all possible information channels

---

3   Source: modified from Luukka, 2006, p. 113.

considered. The recommended data collection strategies are interviews, surveys, observation, crowdsourcing, collaborative data collection and auto-ethnography. It is important to keep in mind the needs of the end-users in order to create something valuable and useful for them. Brainstorming and other workshops could also be organised as well (Ojasalo et al., 2014).

4.1 Interviews

Interviews as a data collection method can be divided into two main groups. Firstly, interviews are either individual interviews or focus groups, and secondly interviews can be conducted face-to-face or digitally. When the research is influenced by a qualitative research methodology, the most common way of data collection is an open interview discussing about in advance identified themes. These interviews are usually conducted individually and face-to-face (Kananen, 2013). A theme interview is flexible and one of the aims is to create a relaxed discussion between the interviewer and interviewee. The themes identified in advance should be derived from the literature review. It is sometimes beneficial to send the themes of the interview beforehand to the interviewee. Since the interviews of the themes are flexible and there is no requirement that the theoretical framework must be completely ready before the interview starts.

The basic idea of the theme interview is to gain a deep understanding of chosen phenomena and practices. Figure 4 shows an example of a theme interview aimed at understanding customer needs for developing new tourist products for Finnish high school students. A sufficient number of themes are generally between six and ten, but more detailed questions can be asked to clarify unclear issues during the interview. People with knowledge and experience are chosen for the interviews and the interview goes on until the saturation point is reached. In qualitative inspired research, saturation means that the last interviews conducted have not brought new information for understanding the phenomenon (Kananen, 2013). The minimum number of interviews cannot be set in advance, but normally the starting point is 4–6 interviews (Ojasalo et al. 2014, p. 108). Theme interviews can be conducted also by phone or by tools such as Skype and Adobe Connect Pro.

E-mail is not usually a sufficient tool to collect interview data. Traditionally e-mail is not used for interviewing, but if this is the only option, the data collection must be a process of several e-mails otherwise it is unlikely to get enough information from the interviewee (Kananen, 2015).

Figure 4: Example of Theme Interview Guide[4]

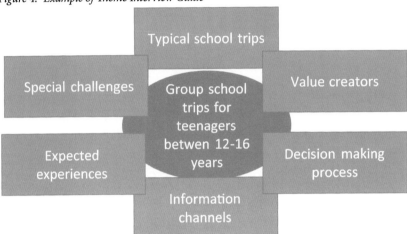

A focus group is usually conducted with a group of 6–12 people. A focus group is normally led by two researchers, one leads the discussion and the other observes the interviewees. The aim is to get the participants of the focus group to discuss topics the interviewers have decided in advance. A focus group is a common strategy for data collection in a development project. The main benefit is that different angles of a phenomenon can be highlighted by a group of people with different backgrounds. Time can also be saved when the researchers do not have to meet different interviewees separately (Ojasalo et al., 2014).

4.2 Surveys

Survey is a research method where a questionnaire is used for the data collection (Veal, 2006). The questionnaire is distributed to a sample of people, today usually electronically (Ojasalo et al., 2014). Response rates to electronic surveys are though usually very low, thus Veal (2006) suggests that a strategy where the questionnaire is filled out by an interviewer is recommended. Ojasalo et al. (2014) highlight surveys as a fast and efficient way to collect data. In constructive research, it can be used to obtain development ideas from a large group, for example, customers. A typical research process of survey research is presented in Figure 5.

---

4   Source: based on Kananen, 2013.

Figure 5: Process of Survey Research[5]

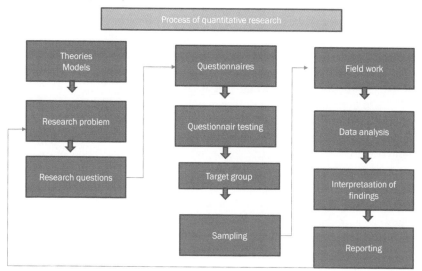

4.3 Observations

Two main strategies to use *observation* as a data collection method are the structured and the unstructured observation. A structured observation is done systematically with a clear scheme (usually a table) of what should be observed, whereas an unstructured observation is conducted in a less formal way. In tourism, observations can be used for instance for studying tourist behaviour at sites such as museums and amusement parks, and for testing service quality by mystery shopping (Veal, 2006). Observations are also divided into direct and participatory observations. Direct observations can be conducted for instance in a zoo, a spa, or a shopping mall, and the focus can be both on the behaviour of human beings as well as facilities such as workspaces. The researcher conducting the direct observations undertakes this as an external and anonymous expert. In participatory observation, the researcher is not a passive observer but an active facilitator of the events or processes in focus for the observations (Yin, 2013).

---

5   Source: Kananen, 2013, p. 133.

4.4 Collaborative Data Collection Methods

Collaborative methods for data collection are used for creative problem solving and innovations. An open and positive atmosphere is a pre-condition for problem solving. Group work and networking are crucial elements. It is important to separate the creative sessions and the evaluation phase. If the idea phase starts too early it will influence in the interest of the participants, and delimit the possibilities to find new angles. The amount of ideas will have a positive impact on quality (Ojasalo et al., 2014). Brainstorming is one of the most used methods. Normally, a group of people will be given about 10 minutes to come up with as many ideas as possible. After this phase follows the categorisation of the ideas which then results in the evaluation phase, when some of the ideas are chosen for further development (Winstanley, 2005). Other possible collaborative techniques are for example six thinking hats, distant thinking models, excursion techniques, Osborn's question list, bodystorming and learning cafes (see Mycoted, 2017; Ojasalo et al., 2014).

4.5 Crowdsourcing

In crowdsourcing, the main idea is to take the customers and end-users into the development process. Usually, crowdsourcing is used for product development processes that earlier were internal to an organisation (Ojasalo et al., 2014). Web 2.0 has made it possible to quickly and cheaply involve many customers, for example in the product development process. The main advantage is that an organisation is able to focus its product and service development on products and services customers really want. One of the main challenges though is how to motivate people to contribute. When enough comments have been collected for instance online in discussions on Facebook or other channels of social media, content analysis can be used for data analyses (Puurtinen, 2010).

4.6 Netnography

Observations can also be conducted to observe phenomena on the Internet (Kananen, 2015). Data analysis can be conducted with both quantitative and qualitative methods. For instance, how often per week members of an Internet group are active versus what are the main themes discussed can be a focus of research. If the focus of the research is on the social behaviour of individuals on the Internet, the method is often referred to as netnography. The researcher chooses whether he/she stays passive only by observing the communication as an outsider or whether he/she actively participates in the communication. For his/her own research, the researcher can also start their own forum as a research forum or platform (Bowler, 2010; Ojasalo et al., 2014).

According to Ojasalo et al. (2014), the special features of netnography are computer mediating and anonymity. It is not restricted by physical distances or time. The research data remains online normally for a long time, resulting in easy access to older data. The data in netnography is often created by the members of the forums on focus like blogs, expressions of opinions, photos, and videos to name a few. The netnographic analysis is close to content analysis where the researcher concentrates on the discussions and members' roles in them. Even though, netnography can seem very informal the researcher must be systematic in the data collection and analysis process.

4.7 Auto-ethnography

Ellis & Bochner (2000) describe auto-ethnography as a method to collect empirical data. They continue that auto-ethnographic data includes texts that are usually written in the first person, featuring emotions and self-consciousness. Often, the empirical data are stories or narratives written by the researchers of the study. Auto-ethnography is a genre of research that connects a person to culture and places within a social context (Reed-Danahay, 1997). In auto-ethnographical study, researchers or authors use their own experiences to obtain a deeper understanding of the phenomenon of focus. That is to say, auto-ethnography is a method where a researcher describes and analyses personal experiences to comprehend a cultural experience (Ellis, 2004). Auto-ethnography means aesthetic descriptions of personal and sometimes interpersonal experiences through notes or stories that are used for improving service processes and developing experiences (see Holmberg & Ritalahti, 2016).

4.8 Benchmarking

As a development method, the basic idea of benchmarking focuses on improvement of activities, products or services. When benchmarking is used as an analysing tool, the focus is to study best practices in the industry or related industries. Typically, benchmarking involves at least the following steps as outlined by Stapenhurst (2009)

1. Define the activity to be improved
2. Find an organisation that does do this activity better than the company you are involved with

3. Find out what practices the organisation relies on
4. Learn and adapt the best practices.

Benchmarking is however, not a data collection method but rather a starting point for analysis. Usually, the researcher must conduct interviews or observations in order to be able to learn about the best practices for instance when it comes to digital marketing or increasing the level of motivation of employees.

4.9 Service Design

Service design is a popular approach in use when developing organisations. The main aim is to improve the quality of service. The growing popularity of the approach is based on the extended needs to improve customer-oriented value thinking. The development tasks or improvements are directed at both the users and staff of the organisation in focus. Service design offers a clear process, easy methods and tools that bring the customers into the core when new service concepts are developed and tested. As such, service innovation is not anything new. Every organisation that provides services should think seriously about improving the quality of its service due to the fierce competition in most fields. In service design, the starting point is to identify the needs and requirements of users and look for solutions together with the users and sometimes also with other stakeholders (Ojasalo et al., 2014).

Service design exploits the heritage of different academic disciplines, such as ethnography, consumer research, interaction design, product design, industrial design, service marketing and corporate strategy, in the process. The methods used in service design to gather customer insights are numerous. To name a few from the long list are for example contextualised interviews, content analysis, customer profiles, storytelling, scenarios, customer paths, visualisation, prototypes, and role plays. One of the main ideas is to engage all the stakeholders in the development process, especially the customers (Ojasalo et al., 2014).

In research aimed at the development of real-life challenges, it is recommended to collect data throughout the development process. In the initial phase, it is usually beneficial to collect as much data as possible from different stakeholders for instance by a survey or by crowdsourcing. Brainstorming and netnography can also be used in order to come up with ideas outside the box. When the project proceeds, it is often worthwhile to organise workshops or focus groups with experts who possess some understanding of the construct being developed. Observations of good practices as well as benchmarking can be used along the process in order to further improve the features of the construct in focus for development.

5 Trustworthiness of a Constructive Research Project

The concepts of reliability and validity are critical when assessing a scientific research project (Veal, 2006; Saunders, Lewis, & Thornhill, 2009), especially in quantitative research. These concepts have been transferred to qualitative research as well (Flick, 2009; Decrop, 2004). In applied research, it is rarely possible to assess the trustworthiness of a project with the same criteria as those used in the scientific research. As a starting point for development project, the data is collected and analysed in order to find a practical solution rather than elaborating on which a tradition of philosophy of science has influenced the research. This approach advocates a need for new thinking. Ojasalo et al. (2014) suggests triangulation as a strategy for improving the trustworthiness of applied research. Triangulation is a concept developed in case study research (Yin, 2013) highlighting that the quality of the research can be improved if different types of data (e.g. interviews and documents) are collected and analysed. The reliability of this approach is improved by adopting investigator triangulation (several researchers look into the same data), theoretical triangulation (using multiple perspectives in data analysis) and longitudinal triangulation (data collection over several points of time) (Decrop, 2004). Thus it is recommended to combine a survey with interviews, focus groups or brainstorming sessions to provide multiple perspectives on the research.

Another important aspect of assessing the quality of an applied research project is the transparency of the research process. Transparency is a concept used in qualitative research (Hiles & Cermék, 2007; Moravscik, 2017) emphasising that the research process should be clearly and openly described. In practice, this means that there is a need for extensive discussion about how the research and development process was initiated, planned and implemented. It is important to highlight how the data collection instruments were prepared and tested as well as by whom, how and when data was collected and analysed. The most important findings from the different phases of data collection should be reported as well as how these findings influenced the chosen paths of the development process.

6 Practical Examples of Constructive Research Projects

The adoption of a constructive research approach in a Bachelor or Master thesis can very often give a more scientific structure to a topic or theme that is focused on development. Even though, a thesis commissioner is very often only looking for the outcome: product, service, or another construct, the student cannot base his/her choices only on opinions. The constructive approach provides a framework for understanding product or service development or service design by offering tools to collect customer or user insights and is as an approach for practical themes in thesis work. Examples of theses with the constructive approach are presented below to provide a clearer picture of the opportunities available to adopt this research approach.

Food Helsinki HELL YEAH! was a thesis project of Heinrichs (2014) who developed a food brochure for Helsinki. To enhance or promote the awareness of Finnish food, Helsinki got its first printed food brochure for tourists as an outcome of the thesis project. The main aim of the thesis project was to raise customer awareness of Finland's capital Helsinki's food brand. Helsinki has a versatile food culture but unfortunately, the city doesn't still have a known food identity. The theoretical framework of the thesis consisted of three main themes: food tourism, place branding and marketing, and consumer behaviour. The empirical part of the thesis adopted a constructive research approach using service design tools to encourage co-creation with complementary focus groups.

Brochures, handbooks and manuals can also be developed in constructive research projects. The travel agency Aventura commissioned a student to create a booklet describing the most unique experiences in Peru for tourists. The theoretical framework of the thesis was focusing on experiences and the importance of experiences in tourism. The content of the booklet was based on the observations the student did during her exchange in Peru, and a survey sent to locals in Peru (Korpela, 2015). During the development phase, the booklet was brought in to a class of third-year tourism students in order to get the final feedback for how the booklet could be improved both visually and content-wise.

Another example of a constructive research process was the preparation of a webpage. Heimonen (2016) did her thesis work for a company offering boat trips for tourists. The theoretical framework was comprised of defining digital marketing and building a company's webpage as a part of digital marketing strategy. The first phase of the data collection was the discussions of requirements of the webpage with the commissioner. Thereafter, benchmarking webpages of similar companies took place. During the development phase, the plans for the new webpage were shown to digital marketing experts and the commissioner in order to get ideas for how the preliminary ideas could be further developed.

A constructive approach can also be used for developing new tourism services and products. For instance, Tapola (2017) developed camp school packages for one of the main cruising companies in the Baltic sea. In this thesis, the theoretical framework focused on tourism services, experiences and service development. The development process was started by benchmarking similar packages offered by competitors. Afterwards, interviews were conducted with teachers responsible for organising these kinds of trips. From the interviews, some key features related to the experiences of camp schools were identified. Based on these ideas, a brainstorming session was organised at the commissioning company to get a clear structure for the products to be offered. The theoretical framework was used as a working tool to guarantee that all the services needed were acknowledged in the service system as well as making sure that the products comprised of real unique experiences. An example of this can be seen in Figure 6.

Figure 6: The Experience Triangle and the One-Day School Camp Trip to Tallinn[6]

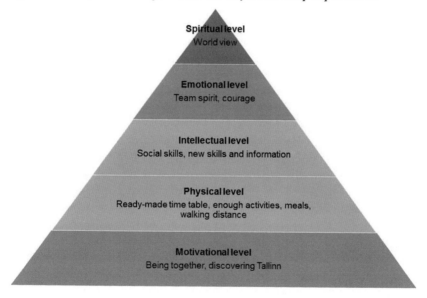

The final phase of this project done for Tallink Silja, the pilot products, were then presented to potential customers, and after the final revisions the products were taken into the product line.

---

6   Source: Tapola, 2017.

7 Discussion

Organisational development work is an ongoing process. Products and services must constantly be improved to meet the expectations of demanding customers in an increasingly competitive marketplace. Constructive research is one answer to this challenge, involving different stakeholders such as end-users and internal working groups in the development of new products and services. It is likely that the renewed product/service offer will correspond to the needs of the market.

Figure 7 summarises the process of a normal constructive research process. The process starts with identifying the preliminary aims and continues with a look into literature and other project-related materials in order to further define the scope of the research. The next step is to summarise the theoretical framework, and based on this outline the plans for data collection Data are then collected in various phases and with different methods in order to gain as much insight as possible before the final product or service is offered to customers. During the final phases, the report is written and the results are disseminated both internally in the organisation as well as externally to customers and other possible stakeholders. The fact that the prepared construct should be commercialisation and/or adopted by the company/organisation is left out from the figure since it is up to the commissioner ordering the project what will happen when the research process is finished.

Constructive research as an approach is especially suitable for students in tourism and hospitality because the maturity of the companies in the field are small and medium-sized companies with limited resources to do development work by themselves. Challenges related to product and service development, digital marketing as well as some human-resource related issues are especially suitable to be solved with the constructive research approach. From the researcher's point of view, it is motivational to be involved in a research problem aiming at solving real organisational problems instead of doing descriptive research common in case study research. Compared to action research which is focusing on organisational development requiring intensive co-operation within the organisation, constructive research focuses more on corresponding to needs outside the business. For someone not working in the organisation where the development work take place, the data collection is less challenging in a constructive research project than in action research.

Figure 7: Summary of the Typical Constructive Research Process

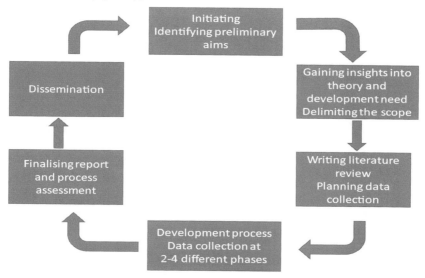

8 Conclusions

The aim of this chapter was to present constructive research as an approach for practical problem-solving at the University of Applied Sciences. Constructive research was in Finland developed in the 1990s, but it took almost two decades before the approach was acknowledged as a suitable strategy providing practical projects with a more academic approach. The need for systematic data collection in these constructive development projects was stressed to ensure good quality project work. In future, the Universities of Applied Sciences will be increasingly dependent on projects funded by external organisations. To some extent, they can develop their own products and services that can be commercialised not only for students but also as a constructive research approach that can be one way of developing a trustworthy development processes for this work.

References

Bowler, G. M. (2010). Netnography: A method specifically designed to study cultures and communities online. *The Qualitative Report*, 15(5), 1270–1275.

Decrop A. (2004). Trustworthiness in qualitative research. In J. Phillimore & L. Goodson (Eds.). *Qualitative research in tourism – ontologies, epistemologies, methodologies* (pp. 156–165). London, England: Routledge.

Ellis, C. (2004). *The ethnographic I: A methodological novel about autoethnography.* Walnut Creek, CA: AltaMira Press.

Ellis, C., & Bochner, A. P. (2000). Autoethnography, personal narrative, reflexivity: Researcher as subject. In K. N. Denzin & Y. Lincoln (Eds.), *The SAGE handbook of qualitative research* (2nd ed., pp. 733–768). Thousand Oaks, CA, USA: Sage.

Flick, U. (2009). *An Introduction to qualitative research.* London, England: Sage.

Goodson, J., & Phillimore, J. (2004). The inquiry paradigm in qualitative tourism research. In J. Phillimore & L. Goodson (Eds.), *Qualitative research in tourism - ontologies, epistemologies, methodologies* (pp. 30–45). London, England: Routledge.

Heimonen, M. (2016). Website as a communication channel – Case SVV Oy. (Unpublished Master's Thesis, Haaga-Helia University of Applied Sciences, 2016).

Heinrichs, E. (2014). Capital city food branding building – Case food Helsinki? HEL YEAH! Retrieved February 14, 2017 from https://www.theseus.fi/bitstream/handle/10024/84012/Capital%20City%20Food%20Brand%20Building%20Case%20Food%20Helsinki%20HEL%20YEAH%20Masters%20Thesis%20Elisabeth%20Heinrichs.pdf?sequence=1.

Hiles, D., & Cermák, I. (2007). Qualitative research: Transparency and narrative oriented inquiry. Retrieved February 17, 2017 from http://is.muni.cz/el/1423/jaro2011/PSY027/um/Hiles___Cermak__2007__QR_-_Transparency_and_NOI.pdf.

Holmberg, E., & Ritalahti, J. (2016). National Parks as experience spaces – An auto-ethnographic study in two Finnish Parks. In M. Lück, J. Ritalahti, & A. Scherer (Eds.), *International Perspectives on Destination Management and Experiences* (pp. 157–176). Frankfurt am Main, Germany: Peter Lang.

Kananen, J. (2013). *Design research (applied action research) as thesis research.* Jyväskylä, Finland: JAMK.

Kananen, J. (2015). *Online Research for preparing your thesis.* Jyväskylä, Finland: JAMK.

Kasanen, E., Lukka, K., & Siitonen, A. (1993). The constructive approach in management accounting. *Journal of Management Accounting Research,* 5, 242–264.

Korpela, J. (2015). ¡Qué chévere! – Opas Perun elämysmatkailuun, Retrieved February 14, 2017 from https://publications.theseus.fi/bitstream/handle/10024/102005/korpela_janika.pdf?sequence=1.

Luukka, K. (2006). Konstruktiivinen tutkimusote: luonne, prosessi ja arviointi. In K. Rolin, M.-L. Kakkuri-Knuuttila, & E. Henttonen (Eds.), *Soveltava yhteiskuntatiede ja filosofia* (pp. 111–123). Helsinki, Finland: Gaudeamus.

Ojasalo, K., Moilanen, T., & Ritalahti, J. (2014). *Kehittämistyön menetelmät,* Helsinki, Finland: SanomaPro.

Moravcsik, D. (2017). Transparency: The Revolution in qualitative research. Retrieved February 11, 2017 from http://www.princeton.edu/~amoravcs/library/transparency.pdf.

Mycoted. (2017). Creativity, innovation, tools, techniques, books, discussions, puzzles, brain teasers, training. Retrieved February 11, 2017 from https://www.mycoted.com/Main_Page.

Puurtinen, M. (2010). Crowdsourcing. Retrieved February 11, 2017 from http://www2.uiah.fi/~mmaenpaa/lectures/Crowdscoursing.pdf.

Reed-Danahay, D. (1997). *Auto/ethnography: Rewriting the self and the social.* Oxford, England: Berg.

Ritalahti, J. (2015). Inquiry learning in tourism. In P. Sheldon & S. Hsu (Eds.), *Tourism education: Global issues and trends* (pp. 135–151). Somerville, MA: Emerald Group Publishing Limited.

Saunders, M., Lewis, P., & Thornhill, F. (2009). *Research methods for business students.* London, England: Pearson.

Silvermann, D. (2013). *Doing qualitative research.* Los Angeles, CA: Sage.

Stapenhurst, S. (2009). *The benchmarking book.* London: Elsevier.

Suvanto, M. (2014). Uusia malleja työelämän kehittämiseen: Tutkimuksellinen kehittämistyö ylempi AMK-tutkinnossa. Retrieved February 11, 2017 from https://www.theseus.fi/handle/10024/85931.

Tapola, H. (2017). Tourism product development; camp schoole packages to Tallinn and Åland for Tallink Silja Oy, Retrieved July 10, 2017 from https://www.theseus.fi/handle/10024/123095.

Tripp, D. (2005). Action research: A methodological introduction. Retrieved February 11, 2017 from http://www.scielo.br/pdf/ep/v31n3/en_a09v31n3.pdf.

Veal, A. J. (2006): *Research methods for leisure and tourism.* Harlow, England: Prentice-Hall.

Winstanley, D. (2005). *Personal effectiveness: A guide to action.* London, England: CIPD.

Xiao, H., & Smith, S. L. J. (2006). Cases studies in tourism research: A state-of-the-art analysis. *Tourism Management, 27*(5), 738–749.

Yin, R. K. (2013). *Case study research: Design and practice.* Thousand Oaks, CA, USA: Sage.

Michael Lück, Brooke Porter

Profiling Pelagic Birdwatchers: The Case of *Albatross Encounter*, Kaikoura, New Zealand

1 Introduction

Birdwatching is defined as 'the activity of spotting, observing and listening for birds in their natural habitats for the purposes of recreation, wildlife appreciation, education and photography' (Vas, 2017, p. 1). Cordell & Herbert (2002) suggest birding as a catalyst for ecotourism. Acorn Consulting (2008, p. 10) looked at birdwatching from a tourism perspective, and defined it as

> Tourist travel for the specific purpose of observing wild birds, otherwise known as *avitourism* or *birding*. People at all levels of fitness and ornithological knowledge can participate. Many countries have thriving bird watching societies, which promote and sponsor trips to destinations where there is an abundance of bird life.

Birding has grown from a small niche activity for highly specialised enthusiasts into a widespread leisure and tourism activity. Acorn Consulting (2008) estimates that 3 million trips are taken annually with the main focus of birdwatching. Given that approximately 17–20 million United States (US) Americans took a birdwatching trip in 2007, the related estimated annual spend is over US $2.5 billion (Acorn Consulting, 2008; Centre for Responsible Travel [CREST], n.d.). Combined with the number of people watching birds from their home, the US Fish and Wildlife Service contends that a total of approximately 46.7 million people watched birds at home and on trips in 2011. Growth rates have been phenomenal, and the US Department of Agriculture Forest Service found that it is 'the most steadily growing [recreational] activity in the United States, growing 287% from 1982 to 2009' (CREST, n.d., p. 1). According to Acorn Consulting (2008), the Royal Society for the Protection of Birds in the United Kingdom has a membership of over one million. These figures are impressive, and suggest that there is a substantial market for birdwatching globally, despite it being classed as a niche (tourism) activity. The comedy The Big Year, released in 2011 and featuring Steve Martin, Jack Black and Owen Wilson, put birdwatching and a major birdwatching competition (Big Year) firmly on the map of the general public, despite at the same time ridiculing this activity.

Within the literature, there has been an emphasis on terrestrial birdwatching activities; however, pelagic bird viewing as a coastal and marine tourism activity, and marine bird tourists have received little attention. Exceptions include Schänzel & McIntosh's (2010) work on the personal and emotive contexts of penguin watching in New Zealand; Kuehn, Sali, & Schuster's (2010) work on shoreline birdwatcher motivations in New York; and Muir & Chester's (1993) study on the management of tourism at a nesting seabird island in North Queensland, Australia.

2 Birdwatcher Specialisation

Compared to other forms of wildlife watching, there is a good deal of terminology available to describe viewing birds; for example, the three terms 'birdwatching', 'birding', and 'twitching'. According to Connell (2009), 'birdwatching' is the umbrella term, while 'birding' is an American term and 'twitching' is primarily British. Various studies have profiled birdwatchers (Connell, 2009; Eubanks, Stoll, & Ditton, 2004; Hvenegaard, 2002; Lee & Scott, 2004; Miller, Hallo, Sharp, Powell, & Lanham, 2014; Moore, Scott, & Moore, 2008; Sali, Kuehn, & Zhang, 2008; Scott & Thigpen, 2003; Scott, Ditton, Stoll, & Eubanks, 2005; Vas, 2017), and mostly agree that birders are predominately from North America and the United Kingdom, middle-aged, male, well-educated and affluent.

A survey of birding literature and websites reveals technology and associated gear that has been specially designed to aid the activity. This degree of specialisation is not observed in other wildlife fields beyond basic photographic equipment and sun protection (e.g., marine mammal viewing). Online evidence shows that a journal or checklist of species is common item carried by birders, but not by other types of wildlife watchers. For instance, a Boolean search of 'bird checklist' reveals hundreds of such lists, whereas a 'dolphin checklist' search reveals less than five checklists of dolphin species. Scott et al. (2005) note the importance of 'listing' or keeping a checklist among bird enthusiasts. Birding equipment ranges from common cameras to specific bird finders and specialised clothing. Based on observed birdwatching and travel behaviour, as well as the equipment used, some studies profile birdwatchers. For example, Scott et al. (2005) identify three groups of birdwatchers and their characteristics:

The Committed Birder
• Travels on short notice to see a rare bird
• Subscribes to a number of birding magazines
• Specialises in identification and keeps logs
• Leads field trips and seminars for local clubs
• Purchases a lot of equipment

The Active Birder
- Travels infrequently to watch birds
- May or may not belong to a birding club
- Subscribes to general interest bird magazines and keeps a log
- Participates in, but does not lead, local field trips and seminars
- Birding is an important, but not exclusive outdoor activity

The Casual Birder
- Birding is incidental to other travel and outdoor interests
- May not belong to a local birding organisation
- Does not subscribe to birding magazine, but may read newspaper articles on birds, and does not keep a lifelong log
- Birding is an enjoyable yet inconsistent outdoor activity

This chapter reports on a study of pelagic birdwatchers in Kaikoura, New Zealand. It will profile birdwatchers on these tours, and investigate their satisfaction with the tour, employing an Importance-Performance Analysis (IPA).

3 Methods

The methods used in this study included a paper-and-pen questionnaire distributed on pelagic birdwatching tours (*Albatross Encounter*) in Kaikoura, New Zealand over the 2012 to 2015 period. *Albatross Encounter* commonly offers three daily boat departures (9 am, 1 pm, 6 pm), but also accommodates groups that require customised departure times. The tours include an eight-minute bus transfer from Kaikoura to South Bay (where the jetty is located), the actual tour, the transfer back, and an information pack. The information pack contains a checklist of birds potentially encountered during the trip (Figure 1); information about albatross, organisations involved in their protection, and the operator; as well as a postcard of *Albatross Encounter*. After departing from the jetty, the vessel travels offshore where the skipper releases a bait ball containing frozen fish, in order to attract marine birds. The bait ball remains a few metres behind the vessel during the birdwatching part of the tour, allowing for close-up photo opportunities (Figure 2).

The survey form comprised five sections:

a) The characteristics of your birding experience in Kaikoura' ('characteristics');
b) About your expectations/motivations of participating in a marine birding tour' (motivations');
c) About your impression on the facilities and equipment' ('facilities');

d) About yourself and your holidays' ('holidays'); and
e) Background information' ('demographic data').

Figure 1: Albatross Encounter Bird Checklist

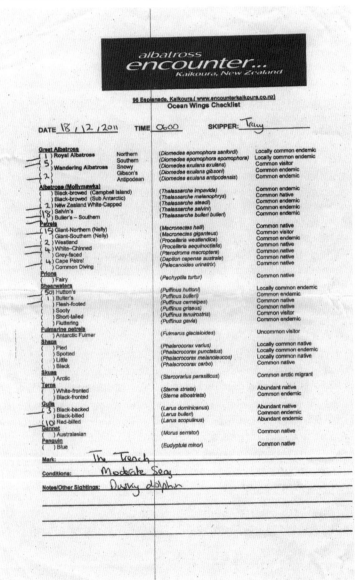

*Figure 2: Seabirds Gathering around the Bait Ball at the Stern of the Albatross Encounter
Vessel (Photo: M. Lück)*

With the exception of the demographic questions, the majority of questions were closed-ended, in a Likert-type format, ranging from 1 = 'not important'/'not satisfied'/'totally disagree' to 5 = 'very important'/'very satisfied'/'totally agree'. Some questions offered open-ended opportunities for respondents, and at the end of the survey plenty of space was provided for respondents to comment on whatever they liked.

A total of 186 usable questionnaires were completed during the survey period. The data (excluding demographic data) were tested for reliability, employing Cronbach's alpha (Salkind, 2004). This test resulted in a reliability coefficient of $\alpha = .725$, indicating a relatively high internal consistency ($\alpha > .70$), and thus reliable results (Sirakaya-Turk, Uysal, Hammitt, & Vaske, 2011). A variety of statistical tests (e.g., frequencies, means, t-tests) were used to analyse the data, employing IBM SPSS, version 22.

The Importance-Performance Analysis

This study employed an IPA, in order to identify attributes and items that require attention from the operator (Huan, Beaman, & Shelby, 2002; Lacher & Harrill, 2010; Lück, 2011). A survey for an IPA is comprised of two sections: one in which the respondent rates the importance of a number of items; and one in which he/she rates the performance of the same items. The items in both sections are rated on a five-point Likert-type scale, from 1 = 'not at all important' to 5 = 'very important', and from 1 = 'poor' to 5 = 'excellent', respectively. The mean of each performance attribute is then matched with the mean of the corresponding importance attribute, and plotted into a scatter-gram (action grid), with the performance value on the x-axis, and the importance value on the y-axis. Finally, the crosshairs are determined by using the grand means of both sections. Previous studies have positioned the crosshairs variously, at either the middle point of the two scales (e.g., Mengak, Dottavio, & O'Leary, 1986, as cited in Bennett, Dearden, & Rollins, 2003), the grand means (e.g., Hollenhorst, Olson, & Fortney, 1992), or at some arbitrary point (e.g., Guadagnolo, 1985). The crosshairs subdivide the graph into four quadrants. Which quadrant the factors fall within indicates how the respective tour operators should deal with them, such as if they should improve them, put more or less effort into these items, and so on, as follows:

- The top-right quadrant shows items that rated high in both importance and performance, indicating that the operator performs well in these areas and should 'keep up the good work'.
- The top-left quadrant represents items that are rated high in importance, but low in performance, suggesting that management 'concentrate here' to improve these items.
- The bottom-right quadrant shows items that are low in importance, but high in performance, so despite the high performance, the operator might waste time and energy on these items because they are of low importance or 'possible overkill' for guests.
- The bottom-left quadrant shows items that are 'low priority' in both importance and performance, and should be of least concern to management (Guadagnolo, 1985; Hollenhorst et al., 1992; Lai & Hitchcock, 2015; Martilla & James, 1977).

While the action grid can be useful for managers in evaluating the success of their operation (Bennett et al., 2003) giving them information about both their clients' motivations (importance) and satisfaction (performance), Ziegler, Dearden & Rollins (2012) suggest the use of the 45° iso-rating line. The diagonal iso-rating line separates the graph into two areas, with the line itself representing the points where the importance values are equal to the performance values. The distance of the items from the iso-rating line indicates how large the gaps between the importance and the performance scores are (Abalo, Varela, & Manzano, 2007; Sethna, 1982). Ziegler et al. (2012) argue that

[t]he iso-rating line approach appears to be a more sensitive method of identifying areas of concern because it focuses on differences in satisfaction and performance ratings, rather than subjective category selection (p. 695).

Consequently, this study employed a combination of the crosshairs method and the iso-rating line method.

4 Results and Discussion

4.1 A Demographic Profile

This section provides a basic demographic profile of pelagic birdwatchers in Kaikoura (Table 1). The majority of respondents were female (54.1%), with 45.9% male respondents. Tour participants were of all age groups, but it was noticeable that two-thirds of respondents were over 50 years of age. Only 9.3% were between 18 and 29 years old, 16.9% were 30–39 years old, and 7.7% were 40–49 years old. When it comes to the employment status, the majority of respondents were employed full time (35.7%), part time (8.8%), or self-employed (5.5%). However, the single largest group were retired (38.5%) and only 3.8% were students, 2.2% students who worked part-time, 1.1% working and travelling, 1.1% homemakers, and 1.6% was not currently employed. The participants in pelagic birdwatching tours were highly educated, with 82.5% having a university degree (39.6% undergraduate and 42.9% postgraduate), 5.5% a polytechnic qualification, 6.6% a high school qualification, and 4.4% had a trade, vocational or professional qualification. Only 1.1% indicated that they had no formal qualification. Corresponding with the high level of education, the annual household income was high as well: almost half of the respondents (46.2%) had an annual household income of more than $NZ100,000, 39.8% had an annual household income between $NZ40,000 and $99,999, and only 13.9% had an annual household income of less than $NZ40,000. The distribution of nationalities show that three regional groups dominated the sample: respondents from the United Kingdom (33.1%), North America (30.4%) and Australia/New Zealand/South Pacific (24.9%). Only 10.3% hailed from the rest of Europe, and 1.7% from South America.

These results are comparable with the terrestrial birdwatcher profiles in previous studies (see Section 2), with the exception of the gender distribution: in contrast to previous studies, this survey revealed that the majority (54.1%) of pelagic birdwatchers was female.

Table 1: Demographic Details of Respondents

Aspect	%
Gender (n = 183)	
Male	45.9
Female	54.1
Age (n = 183)	
18–29	9.3
30–39	16.9
40–49	7.7
50–59	19.1
60–69	35.0
>70	12.0
Employment status (n = 182)	
Self-employed	5.5
Employed full time	35.7
Employed part-time	8.8
Student	3.8
Student & working part-time	2.2
Work & travelling	1.1
Homemaker	1.1
Retired	38.5
Not currently employed	1.6
Other	1.5
Education (n = 182)	
No formal education	1.1
High school certificate/diploma	6.6
Polytechnic certificate/diploma	5.5
University degree	39.6
Postgraduate degree	42.9
Vocational/trade/professional qualification	4.4
Income in $NZ (n = 158)	
>20,000	6.3
20,000–39,999	7.6
40,000–59,999	13.9
60,000–79,999	13.9
80,000–99,999	12.0
100,000–150,000	20.3
>150,000	25.9

Aspect	%
Nationality (n = 181)	
New Zealand/Australia/South Pacific	24.9
North America	30.4
South America	1.7
Europe	10.3
United Kingdom	33.1

4.2 Interest in Birdwatching

Respondents were asked a variety of questions about their general interest in and experience with birdwatching. The vast majority (95.2%) had been on a wildlife tour before, and 73% had been birding before. Of these, the majority had been on up to 10 tours in the last five years, with some very engaged birdwatchers having been on up to 150 tours in the past five years (Table 2).

Table 2: How Many Times have you been on a Birding Tour in the Past Five Years? (n = 118)

Number of birding trips	Frequency	Percent
1	22	18.6
2	24	20.3
3	15	12.7
4	8	6.8
5	12	10.2
6	5	4.2
10	19	16.1
12	2	1.7
13	2	1.7
14	2	1.7
20	3	2.5
25	2	1.7
125	1	0.8
150	1	0.8

As discussed in the literature review, birdwatchers around the world are described using different terms: in North America, the term 'birder' is more commonly used, whereas in the United Kingdom, 'twitcher' is a familiar term. When the birdwatchers in this study were queried, the largest number identified with the term 'birdwatcher' (37.3%), followed by 'birder' (28.8%), and 27.7% were not sure or were unfamiliar with these terms (Figure 3). A mere 1.7% identified with the term 'twitcher', despite one-third of the respondents being from the United Kingdom.

Figure 3: Self-Identification with Birdwatching Labels

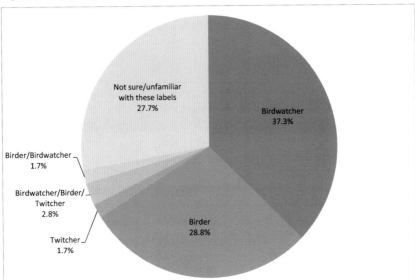

Respondents were asked a variety of questions about their general birdwatching experiences and behaviours. Results show that 45% of respondents totally agreed or agreed that they had not seen albatross prior to this trip (Figure 4). When it came to specific birdwatching behaviour, 56.7% totally agreed or agreed that they maintain a log or checklist of bird species they have seen and 73% totally agreed or agreed that seeing rare species of birds is important to them. A total of 23.3% of the respondents described themselves as expert birdwatchers, but only 5% indicated that their level of bird knowledge exceeded that of the guide.

Figure 4: Travel Motivations and Birdwatching Experience

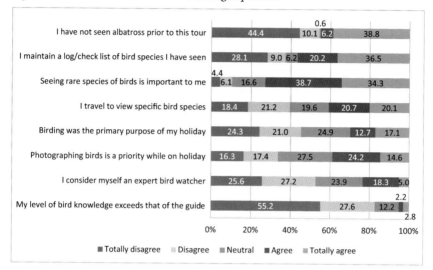

In terms of travel behaviour, 40.8% of respondents totally agreed or agreed that they travel to view specific birds, and 29.8% totally agreed or agreed that the primary purpose of their holiday was indeed birdwatching. More specifically, 27% indicated that they came to Kaikoura specifically to watch birds, and 33% to see particular species (more than one answer to this question was possible). Kaikoura is famous for its sperm whales (*Physeter macrocephalus*) and Dusky dolphins (*Lagenorhynchus obscrurus*), as well as other marine mammals, so it is not surprising that 9% came specifically for whale and dolphin watching, and 75% indicated that they came to Kaikoura specifically for a combination of birdwatching, whale/dolphin watching, and other wildlife watching. Photographing birds was a priority for 38.8% of the respondents.

4.3 Special Equipment for Birdwatching

Respondents were asked whether they carried a variety of equipment and specialised clothing on the *Albatross Encounter* tour in Kaikoura (Figures 5 and 6). The results show that among the most carried items were binoculars (71%), and cameras and camera accessories. A quarter of the respondents (24.7%) carried a journal or log, and 22% a species checklist. Highly specialised equipment, such as bird calls, bird finders, MP3 players and speakers, and oil-filled heads were among the least carried items (Figure 5).

Figure 5: Birdwatching Equipment Carried on the Albatross Encounter Tour

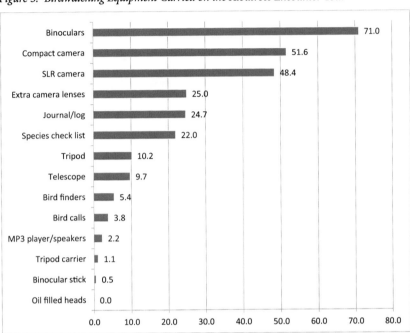

Figure 6: Specific Clothing Carried on the Albatross Encounter Tour

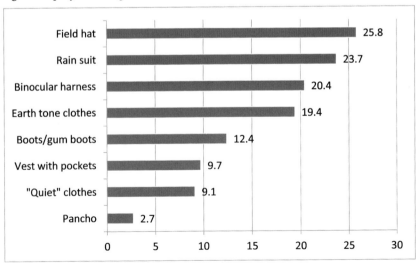

Respondents also carried a variety of specialised clothing on their tour, most commonly a field hat (25.8%), a rain suit (23.7%), a binocular harness (20.4%) and earth-tone clothes (19.4%). The stereotypical birdwatcher vest with a number of pockets was carried by only 9.7% of the respondents (Figure 6).

4.4 The Importance-Performance Analysis

Overall, satisfaction with the tour was very high: A total of 68% stated that the tour exceeded their expectations, 31.5% thought it was as expected, and only 0.6% found that the tour was not as good as expected. However, in order to gain some more insight into the components of the tour that contributed to the overall satisfaction, respondents were given the opportunity to indicate how important a number of attributes were in motivating them to participate in the *Albatross Encounter* tour in Kaikoura. They were asked to rate the attributes on a five-point Likert-type scale, ranging from 1 = 'not at all important' to 5 = 'very important'. Table 3 shows the means of the attributes for both the importance (= motivation) and the performance (= satisfaction) scores. Based on the results, the top three motivational attributes were:

1. Have a knowledgeable marine guide (mean = 4.79; n = 184)
2. Having an experienced captain/skipper (mean = 4.78; n = 183)
3. Opportunity to see albatross (mean = 4.75; n = 187)

At the other end of the ranked attributes were the three least important motivations:

1. Opportunity to feed marine birds (mean = 2.16; n = 164)
2. Have a gift shop (mean = 2.21; n = 176)
3. Sunny weather (mean = 2.81; n = 176)

The results indicate that most attributes were at least moderately important to the respondents. However, the opportunities to feed marine birds and to see other marine wildlife were not as important to the participants. Equally, sunny weather was not important, nor was a gift shop. This suggests that respondents booked the tour specifically to view albatross and other pelagic birds, and were not particularly interested in other wildlife viewing opportunities that may have unfolded during the tour. Table 3 also illustrates the performance of these items, and based on the results the attributes with the highest satisfaction scores were:

1. Having an experienced captain/skipper (mean = 4.93; n = 183)
2. Have a knowledgeable marine guide (mean = 4.89; n = 184)
3. Opportunity to see albatross (mean = 4.86; n = 187)

The items with the lowest performance scores were:

1. Opportunity to feed marine birds (mean = 3.50; n = 164)
2. Have a gift shop (mean = 3.74; n = 176)
3. Sunny weather (mean = 4.11; n = 176)

A gap analysis resulted in entirely positive gap values, indicating that all performance scores exceeded the importance scores, which means that the performance of the operator overall is very positive. This is illustrated by the fact that all items are below the 45° iso-rating line in the IPA graph (Figure 7). However, the performance gap of the item 'Opportunity to view different species of birds' was not statistically significant, with a p-value of .754.

Figure 7: Importance-Performance Graph of the Albatross Encounter Tour

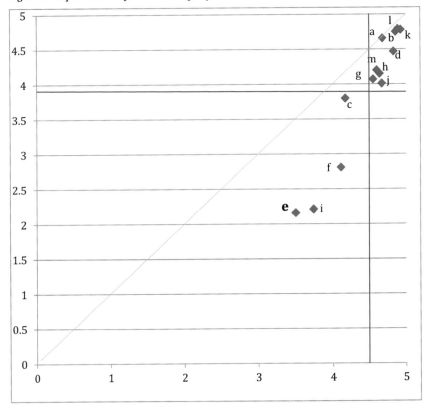

Table 3: Importance-Performance Analysis of the Albatross Encounter Tour

		Importance		Performance		Gap (I-P)	df	p
		mean	sd	mean	sd			
	Keep up the Good Work							
a	Opportunity to view different species of birds (n = 181)	4.66	.669	4.68	.584	0.02	180	.754
k	Have a knowledgeable marine guide (n = 184)	4.79	.448	4.89	.367	0.10	183	.008*
b	Opportunity to see albatross (n = 187)	4.75	.542	4.86	.442	0.11	186	.004*
l	Have an experienced captain/ skipper (n = 183)	4.78	.431	4.93	.269	0.15	182	.000*
d	Being able to get close to pelagic birds (n = 182)	4.47	.798	4.83	.545	0.36	181	.000*
m	Understand safety rules and procedures (n = 181)	4.20	.905	4.60	.638	0.40	180	.000*
g	Good value for money (n = 176)	4.07	.892	4.55	.762	0.48	175	.000*
h	Opportunity for photography (n = 177)	4.15	1.163	4.64	.733	0.49	176	.000*
j	Have clean and comfortable boat (n = 184)	4.01	.890	4.67	.612	0.66	183	.000*
	Low Priority							
c	Opportunity to see other marine wildlife (n = 182)	3.80	.915	4.17	.968	0.36	181	.000*
i	Have gift shop (n = 176)	2.21	1.208	3.74	1.224	1.53	175	.000*
f	Sunny weather (n = 176)	2.81	1.311	4.11	1.164	1.30	175	.000*
e	Opportunity to feed marine birds (n = 164)	2.16	1.335	3.50	1.308	1.34	163	.000*

*significant at the 0.05 level, based on paired samples t-test

The results of the IPA show that no items fell into the 'concentrate here' and the 'possible overkill' quadrants. Nine items were in the 'keep up the good work' quadrant, and four items were of 'low priority'. This is a very positive result for the tour operator, since they appear to understand their customers well, and provide the product these birdwatchers expect. Among the 'low priority' items was 'sunny weather', which cannot be influenced by the operator. A gift shop is common for most tourism businesses in order to generate extra revenue, but it appears that it is not very high on the importance list of birdwatchers. On *Albatross Encounter* tours, participants do not have the opportunity to feed the birds, but the operator uses a bait ball in order to attract a variety of marine birds to the boat. While this procedure is vital to the success of the tours, participants do not feel that they would like to individually feed birds. Lastly, the low importance score of 'opportunity to see other marine wildlife' reinforces the data about the birdwatchers' expertise and travel behaviour, i.e., that they are highly specialised on birdwatching, own the appropriate equipment, and keep logs and journals. The fact that many indicated that they came to Kaikoura to also watch other marine wildlife suggests that they have booked this tour specifically to watch birds, and that they may have booked other tours to view whales, dolphins, seals and other marine wildlife.

5 Conclusions

The research presented in this chapter offers new and interesting insight into the profile of the pelagic avitourist. The findings demonstrate that, in general, the operator was meeting and/or exceeding pelagic avitourists' expectations. These findings suggest that future research focused on the modelling of the *Albatross Encounter* tour may be beneficial to the pelagic avitourism industry (see also Lück & Porter, 2016).

Perhaps of more specific interest are the findings reinforcing ideas about birder specialisation. Nearly all respondents indicated a level of satisfaction with only seeing pelagic birds. With the increasing diversification of tourist activities and opportunities, this concept of tour specialisation may be viewed as a simplification of a tourist product. This finding is important for other marine tour operators looking to access a pelagic avitourism market, demonstrating that a separate tour product may be more valuable than the diversification of an existing tour product (e.g., combination with marine mammal viewing tour).

Acknowledgements

We would like to thank the owners and team at *Albatross Encounter*, Kaikoura, for their unconditional support of this study. We also owe great gratitude to Trish Brother (Auckland University of Technology) for her meticulous work in copy-editing this chapter.

References

Abalo, J., Varela, J., & Manzano, V. (2007). Importance values for Importance-Performance Analysis: A formula for spreading out values derived from preference rankings. *Journal of Business Research*, 60, 115–121. doi: 10.1016/j. jbusres.2006.10.009.

Acorn Consulting. (2008). *Developing a niche tourism market database for the Caribbean: 20 nice market profiles*. A report for the Caribbean Tourism Organisation. Flimwell, UK: Acorn Consulting Partnership Ltd.

Bennett, M., Dearden, P., & Rollins, R. (2003). The sustainability of dive tourism in Phuket, Thailand. In H. Landsdown, P. Dearden, & W. Neilson (Eds.), *Communities in SE Asia: Challenges and responses* (pp. 97–106). Victoria, Canada: University of Victoria, Centre for Asia Pacific Initiatives.

Centre for Responsible Travel (CREST). (n.d.). Market analysis of bird-based tourism: A focus on the U.S. market to Latin America and the Caribbean including fact sheets on The Bahamas, Belize, Guatemala, Paraguay. Online report. Retrieved January 24, 2016 from http://www.responsibletravel.org/resources/documents/birdstudyreport_71615.pdf.

Connell, J. (2009). Birdwatching, twitching and tourism: Towards an Australian perspective. *Australian Geographer*, 40(2), 203–217. doi: 10.1080/00049180902964942.

Cordell, H.K., & Herbert, N.G. (February, 2002). The popularity of birding is still growing. *Birding*, 54–61.

Eubanks, T.L., Stoll, J.R., & Ditton, R.B. (2004). Understanding the diversity of eight birder sub-populations: Socio-demographic characteristics, motivations, expenditures and net benefits. *Journal of Ecotourism*, 3(3), 151–172. doi: 10.1080/14664200508668430.

Guadagnolo, F. (1985). The Importance-Performance analysis: An evaluation and marketing tool. *Journal of Park and Recreation Administration*, 3(1), 13–22.

Hollenhorst, S., Olson, D., & Fortney, R. (1992). Use of Importance-Performance Analysis to evaluate state park cabins: The case of the West Virginia State Park system. *Journal of Park and Recreation Administration*, 10(1), 1–11.

Huan, T.-C., Beaman, J., & Shelby, L.B. (2002). Using action-grids in tourism management. *Tourism Management*, 23, 255–264.

Hvenegaard, G.T. (2002). Birder specialization differences in conservation involvement, demographics, and motivation. *Human Dimensions of Wildlife*, 7(1), 21–36. doi: 10.1080/108712002753574765.

Kuehn, D.M., Sali, M.J., & Schuster, R. (2010). Motivations of Male and Female Shoreline Bird Watchers in New York. *Tourism in Marine Environments*, 6(1), 25–37.

Lacher, R.G., & Harrill, R. (2010). Going beyond sun, sand, and surf? An Importance-Performance analysis of activities in a 3S resort destination. *e-Review of Tourism Research*, 8(4), 57–68.

Lai, I.K.W., & Hitchcock, M. (2015). Importance-performance analysis in tourism: A framework for researchers. *Tourism Management*, 48, 242–267. doi: 10.1016/j.tourman.2014.11.008.

Lee, J.-H., & Scott, D. (2004). Measuring birding specialization: A confirmatory factor analysis. *Leisure Sciences*, 26(3), 245–260. doi: 10.1080/01490400490461387.

Lück, M. (2011). An Importance-Performance Analysis of backpackers at Robinson Crusoe Island resort, Fiji. *ARA Journal of Tourism Research*, 3(1), 43–53.

Lück, M., & Porter, B. (2016, November 29–December 1). Encounters with albatross: Who is watching them? Paper presented at the New Zealand Hospitality and Tourism Research Conference (NZTHRC): Sustainable consumption in tourism & hospitality: Fact, faith or fiction? Department of Marketing and Entrepreneurship, University of Canterbury, Christchurch, New Zealand.

Martilla, J.A., & James, J.C. (1977). Importance-Performance analysis: An easily applied technique for measuring attribute importance and performance can further the development of effective marketing programs. *Journal of Marketing*, 41(1), 77–79.

Miller, Z.D., Hallo, J.C., Sharp, J.L., Powell, R.B., & Lanham, J.D. (2014). Birding by ear: A study of recreational specialization and soundscape preference. *Human Dimensions of Wildlife*, 19(6), 498–511. doi: 10.1080/10871209.2014.921845.

Moore, R.L., Scott, D., & Moore, A. (2008). Gender-based differences in birdwatchers' participation and commitment. *Human Dimensions of Wildlife*, 13(2), 89–101. doi: 10.1080/10871200701882525.

Muir, F., & Chester, G. (1993). Managing tourism to a seabird nesting island. *Tourism Management*, 15(2), 314–329.

Sali, M.J., Kuehn, D.M., & Zhang, L. (2008). Motivations for male and female birdwatchers in New York State. *Human Dimensions of Wildlife*, 13(3), 187–200. doi: 10.1080/10871200801982795.

Salkind, N.J. (2004). *Statistics for people who (think they) hate statistics* (4th ed.). London, England: Sage Publications.

Schänzel, H.A., & McIntosh, A.J. (2010). An insight into the personal and emotive context of wildlife viewing at the Penguin Place, Otago Peninsula, New Zealand. *Journal of Sustainable Tourism*, 8(1), 36–52. doi: 10.1080/09669580008667348.

Scott, D., Ditton, R.B., Stoll, J.R., & Eubanks, T.L. (2005). Measuring specialization among birders: Utility of a self-classification measure. *Human Dimensions of Wildlife*, 10(1), 53–74. doi: 10.1080/10871200590904888.

Scott, D., & Thigpen, J. (2003). Understanding the birder as tourist: Segmenting visitors to the Texas hummer/bird celebration. *Human Dimensions of Wildlife*, 8(3), 199–218. doi: 10.1080/10871200304311.

Sethna, B.N. (1982). Extensions and testing of importance-performance analysis. *Business Economics*, 20, 28–31.

Sirakaya-Turk, E., Uysal, M., Hammitt, W., & Vaske, J.J. (Eds.). (2011). *Research methods for leisure, recreation and tourism*. Wallingford, England: CABI.

Vas, K. (2017). Birding blogs as indicators of birdwatcher characteristics and trip preferences: Implications for birding destination planning and development. *Journal of Destination Marketing & Management*, 6(1), 33–45.

Ziegler, J., Dearden, P., & Rollins, R. (2012). But are tourists satisfied? Importance-performance analysis of the whale shark tourism industry on Isla Holbox, Mexico. *Tourism Management*, 33(3), 692–701. doi: 10.1016/j.tourman.2011.08.004.

Ismael Castillo Ortiz

Historical Perspective on Factors related to Tourists' Behavioural Intentions in Hotel Restaurants

1 Introduction

Tourism is the most important economic activity in the global service sector economy. Transportation, accommodation, information, gastronomy, marketing, financial services, insurance, etc., include the wide range of services that are integrated into the tourist system. The grouping of these services supports the production of tourist experiences (OECD, 2012). Tourism is an important part of the economy of the contemporary experience, in which food plays a relevant role. Food offers much more than the satisfaction of a need; it is also a fundamental part of all cultures, an important element of the world's intangible heritage, and an increasingly important attraction for tourists. The links between food and tourism also provide a platform for local economic development, which can be enhanced by the use of branded food experiences and destination marketing (OECD, 2012).

Food tourism has gained increasing attention over the past years. Tourists are centering their product development and marketing accordingly. With food so deeply connected to its origin, this focus allows destinations to market themselves as truly unique, appealing to those travellers who look to feel part of their destination through its flavours (OMT, 2012).

For many of the world's billions of tourists, returning to familiar destinations to enjoy tried and tasted recipes or traveling further afield in search of new and special cuisine, gastronomy has become a central part of the tourism experience (OMT, 2012). Food plays a particularly important role in the development of tourism services, as it often comprises 30% or more of tourism spending (OECD, 2012), and this money is regularly spent directly with local businesses. In order to use food and tourism as an economic development strategy, it is important to encourage visitors to arrive, spend and stay longer. Short, medium and long-term strategies include a range of options designed to keep costs, networks and relationships (with local businesses and organisations, as well as other regional actors) supportive of visitors and the development of intellectual capital for the purpose to improve the regional knowledge base and to create attractive food experiences.

Tourist motivations constitute a key concept for the design and creation of products and services that add value for tourists. Motivations are related to consumer satisfaction and are considered a key component in understanding the decision-making process of visitors (OMT, 2012). Destinations that want to promote food tourism have to work on various levels in the field of quality: the protection and recognition of local products, the development of a competitive offering, the professionalism of human resources throughout the value chain of food tourism through training and retraining, and consumer protection and reception in order to increase visitor satisfaction. Motivations are related to consumer satisfaction and are considered a key component in understanding the decision-making process of visitors. Tourists are increasingly looking for local, authentic and innovative experiences intrinsically linked to the places they visit. Both nationally and regionally, food can become unique elements of the brand image of places and help create a distinctive character. This is why hotel restaurants form a fundamental part of the tourist experience and are the tourist's first contact with the gastronomic offer of the locality. This work aims to understand the historical relationship between quality dimensions in restaurants (physical environment, food and service), satisfaction and associated behavioural intentions of tourists.

2 Literature Review

Gastronomy and tourism seem to have found a mutually beneficial relationship for both sectors; tourism offers gastronomic producers added value to their products by creating experiences around raw materials (products such as cheeses, wine, spirits, etc.) and in turn the gastronomic experiences add value to the tourist offering a link with the local culture, the landscape, the food and the drinks; creating an essential atmosphere for a memorable and satisfying holiday experience.

The causes of previous academic neglect of gastronomy have led to a reappraisal of the ideas of Brillat-Savarin (1999) in a postmodern framework. It has been argued that gastronomy is a subculture (Scarpato, 2000) and gastronomy studies are based on premises to give voice to gastronomic identities; who are culinary professionals who participate in the conception, preparation, promotion, and presentation of food, such as wine writers and cooks, consultants, researchers, educators; as well as those working in gastronomic agencies from restaurants to tourist centres.

Good food is commonly seen as an essential component of customer satisfaction and repeat sponsorship decisions in the catering sector (Namkung & Jang, 2007; Sulek & Hensley, 2004). Today, an exotic experience exclusively based on food may not be enough to attract and keep consumers to a restaurant. The relationship of food research to society, culture, and economics is largely developed by social scientists, such as sociologists, historians, and philosophers (Beardsworth & Keil, 1997; Tannahill, 1988; Visser, 1991; Wood, 1995); its works are influenced by a humanistic gastronomic perspective that offers little practical and productive sense. There is emptiness in their contributions to food guides that needs to address the imagination, production, transformation, distribution, sale and consumption of food.

On the other hand, there are studies (Heung & Ngai, 2008; Ryu, Lee, & Gon Kim, 2012) that mention the constructs that compose the experience of diners in restaurants. Physical environment, food, service, image, perceived value, satisfaction and behavioural intentions are key descriptors for relevant information about experiences in restaurants. Thus it is necessary to recognize from a practical and applicable perspective, the appropriate strategies and areas to improve the quality of the culinary experience of tourists visiting new destinations.

2.1 Factors Related to the Tourist Behavioural Intentions in Hotels Restaurants

Service quality and customer satisfaction have become the most fundamental marketing priorities, as they are prerequisites of consumer loyalty, often evaluated based on repeat sales and positive recommendations by word of mouth (Han & Ryu, 2009; Liu & Jang, 2009a). In today's highly competitive market, the key to gaining an advantage lies in providing a high-quality service that, in turn, leads to satisfied customers (Ryu & Han, 2011).

In particular, in the restaurant sector, customers typically use food, physical environment and employee services as key components of the restaurant experience in evaluating the quality of restaurant service (Chow, Lau, Lob, Sha, & Yun 2007; Namkung & Jang, 2008; Ryu, Han, & Jang, 2010). An appropriate combination of these vital attributes results in the perception of high-quality restaurant customer service, which in turn enhances satisfaction and loyalty in the restaurant industry.

However, little research has been carried out to investigate the influence of multiple components related to tourist behavioural intentions in hotel restaurants, such as food quality, physical environment, service quality, and satisfaction, which make it relevant to know and understand the influence of these factors on the behavioural intentions of the tourists who visit hotel restaurants. All this is important because it offers relevant information on how to offer better products and services to tourists visiting new destinations to increase the competitiveness and flow of tourism and the development of economies.

2.2 Physical Environment Quality

Gregoire, Shanklin, Greathouse, & Tripp (1995) observed that the cleanliness of a restaurant is an important factor for consumers when deciding where to dine. Additionally, cleaning of the toilet facility was used as an indispensable attribute for restaurant customer selections, restaurant customers remember cleaning deficiencies longer and are more likely to avoid these restaurants in the future (Wakefield & Blodgett, 1996). Dulen (1999) states that physical environment is the main feature, as well as food and service, in increasing customer satisfaction.

Bitner (1990) proposed that the physical environment can significantly affect the final customer satisfaction. On the other hand, Bitner (1992) discusses the effect of the tangible physical environment in the general development of the quality of service image. She coined the term SERVICESCAPE to describe the combined effect of all physical factors that can be controlled by customer service organizations and improve employee behaviors.

Although food and service must be of acceptable quality, the physical environment (e.g. music) can largely determine the degree of overall satisfaction and subsequent behaviour in the restaurant industry; services are primarily intangible and often require the customer to be present during the process. The physical environment can have a significant impact on the perception of the overall quality of the service encounter, which in turn affects customer satisfaction in the restaurant industry (Bitner, 1990; 1992; Brady & Cronin, 2001; Kotler, 1973; Parasuraman, Zeithaml, & Berry, 1988; Ryu & Jang, 2008).

The importance of the physical environment to create an image and to influence the behaviour of the client is especially relevant in the catering sector (Hui, Dube, & Chebat 1997; Millman, 1986; Raajpoot, 2002; Robson, 1999). Since the service is generally produced and consumed at the same time, the consumer is 'in the factory', they often experience total service within the physical property facilities (Bitner, 1992).

Research suggests a direct relationship between physical environment and outcomes, such as customer satisfaction (Chang, 2000). For example, Wakefield and Blodgett (1996) examined the effects of accessibility design, aesthetics of facilities, electronic equipment, seating comfort, and cleanliness in terms of the perceived quality of the SERVICESCAPE. The results revealed that the perceived quality of the physical environment significantly affects a client. In addition, Chang (2000) suggests that the physical environment was in general a direct indicator of a satisfied customer, suggesting that customer satisfaction was directly and positively associated with aspects of positive approach behaviours. Therefore, restaurateurs could have another tool with which to manage customer satisfaction and subsequent behaviour.

Kivela, Inbakaran, & Reece (2000) found that 'excellence in the environment' was one of the most important predictors of revisiting the establishment and Sparks, Bowen, & Klag (2003) found in their study; that more than 55% tourists in restaurants were positively affected by an attractive decor. When it comes to dining out, people are constantly looking for comfort as well as quality and a pleasant and affordable atmosphere away from their everyday life. Soriano (2003) states that providing good food and good service is not enough to attract consumers; restaurants should offer good value meals in a favourable environment. Cullen (2004), Erik & Nir (2004) and Bartha (2008) pointed out that attractive décor and the environment influence consumers' choice of where to dine. Henson, Majowicz, Masakure, Sockett, Jones, & Hart (2006) found that cleanliness was the most important determinant for consumers in the food safety assessment of the restaurant.

Although food quality is basic in a restaurant perception, the ambience and service performance greatly influence a customer's evaluation of a particular establishment (Wall & Berry, 2007). Lin & Mattila (2010) examined the relative impact of physical surroundings and customer-employee interactions on customers' emotions and satisfaction; they found that the servicescape and the service encounter influence pleasure and satisfaction. In addition, perceived congruency (i.e., matching the restaurant theme with food served and matching the exterior look with the interior décor) had a positive impact on pleasure level, while such impact on arousal was minimal. Further, perceived congruency and pleasure had a joint impact on satisfaction.

Kisang, Hye-Rin, & Woo Gon (2012) found that the quality of the physical environment, food, and service were significant determinants of restaurant image. The quality of the physical environment and food were significant predictors of customer perceived value, and the restaurant image was found to be a significant antecedent of customer perceived value.

Hwang & Ok (2013) explained that physical environment quality had a significant effect only on hedonic attitude and interactional and outcome qualities had significant effects on utilitarian and hedonic attitudes toward restaurant brands. Ha & Jang (2013) investigated the moderating role of personality characteristics and overall loyalty level toward a restaurant in the relationship between variety drivers and variety seeking intentions. Their results showed that atmospheric quality, overall boredom, and boredom with atmospheric attributes significantly influence variety seeking intentions. Marinkovic, Senic, Ivkov, Dimitrovski, & Bjelic

(2014) confirmed the significant impact of atmosphere and quality of interaction on guest satisfaction.

Jin, Goh, Huffman, & Yuan (2015) showed that perceived image of restaurant innovativeness (perceived innovativeness of environment quality) influences both brand credibility and brand preference. Ali, Amin, & Ryu (2016) revealed that the physical environment is a significant predictor of consumption emotions and price perceptions, which in turn affect customer satisfaction. Moreover, consumption emotions and price perceptions significantly mediate the relationship between physical environment and customer satisfaction.

The hotel restaurant's physical environment quality has evolved. In the decade of the nineties, the variables related to quality were mainly the space, cleanliness, the decoration and the music which generated the atmosphere and ambiance of the establishment. Later, aspects such as comfort, attractive décor and aesthetics were also important. In the new millennium, the perceived congruency and pleasure generated by the perception of the utilitarian and hedonic space itself became relevant; currently followed by the perceived innovativeness of environmental quality.

2.3 Restaurants Food Quality

The quality of the food, the ambience, the variety of the menu, the service of the staff, the cleanliness, style, price, interior design and decor, professional staff appearance, and store location have been identified as components of the image of the shop in the catering sector (Baker, Grewal, & Parasuraman, 1994; Lindquist, 1974; Prendergast & Man, 2002).

Clark & Wood (1999) observed that food quality was the most influential predictor of consumer loyalty in restaurant choice. MacLaurin & MacLaurin (2000) explored nine factors in thematic restaurants in Singapore and food quality was included as one of the important elements in addition to thematic concept, quality of service, menu, environment, comfort, and the merchandise of products and prices.

Fu & Parks (2001) examined the quality of service dimensions that influence diners towards their intention to return to a family-style restaurant. They used 'food quality' as one of the 24 items of the questionnaire to measure 'perceived quality of restaurant service'. Mattila (2001) indicated that the three main reasons for customers to frequent their restaurants were quality of food, service and atmosphere. Specifically, the quality of the food was the most important attribute of the quality of the restaurant service.

Some research showed that the most important factor in determining whether a customer is returning to the restaurant was food quality (Soriano, 2003; Sulek & Hensley, 2004). In addition, food quality and freshness of ingredients have been rated as the most important reasons customers return to a restaurant (Brumback, 1999; Sulek & Hensley, 2004). Taste is one of the attributes most used to measure consumer preference in the selection of a restaurant.

Namkung & Jang (2007) describe how overall food quality significantly affects customer satisfaction and behavioural intentions and revealed that the relationship between food quality and customer behavioural intentions is mediated by satisfaction; also taste and presentation were the two greatest contributors to customer satisfaction and behavioural intentions. Food is considered as one of the most important attributes of customer satisfaction in restaurants (Heung & Ngai, 2008).

Liu & Jang (2009b) indicated that food quality, service reliability and environmental cleanliness are three pivotal attributes to create satisfied customers and positive post-dining behavioural intentions. Ha & Jang (2010) found that providing quality food is particularly critical for creating customer satisfaction in ethnic restaurants where atmospherics are not satisfactory. Kwun (2011) confirm that enhanced performance in product quality, menu, and facility have favourable effects on perceived value, satisfaction and, ultimately, on consumer attitude. Jang, Liu, & Namkung (2011) revealed that menu presentation is a significant predictor of positive emotions.

Ryu, Lee, & Gon Kim (2012) showed that the quality of food is a significant determinant of restaurant image. In addition, the quality of food is also a significant predictor of customer perceived value. Also Jin, Lee, & Huffman (2012) mentioned that a restaurant's food quality positively influences brand image and customers' satisfaction. Teng & Chang (2013) indicated that the relationship between food quality and affective responses increases with employee hospitality.

Lee, Jin, & Lee (2014) found that food quality have significant interaction on the relationship between perceived value and attitudinal/behavioural loyalty in a touristic water park. Dutta, Parsa, Parsa, & Bujisic (2014) found out that restaurateurs have a strategic advantage when they choose high-quality food. Lin (2014) studied the effects of cuisine experience and psychological well-being on hot springs tourists'; his results indicated that cuisine experience and psychological well-being influence hot springs tourists' revisit intentions and only cuisine experience affects psychological well-being.

Joung, Choi, & Goh (2015) examined relationships among food quality and behavioural intention regarding dining experiences in continuing care retirement communities in the United States. Their results show that food quality has positive impacts on residents' satisfaction and positively influenced behavioural intention. Bufquin, DiPietro, & Partlow (2016) confirmed in an independent casual-dining restaurant that food quality has an influence on customers' satisfaction, which in turn affects their behavioural intentions.

Kim & Baker (2017) find that using an ethnic menu name and possessing employees of referent ethnic origin have the largest impacts on customer perceptions of authenticity. Additionally, food authenticity has the largest impact on revisit intention, and culture and employee authenticity have the largest impact on willingness to pay more.

The quality of the food was, is and will be a fundamental aspect of tourists' expectations. The evolution of food quality has examined the quality of the ingredients, the flavour, the presentation of the food and the drinks as tangible elements that are complemented by intangible relationships such as identity, relevance (authenticity) and lifestyle (well-being).

2.4 Service Quality

There have been mixed results about the causal link between quality of service and customer satisfaction. The most common explanation for the difference is that perceived quality of service is described as a form of attitude, a long-term global evaluation of a product or service; while satisfaction is a specific evaluation of the transaction (Bitner, 1990; Cronin & Taylor, 1992; Oliver, 1981; Parasuraman et al., 1988).

Based on these conceptualisations, the incidents of satisfaction over time lead to the perception of quality of service. Many other researchers empirically support the influence of perceived service quality on customer satisfaction (Cronin & Taylor, 1992; Spreng & Mackoy, 1996). For example, Cronin & Taylor (1992) developed the SERWERF instrument based on SERVQUAL and examined the conceptualization and measurement of service quality and the relationship between quality of service, consumer satisfaction, and purchase intentions their findings suggest that service quality was a precedent of consumer satisfaction, while consumer satisfaction was not a significant predictor of service quality. Later, Bojanic & Rosen (1994) introduced a modified SERVQUAL model and identified six factors determining the service quality of restaurant customers: assurance, reliability, tangibles, access, knowing customers, and responsiveness.

Stevens, Knutson, & Patton (1995) proposed 'Dineserv' a tool for measuring service quality in restaurants as a reliable, relatively simple tool for determining how consumers view a restaurant's quality. The 29-item Dineserv questionnaire comprises service quality standards that fall into five categories: assurance, empathy, reliability, responsiveness and tangibles. Lee and Ulgado (1997) used the SERVQUAL instrument to examine the differences between the United States and Korean fast food consumers, comparing their expectations and perceptions of McDonald's as a Fast Food Restaurant. In addition to the original five dimensions of service quality, they added another three items dealing with food prices, service time, and location to expand the study of the underlying factors of overall perceived service quality.

Lee, Lee, & Yoo (2000) examined the causal relationship between quality of service and satisfaction. The results showed that the perceived quality of service was a precedent of satisfaction, not the other way around. Consistent with these findings, they suggested that service quality better explains customer satisfaction, and the coefficient of service quality path to customer satisfaction is greater than the coefficient of the path of customer satisfaction with quality of service.

Fu & Parks (2001) analysed the relationship between service quality dimensions and restaurant loyalty among elderly customers at two family-style restaurants using the SERVQUAL instrument; their major findings were that friendly service and individual attention were more important factors than tangible aspects of service in influencing elderly customers' behavioural intentions. Law, Hui, & Zhao (2004) conducted a study to model repurchase frequency and customer satisfaction for fast food restaurants, and they identified the following underlying factors in the determination of return frequency: difference between expected and actual waiting time, satisfaction with waiting, food price, employee attitudes, food quality, food variety, convenience, environment and availability.

Jain & Gupta (2004) conducted a survey of consumers in fast food restaurants in India and compared weighted and unweighted versions of the SERVQUAL and SERWERF instruments. They found that SERVPERF is more effective in explaining service quality constructs and variations in overall service quality scores. Therefore, in this study, performance perceptions alone were used to measure service quality, and the items of service quality would be adapted to the fast food restaurants context.

Lee, Park, Park, Lee, & Kwon (2005) discovered that the greater the tangibles, assurance, and sensory dimensions of service quality, the greater are the perceived service values by the customers. Hau-siu Chow, Lau, Wing-chun Lo, Sha, & Yun (2007) supported the significant links between service quality and customer satisfaction, service quality and repeat patronage, but not customer satisfaction and repeat patronage. Susskind, Kacmar, & Borchgrevink (2007) explained the relationship between guest service employees' work-related perceptions and attitudes;

they are all connected to guests' reported satisfaction. Their results show that employees' perceptions of the presence of organisational standards for service delivery were strongly related to their perceptions of receiving adequate support from co-workers and supervisors to perform their jobs. Employees' perceived support from co-workers was significantly related to service providers' guest orientation (commitment to their guests), while perceived support from supervisors proved to be a weak influence on guest orientation. Ultimately, service providers' guest orientation was strongly related to guests' satisfaction with their service experience in the restaurant.

Qin & Prybutok (2009) indicated that five dimensions in restaurant service were significant: tangibles, reliability/responsiveness, recovery, assurance, and empathy service quality was determinant of customer satisfaction. Gazzoli, Hancer, & Park (2010) suggested that empowerment and job satisfaction have a significant impact on customers' perception-of-service quality. Ryu, Han, & Jang (2010) showed that quality of service was a significant determinant of customer satisfaction. Sunghyup (2010) found that service quality was the only attribute to directly and indirectly affect trust.

Namkung & Jang (2010) studied diners in the United States assessed customer reaction to failures in the following four service stages: (1) reception, (2) ordering, (3) meal consumption, and (4) checkout. The study found that in both casual dining and fine dining restaurants, service failure in stage 3 (consumption) most strongly diminishes overall customer satisfaction, followed by stage 4 (payment and exiting), stage 2 (order taking and delivery), and finally stage 1 (greeting and seating). The relative impact of service failure on behavioural intentions varies by service stage and restaurant type. In casual dining restaurants, service failure in stage 3 had the most effect in diminishing diners' intent to come back and willingness to recommend the restaurant to others, followed by service failure in stage 4. On the other hand, for fine dining restaurants, service failure in stage 2 was the most critical influence on diners' likelihood of returning. Additionally, stage 4 was the most important determinant in fine restaurant diners' willingness to recommend the restaurant to others.

Mathe & Slevitch (2013) studied the interaction between employee involvement climate and supervisor undermining; their results suggest that a significant interaction exists between these two constructs and are key predictors in increasing or decreasing customer perceptions of service quality. Marinkovic et al. (2014) confirmed the significant impact of quality of interaction on guest satisfaction, and satisfaction, along with the atmosphere and perceived price emerged as a significant trigger of revisit intentions. Lai (2015) found that service quality positively influences perceived value, customer satisfaction, and customer loyalty and customers rate food and service attributes as most important when dining out.

Rhee, Yang, & Kim (2016) show that service is considered as substantially important criteria in selecting restaurants. Kuo, Chen, & Cheng (2016) analysed the DINESERV framework to compare revisiting customers with first-time customers, showing there was no significant difference in the service constructs of empathy, assurance, and reliability. However, the satisfaction of first-time customers is influenced more by the responsiveness of front-line service staff, whereas revisiting customers care more about the dining atmosphere. Djekic, Kane, Tomic, Kalogianni, Rocha, Zamioudi, & Pacheco (2016) found that consumers from different cities showed different perceptions regarding service quality in restaurants. The gender of consumers plays a significant role in the perception of interior, restroom and servicing factors in restaurants.

Arroyo-López, Cárcamo-Solís, Álvarez-Castañón, & Guzmán-López (2017) corroborated that training becomes relevant to develop proper service skills and customer orientation. The effectiveness of training in the improvement of service quality was evident after the comparison of measures of service quality and perceived price before and after service employees completed the training. Jalilvand, Salimipour, Elyasi, & Mohammadi (2017) found that personal interaction quality influence word-of-mouth behaviour of customer in an indirect way through relationship quality.

From SERVQUAL were generated multiple instruments to adapt it to the food and beverage service industry. Later, the influence of the satisfaction of the staff with the satisfaction of the tourists was studied, the service was conceived as a process divided in stages and the importance of the training and the influence of the leaders in the satisfaction of the clients was denoted. Recently, differences between the perceptions and expectations of first-time customer to restaurants and those that repeat the experience have been studied.

2.5 Satisfaction

It should be kept in mind that different cultures have different perceptions of satisfaction and evaluation of gastronomy and that high quality of service can result in dissatisfaction among consumers if their expectations had been too high, quality in hotel's restaurant is a decisive factor in satisfaction, as it produces a lasting memory about the experience for the tourist.

Customer satisfaction has long been considered a fundamental determinant of long-term customer behaviour (Oliver, 1980; Yi, 1990), so service firms increasingly dedicate substantial energies to tracking customer satisfaction.

Hunt (1977) defined satisfaction as 'an evaluation rendered that the (product) experience was at least as good as it was supposed to be' (p. 459). Similarly, based on the theoretical-empirical evidence to date, Oliver (1997) described it as

> the consumer's fulfilment response. It is a judgment that a product or service feature, or the product or service itself, provided (or is providing) a pleasurable level of consumption-related fulfilment, including levels of under- or overfulfillment (p. 13).

Although researchers struggle to clearly define the concept of customer satisfaction, an essential aspect of customer satisfaction is an evaluation process (Back, 2005). This evaluative process-oriented approach has been regarded as the most effective way to measure the level of customer satisfaction (Oliver, 1997; Yi, 1990).

According to Oliver (1993), satisfaction links purchase/consumption with post-purchase phenomena, such as repeat purchase, positive word-of-mouth advertising, and brand loyalty. Satisfaction occurs when the actual performance is equal to or greater than the expected performance (Oliver, 1981; Yuskel & Rimmington, 1998). Patterson & Spreng (1997) examined the role of perceived value to the customer to explain the behaviour of consumers in a service context and found that perceived customer value was a positive and direct antecedent of customer satisfaction. In addition, customer satisfaction can be explained as a consumption of subsequent evaluation judgment, relating to a product or a service (Yuskel & Rimmington, 1998).

Dabholkar, Shepherd, & Thorpe (2000) found that satisfaction has significant direct effects on customer's behavioural intentions. This study investigated the effect of customer satisfaction on behavioural intentions. Previous studies show that the brand/store have a significant impact on the satisfaction (Andreassen & Lindestad, 1998; Bloemer, Reyter, & Wetzels, 1999, Cretu & Brodie, 2007; Patterson & Spreng, 1997; Ryu et al., 2008). Therefore, maintaining the image of a restaurant differentiated from the competition is an important task for restaurant operators. Managing a consistent and distinct image in the restaurant is an important marketing strategy for restaurant manager's component, which in turn influences satisfaction.

Ryu et al. (2008) examined the relationship between the overall image of fast-casual dining, perceived customer value, customer satisfaction, and intentions and found that overall image of a restaurant was an important determinant of value and perceived customer satisfaction. Chow et al. (2007) investigated the relationship between quality of service, customer satisfaction and frequency of recommendation in the context of full-service restaurants. They captured three dimensions of quality (quality of interaction, physical quality and quality of results). Namkung & Jang (2008) also conducted a study to identify key quality attributes that significantly distinguish highly satisfied diners from those who are not highly satisfied, using the context of medium to high-end restaurants. Three quality factors (food, atmosphere and service) were used to measure perceived quality of diners in relation to experience in the restaurant.

Quality of service and customer satisfaction have become the most basic marketing priorities, as they are prerequisites of consumer loyalty, such as repeat sales and positive word-of-mouth recommendation (Han & Ryu, 2009; Liu & Jang, 2009b). In particular, in the catering sector, customers typically use food, physical environment, and employee services as key components of the restaurant quality assessment experience (Chow et al., 2007; Namkung & Jang, 2008; Ryu, Han, & Jang, 2010).

Moreover, Jang & Namkung (2009) incorporated specific stimuli and measurement of specific emotions in a restaurant. In addition, Ryu & Han (2010) study, examined the relationships between the three determining dimensions of quality (food, service and physical environment), price, customer satisfaction and behavioural intention in casual restaurants fast food. The mediator satisfaction between service quality and behavioural intentions role has been established in the marketing literature. Wansink & van Ittersum (2012) in a fast food restaurant study indicated that softening the lighting and music led people to eat less, to rate the food as more enjoyable, and to spend just as much, a more relaxed environment increases satisfaction and decreases consumption.

Lee, Cho, & Ahn (2012) examined (a) the relationship between customer satisfaction and service quality among elderly consumers, (b) differences in level of satisfaction between older and younger customers, (c) differences in perception-of-service quality between older and younger customers, and (d) differences in perception-of-service quality between elderly male and female customers. Statistically significant differences in levels of satisfaction were discovered between older and younger customers, but no significant relationship was found between level of customer satisfaction and perceived service quality. There were significant differences in perceptions of service quality between older and younger customers, and between male and female older customers.

Choi & Sheel (2012) examined on family restaurants the relationship between the services offered to waiting customers and customer satisfaction in family restaurants. Analysis of the data using exploratory factor analysis identified five key constructs that summarized important areas of waiting service: human service, visual media service, menu service, sitting service, and notice service. They indicated that all five factors influenced customer satisfaction.

Tan, Oriade, & Fallon (2014) investigated customer's perception of Chinese fast food restaurant service quality and its relationship with customer satisfaction. Employing modified DINESERV scale, they proposed a new measurement scale, Chinese Fast Food Restaurants Service Quality Scale (CFFRSERV), contained 28 items across six dimensions: assurance and empathy, food, cleanliness, responsiveness, reliability and tangibles. Their findings revealed that service quality variables have positive influence on customer satisfaction except reliability dimension.

Liu, Huang, & Chen (2014) explored relationships among relationship benefits, customer satisfaction, and customer citizenship behaviour from the viewpoint of organisational citizenship behaviour theory in chain store restaurants. The research result is customer satisfaction has an intervening effect between relational benefits and customer citizenship behaviour. Moreover, customer satisfaction with employees increases positive satisfaction with stores significantly.

Jin, Line, & Merkebu (2015) found that innovative customers are grateful to the restaurant for having their needs for novelty satisfied, were more likely to perceive prices as fair and were more likely to report positive behavioural intentions. Satisfaction in restaurants was conceived for many years as the primary objective of business owners and people dedicated to marketing food and beverage establishments. The studies presented, have dedicated their perspectives and methodologies searching for the causes that generate satisfaction and to explain or predict the repeating satisfaction way through processes and recommendations. The first studies describe the elements that generate satisfaction, then the cause-and-effect relationships are studied in simple models and with few variables, nowadays are studying the relations of multiple factors in complex models that pretend to explain the degree of incidence of each factor in the satisfaction to prioritize and predict them. Attention is now given to behavioural intentions and loyalty because a customer who is satisfied does not necessarily repeat or recommend the consumption of services and products.

2.6 Behavioural Intentions

Behavioural intentions can be defined as forecasting or future planned behaviour of an individual (Swan, 1981). It reflects the expectations of an individual on a particular behaviour in a given environment and can be interpreted as the probability of action (Fishbein & Ajzen, 1975). Behavioural intentions are defined according to four categories: (1) personal communication mouth-to-mouth, (2) purchase intentions, (3) the price sensitivity and (4) the complaint behaviour. The latter two categories contain elements that are not based on the quality of service (Cronin & Taylor, 1992; Zeithaml, Berry, & Parasuraman, 1996).

Repeat purchase is an important outcome measure for organisations, and is seen as an indicator showing whether a customer will stay or leave the company (Zeithaml, Berry, & Parasuraman, 1996). In addition, the effects caused by the change in the retention rate are exponential, a reduction or increase in the retention rate has significant effects on future earnings (Reichheld and Sasser Jr., 1990; Gould, 1995).

Customers frequently develop an attitude toward purchasing based on prior service experience. They also undergo a cognitive decision-making process about whether to stay or leave a service firm (Colgate & Lang, 2001). Oliver (1997) described this attitude as the development of a fairly stable like/dislike of a product based on previous experience. He also indicated that customers can develop an attitude based on prior information without actual experience, so they frequently increase biases for or against providers based on the provider's images in the marketplace. This attitude is strongly related to the customers' intentions to repatronise the service/product and to be engaged in word-of-mouth behaviours. In this sense, Oliver (1997) defined behavioural intentions as an affirmed likelihood to engage in a certain behaviour. Based on this definition, behavioural intention in this study may be described as a stated likelihood to return to the restaurant and to recommend the restaurant to family, friends, and others in the future.

Behavioural intentions involve recommend the company to others, offering positive words, willingness to behave as a partner organization, and the sample of staying true to the company (Brown, Berry, Dacin, & Gunst, 2005; Bowen & Shoemarker, 1998; Reichheld & Sasser, 1990; Reichheld, 1996). Other researchers have included an attitudinal component behavioural intention, which, if positive, can produce customer loyalty (Han & Ryu, 2009). When behavioural components are favourable, which is the goal of service providers, customers positively affirm their chance to reuse services/products provider and share positive to other people with whom they are in contact criticism. When the components of intent are negative, it is likely that the opposite customer behaviour occurs, these values into behavioural intentions involve an attitudinal component of likes and dislikes (Peter & Olson, 2003). Thus, when the valence is positive for both behavioural intentions, customer attitudes are positive towards the service provider and are likely to lead to loyalty to the supplier.

Behavioural intentions include revisits and word-of-mouth intentions (Han & Ryu, 2009; Ryu et al., 2010; Ok, Back, & Shanklin, 2005) that can predict the future consumption behaviour of consumers and their recipient's word-of-mouth intentions. Behavioural intentions are comprised of both attitudinal and behavioural indicators (Othman, Zahari, & Radzi, 2013) and include consumers' willingness to repurchase and spread positive recommendation to others (Giovanis, Tomaras, & Zondiros 2013; Heung & Gu, 2012; Hyun, Kim, & Lee 2011; Lai & Chen, 2011). Depending on consumer experiences and evaluations (Othman, Zahari, & Radzi 2013), behavioural intentions can be positive or negative. Positive behavioural intentions can lead to a willingness to pay premium prices (Chang & Polonsky, 2012) and are often associated with more frequent re-patronage (Liang & Zhang, 2011; Othman, Zahari, & Radzi, 2013). Conversely, negative behavioural intentions are likely to contribute to an increase in consumer complaints and a decrease in the probability of spending money at a service firm (Othman, Zahari, & Radzi, 2013). In the context of restaurant patronage, behavioural intentions represent the likelihood that patrons will visit a restaurant in the future and/or recommend the restaurant to friends or family through word-of-mouth communication (Heung & Gu, 2012; Liu & Jang, 2009b).

Jin, Line, & Merkebu (2015) conducted research to identify drivers of price fairness and post-consumption behavioural intentions within the context of upscale/ fine dining restaurant patronage. The results suggest for innovative consumers, the perception that a restaurant is innovative results in increased perceptions of price fairness and positive post-consumption behavioural intention. Kim & Baker (2017) found that tangible cues are critical indicators of customer perceptions of authenticity and behavioural intentions.

3 Discussion

The tourist today is more cultured than the visitors of 20–30 years ago. They are looking for new experiences, are concerned about the environment, interested in health/wellness lifestyle issues and want to experience the local culture when travelling. It is important to know the trends of gastronomic tourism in order to have a basis on what tourists prefer today in their travel experiences. The main difference lies in what is perceived as quality. There are many studies that attribute different indicators to describe the quality that seems to be a constant —the greater tourists' knowledge about the destination is, the greater their expectation of their visits.

Over the decades there is an evolution of the factors that promote satisfaction, as the years go by it seems that there is a greater complexity on the demand and supply of restaurants. In recent years, the increasing competition and the evolution of tourist profiles promote the search for a more specialised competitive advantage and the development of more sophisticated products compounded with various complements.

A synthesis of existing literature reveals that components of restaurant experience are restaurant interior and atmosphere, social meeting, food and beverage quality, the company of other people and customer satisfaction. Food is the most influential restaurant selection attribute and determinant of tourist satisfaction and retention, and still food and beverage constitute the core of meal experience.

From the tourist demand point of view, it becomes clear that all the factors mentioned have an influence on the tourists' behavioural intentions; clarifying that the different types of tourists have varying levels of expectations. Quality of food and quality of service seems to be the main factors that have the greatest relevance in the culinary experiences of tourists of all types and ages. It is possible to assume that the menu has primary implications for the core component of meal experience and that menu planning attentive to tourists' expectations assures they can receive what they expect in terms of content, variety and expectations.

From the hotel restaurant's offer point of view, another important consideration is the defined concept, its category and the type of service it provides to diners. There are big differences over offers/expectations in a fast food service such as a limited beach menu restaurant, a typical regional food restaurant and a gourmet specialty restaurant.

The review of the studies shows different types of analysis from theoretical conceptual perspectives, descriptive studies, correlation and some that pretend to be explanatory in a very limited context and specific to the restaurant industry. We are in times of advanced research techniques and methods used to generate quality knowledge in the tourism and restaurant industry. The increasing number of studies dedicated to the subject and the era of easy access to the information, allows us to glimpse a more consistent and clear development of the factors related to the tourist behavioural intentions in hotel restaurants.

4 Conclusion

There are multiple aspects that a tourist considers when attending a restaurant, by the nature of the activity, food and service that are the fundamental part of the experience, but there are other factors that become relevant and that are increasingly appreciated and valued by tourists. It is necessary to go deeper into studies that use multivariate techniques and methods that allow establishing descriptive parameters on the main factors that foster satisfaction and positive intentions of behaviour in tourists who attend different hotel restaurants concepts. The biggest challenge is to be able to identify similar groups of tourists, their expectations and needs as they vary according to their age, idiosyncrasy, culture, country of origin, socio-economic and socio-cultural class.

The best way for a tourist to understand the offer of a restaurant in a hotel, is that all factors related to the intentions of behaviour must clearly communicate the concept of the establishment; its gastronomic offer, its service, the environment that is created in the physical place, and the needs that satisfies the establishment.

References

Ali, F., Amin, M., & Ryu, K. (2016). The role of physical environment, price perceptions, and consumption emotions in developing customer satisfaction in Chinese resort hotels. *Journal of Quality Assurance in Hospitality & Tourism*, 17(1), 45–70. https://doi.org/10.1080/1528008X.2015.1016595.

Andreassen, T., & Lindestad, B. (1998). Customer loyalty and complex services. *International Journal of Service Industry Management*, 9(1), 7–23. http://doi.org/10.1108/09564239810199923.

Arroyo-López, P. E., Cárcamo-Solís, M. de L., Álvarez-Castañón, L., & Guzmán-López, A. (2017). Impact of training on improving service quality in small provincial restaurants. *Journal of Foodservice Business Research*, 20(1), 1–14. https://doi.org/10.1080/15378020.2016.1192881.

Back, K. J. (2005). The effects of image congruence on customers' brand loyalty in the upper middle-class hotel industry. *Journal of Hospitality & Tourism Research*, 29(4), 448–467.

Baker, J., Grewal, D., & Parasuraman, A. (1994). The influence of store environment on quality inferences and store image. *Journal of the Academy of Marketing Science*, 22(4), 328–339.

Bartha, A. (2008). Foreign tourist motivation and information source influencing their preference for eating out at ethnic restaurants in Bangkok. *International Journal of Hospitality & Tourism Administration*, 9(1), 1–17.

Beardsworth, A. & Keil, T. (1997). *Sociology on the menu: An invitation to the study of food and society*. London: Routledge.

Bitner, M. (1990). Evaluating service encounters: The effects of physical surroundings and employee responses. *Journal of Marketing*, 54(2), 69–82. doi: 10.2307/1251871.

Bitner, M. (1992). Servicescapes: The impact of physical surroundings on customers and employees. *Journal of Marketing*, 56(2), 57–71. doi: 10.2307/1252042.

Bloemer, J., de Ruyter, K., & Wetzels, M. (1999). Linking perceived service quality and service loyalty: A multi-dimensional perspective. *European Journal of Marketing*, 33(11/12), 1082–1106. http://doi.org/10.1108/03090569910292285.

Bojanic, D. C., & Rosen, D. L. (1994). Measuring service quality in restaurants: An application of the SERVQUAL instrument. *Hospitality Research Journal*, 18(1), 3–14.

Bowen, J. T., & Shoemarker, S. (1998). Loyalty: A strategic commitment. *Cornell Hotel and Restaurant Administration Quarterly*, 39(1), 12–25.

Brady, M. K., & Cronin, J. (2001). Some new thoughts on conceptualizing perceived service quality: A hierarchical approach. *Journal of Marketing*, 65(3), 34–49.

Brillat-Savarin, J. A. (1999). *The Physiology of taste, or, meditations on transcendental gastronomy*, tr. M. F. K. Fisher. Washington, DC: Counterpoint Press.

Brown, T. J., Barry, T. E., Dacin, P. A., & Gunst, R. F. (2005). Spreading the word: investigating antecedents of consumers' positive word-of-mouth intentions and behaviors in a retailing context. *Journal of the Academy of Marketing Science*, 33(2), 123–138.

Brumback, N. (1999). Roaming holiday. *Restaurant Business*, 8(3), 39.

Bufquin, D., DiPietro, R., & Partlow, C. (2016). The influence of the DinEX service quality dimensions on casual-dining restaurant customers' satisfaction and behavioural intentions. *Journal of Foodservice Business Research*, 1–15. https://doi.org/10.1080/15378020.2016.1222744.

Chang, K. (2000). The impact of perceived physical environments on customers: satisfaction and return intentions. *Journal of Professional Services Marketing*, 21(2), 75–85.

Chang, Y.-W., & Polonsky, M. J. (2012). The influence of multiple types of service convenience on behavioural intentions: The mediating role of consumer satisfaction in a Taiwanese leisure setting. *International Journal of Hospitality Management*, 31, 107–118.

Choi, C., & Sheel, A. (2012). Assessing the relationship between waiting services and customer satisfaction in family restaurants. *Journal of Quality Assurance in Hospitality & Tourism*, 13(1), 24–36. https://doi.org/10.1080/1528 008X.2012.643186.

Chow, I. H., Lau, P. V., Lob, T. W., Sha, Z., & Yun, H. (2007). Service quality in restaurant operations in China: Decision- and experiential-oriented perspectives. *International Journal of Hospitality Management*, 26(3), 698–710.

Clark, A., & Wood, R. (1999). Consumer loyalty in the restaurant industry: A preliminary exploration of the issues. *International Journal of Contemporary Hospitality Management*, 10(4), 139–144.

Colgate, M., & Lang, B. (2001). Switching barriers in consumer markets: An investigation of the financial services industry. *Journal of Consumer Marketing*, 18(4), 332–347.

Cretu, A. E., & Brodie, R. J. (2007). The influence of brand image and company reputation where manufacturers market to small firms: A customer value perspective. *Industrial Marketing Management*, 36(2), 230–240. http://doi.org/10.1016/j.indmarman.2005.08.013.

Cronin, J., & Taylor, S. (1992). Measuring service quality: A reexamination and extension. *Journal of Marketing*, 56(3), 55–68.

Cullen, F. (2004). Factors influencing restaurant selection in Dublin. *Journal of Food Service Business Research*, 7(2), 53–84.

Dabholkar, P. A., Shepherd, C. D., & Thorpe, D. I. (2000). A comprehensive framework for service quality: An investigation of critical conceptual and measurement issues through a longitudinal study. *Journal of Retailing*, 76(2), 139–173.

Djekic, I., Kane, K., Tomic, N., Kalogianni, E., Rocha, A., Zamioudi, L., & Pacheco, R. (2016). Cross-cultural consumer perceptions of service quality in restaurants. *Nutrition & Food Science*, 46(6), 827–843. https://doi.org/10.1108/NFS-04-2016-0052.

Dulen, J. (1999). Quality control. *Restaurant & Institutions*, 109(5), 38–52.

Dutta, K., Parsa, H. G., Parsa, R. A., & Bujisic, M. (2014). Change in consumer patronage and willingness to pay at different levels of service attributes in restaurants: A study in India. *Journal of Quality Assurance in Hospitality & Tourism*, 15(2), 149–174. https://doi.org/10.1080/1528008X.2014.889533.

Erik, C., & Nir, A. (2004). Food in tourism: Attraction and impediment. *Annals of Tourism Research*, 31(4), 755–778.

Fishbein, M., & Ajzen, I. (1975). *Belief, attitude, intention and behavior: An introduction to theory and research*. Reading: Addison-Wesley.

Fu, Y.-Y., & Parks, S. C. (2001). The Relationship between restaurant service quality and consumer loyalty among the elderly. *Journal of Hospitality & Tourism Research*, 25(3), 320–326. http://doi.org/10.1177/109634800102500306.

Gazzoli, G., Hancer, M., & Park, Y. (2010). The role and effect of job satisfaction and empowerment on customers' perception of service quality: A study in the restaurant industry. *Journal of Hospitality & Tourism Research*, 34(1), 56–77. https://doi.org/10.1177/1096348009344235.

Giovanis, A. N., Tomaras, P., & Zondiros, D. (2013). Suppliers logistics service quality performance and its effect on retailers' behavioural intentions. *Procedia – Social and Behavioural Sciences*, 73, 302–309.

Gould, G. (1995). Why it is customer loyalty that counts and how to measure it? *Managing Service Quality*, 7(4), 4–26.

Gregoire, M. B., Shanklin, C. W., Greathouse, K. R., & Tripp, C. (1995). Factors influencing restaurant selection by travelers who stop at visitor information centers. *Journal of Travel & Tourism Management*, 4(2), 41–50.

Ha, J., & Jang, S. (Shawn). (2010). Effects of service quality and food quality: The moderating role of atmospherics in an ethnic restaurant segment. *International Journal of Hospitality Management*, 29(3), 520–529. https://doi.org/10.1016/j.ijhm.2009.12.005.

Ha, J., & Jang, S. (Shawn). (2013). Variety seeking in restaurant choice and its drivers. *International Journal of Hospitality Management*, 32, 155–168. https://doi.org/10.1016/j.ijhm.2012.05.007.

Han, H., & Ryu, K. (2009). The roles of the physical environment, price perception, and customer satisfaction in determining customer loyalty in the restaurant industry. *Journal of Hospitality & Tourism Research*, 33(4), 487–510. http://doi.org/10.1177/1096348009344212.

Henson, S., Majowicz, S., Masakure, O., Sockett, P., Jones, A., Hart, R., et al. (2006). Consumer assessment of the safety of restaurants: The role of inspection notices and other information cues. *Journal of Food Safety*, 26, 275–301.

Heung, V., & Gu, T. (2012). Influence of restaurant atmospherics on patron satisfaction and behavioural intentions. *International Journal of Hospitality Management*, 31(4), 1167–1177.

Heung, V., & Ngai, E. W. T. (2008). The mediating effects of perceived value and customer satisfaction on customer loyalty in the Chinese restaurant setting. *Journal of Quality Assurance in Hospitality & Tourism*, 9(2), 85–107.

Hui, M., Dube, L., & Chebat, J. (1997). The impact of music on consumer's reaction to waiting for services. *Journal of Retailing*, 73(1), 87–104.

Hunt, H. K. (1977). *Conceptualization and measurement of consumer satisfaction and dissatisfaction.* Cambridge, MA: Marketing Science Institute.

Hwang, J., & Ok, C. (2013). The antecedents and consequence of consumer attitudes toward restaurant brands: A comparative study between casual and fine dining restaurants. *International Journal of Hospitality Management*, 32, 121–131. https://doi.org/10.1016/j.ijhm.2012.05.002.

Hyun, S. S., Kim, W., & Lee, M. J. (2011). The impact of advertising on patrons' emotional responses, perceived value, and behavioural intentions in the chain restaurant industry: The moderating role of advertising-induced arousal. *International Journal of Hospitality Management*, 30(3), 689–700.

Jain, S. K., & Gupta, G. (2004). Measuring service quality: SERVQUAL vs. SERVPERF scales. *VIKALPA*, 29, 2, 25–37.

Jalilvand, M. R., Salimipour, S., Elyasi, M., & Mohammadi, M. (2017). Factors influencing word of mouth behaviour in the restaurant industry. *Marketing Intelligence & Planning*, 35(1), 81–110. https://doi.org/10.1108/MIP-02-2016-0024.

Jang, S., & Namkung, Y. (2009). Perceived quality, emotions, and behavioural intentions: Application of an extended Mehrabian-Russell model to restaurants.
Journal of Business Research, 62, 451–460.

Jang, S. C., Liu, Y., & Namkung, Y. (2011). Effects of authentic atmospherics
in ethnic restaurants: Investigating Chinese restaurants. *International Journal of Contemporary Hospitality Management*, 23(5), 662–680. https://doi.
org/10.1108/09596111111143395.

Jin, N. (Paul), Goh, B., Huffman, L., & Yuan, J. J. (2015). Predictors and outcomes
of perceived image of restaurant innovativeness in fine-dining restaurants.
Journal of Hospitality Marketing & Management, 24(5), 457–485. https://doi.
org/10.1080/19368623.2014.915781.

Jin, N., Lee, S., & Huffman, L. (2012). Impact of restaurant experience on brand
image and customer loyalty: Moderating role of dining motivation. *Journal of
Travel & Tourism Marketing*, 29(6), 532–551. https://doi.org/10.1080/105484
08.2012.701552.

Jin, N. (Paul), Line, N. D., & Merkebu, J. (2015). Examining the impact of consumer innovativeness and innovative restaurant image in upscale restaurants. *Cornell Hospitality Quarterly*, 57(3), 268–281. https://doi.org/10.1177/
1938965515619229.

Joung, H.-W., Choi, E.-K. (Cindy), & Goh, B. K. (2015). The impact of perceived
service and food quality on behavioural intentions in continuing care retirement communities: A mediating effect of satisfaction. *Journal of Quality Assurance in Hospitality & Tourism*, 16(3), 221–234. https://doi.org/10.1080/15
28008X.2015.1016593.

Kim, K., & Baker, M. A. (2017). The impacts of service provider name, ethnicity,
and menu information on perceived authenticity and behaviors. *Cornell Hospitality Quarterly*, 58(3), 312–318. https://doi.org/10.1177/1938965516686107.

Kisang R., Hye-Rin L., & Woo Gon. K. (2012). The influence of the quality of the
physical environment, food, and service on restaurant image, customer perceived value, customer satisfaction, and behavioural intentions. *International
Journal of Contemporary Hospitality Management*, 24(2), 200–223. https://doi.
org/10.1108/09596111211206141.

Kivela, J., Inbakaran, R., & Reece, J. (2000). Consumer research in the restaurant
environment, Part 3: Analysis, findings and conclusions. *International Journal
of Contemporary Hospitality Management*, 12(1), 13–30.

Kotler, P. (1973). Atmospherics as a marketing tool. *Journal of Retailing*, 49(4),
48–64.

Kuo, T., Chen, C. T., & Cheng, W. J. (2016). Service quality evaluation: Moderating influences of first-time and revisiting customers. *Total Quality Management & Business Excellence*, 1–12. https://doi.org/10.1080/14783363.2016.1209405.

Kwun, D. J. W. (2011). Effects of campus foodservice attributes on perceived value, satisfaction, and consumer attitude: A gender-difference approach. *International Journal of Hospitality Management*, 30(2), 252–261. https://doi.org/10.1016/j.ijhm.2010.09.001.

Lai, I. K. W. (2015). The roles of value, satisfaction, and commitment in the effect of service quality on customer loyalty in Hong Kong-style tea restaurants. *Cornell Hospitality Quarterly*, 56(1), 118–138. http://doi.org/10.1177/1938965514556149.

Lai, W. T., & Chen, C. F. (2011). Behavioural intentions of public transit passengers—The roles of service quality, perceived value, satisfaction and involvement. *Transport Policy*, 18(2), 318–325.

Law, A. K. Y., Hui, Y. V., & Zhao, X. (2004). Modeling repurchase frequency and customer satisfaction for fast food outlets. *The International Journal of Quality & Reliability Management*, 21(5), 545–563.

Lee, H., Lee, Y., & Yoo, D. (2000). The determinants of perceived service quality and its relationship with satisfaction. *Journal of Services Marketing*, 14(3), 217–231.

Lee, M., & Ulgado F. M. (1997). Customer evaluation of fast-food services: A cross-national comparison. *The Journal of Services Marketing*, 11(1), 39–52.

Lee, S., Jin, N. (Paul), & Lee, H. (2014). The moderating role of water park service quality, environment, image, and food quality on perceived value and customer loyalty: A South Korean case study. *Journal of Quality Assurance in Hospitality & Tourism*, 15(1), 19–43. https://doi.org/10.1080/1528008X.2014.855102.

Lee, T. J., Cho, H., & Ahn, T.-H. (2012). Senior citizen satisfaction with restaurant service quality. *Journal of Hospitality Marketing & Management*, 21(2), 215–226. https://doi.org/10.1080/19368623.2010.520822.

Lee, Y. K., Park, K. H., Park, D. H., Lee, K. A., & Kwon, Y. J. (2005). The relative impact of service quality on service value, customer satisfaction, and customer loyalty in Korean family restaurant context. *International Journal of Hospitality & Tourism Administration*, 6(1), 27–51. https://doi.org/10.1300/J149v06n01_03.

Liang, R. D., & Zhang, J. S. (2011). The effect of service interaction orientation on customer satisfaction and behavioural intention: The moderating effect of dining frequency. *Procedia – Social and Behavioural Sciences*, 24, 1026–1035.

Lin, I. Y., & Mattila, A. S. (2010). Restaurant servicescape, service encounter, and perceived congruency on customers' emotions and satisfaction. *Journal of Hospitality Marketing & Management*, 19(8), 819–841. https://doi.org/10.1 080/19368623.2010.514547.

Lin, C.-H. (2014). Effects of cuisine experience, psychological well-being, and self-health perception on the revisit intention of hot springs tourists. *Journal of Hospitality & Tourism Research*, 38(2), 243–265. https://doi. org/10.1177/1096348012451460.

Lindquist, J. (1974). Meaning of image. *Journal of Retailing*, 50, 29–38.

Liu, C., Huang, C., & Chen, M. (2014). Relational benefits, customer satisfaction and customer loyalty in chain store restaurants. *International Journal of Organizational Innovation*, 7(1), 46–56.

Liu, Y., & Jang, S. (2009a). Perceptions of Chinese restaurants in the U.S.: What affects customer satisfaction and behavioural intentions? *International Journal of Hospitality Management*, 28(3), 338–348. https://doi.org/10.1016/j. ijhm.2008.10.008.

Liu, Y., & Jang, S. (2009b). The effects of dining atmospherics: An extended Mehrabian-Russell model. *International Journal of Hospitality Management*, 28(4), 494–503. http://doi.org/10.1016/j.ijhm.2009.01.002.

MacLaurin, D., & MacLaurin, T. (2000). Customer perceptions of Singapore's theme restaurants. *The Cornell Hotel and Restaurant Administration Quarterly*, 41(3), 75–85.

Marinkovic, V., Senic, V., Ivkov, D., Dimitrovski, D., & Bjelic, M. (2014). The antecedents of satisfaction and revisit intentions for full-service restaurants. *Marketing Intelligence & Planning*, 32(3), 311–327. https://doi.org/10.1108/ MIP-01-2013-0017.

Mathe, K., & Slevitch, L. (2013). An exploratory examination of supervisor undermining, employee involvement climate, and the effects on customer perceptions of service quality in quick-service restaurants. *Journal of Hospitality & Tourism Research*, 37(1), 29–50. https://doi.org/10.1177/1096348011413590.

Mattila, A. (2001). Emotional bonding and restaurant loyalty. *The Cornell Hotel and Restaurant Administration Quarterly*, 42(6), 73–79.

Millman, R. (1986). The influence of background music on the behavior of restaurant patrons. *Journal of Consumer Research*, 13(2), 286–289.

Namkung, Y., & Jang, S. (2010). Service failures in restaurants. *Cornell Hospitality Quarterly*, 51(3), 323–343. https://doi.org/10.1177/1938965510364488.

Namkung, Y., & Jang, S. C. (2008). Are highly satisfied restaurant customers really different? A quality perception perspective. *International Journal of Contemporary Hospitality Management*, 20(2), 142–155.

Namkung, Y., & Jang, S. (2007). Does food quality really matter in restaurants? Its impact on customer satisfaction and behavioural intentions.

Journal of Hospitality & Tourism Research, 31(3), 387–409. https://doi.org/10.1177/1096348007299924.

OECD. (2012). *Food and the Tourism Experience: The OECD-Korea Workshop.* OECD Studies on Tourism. Korea: OECD Publishing.

Ok, C., Back, K., & Shanklin, C. W. (2005). Modeling roles of service recovery strategy: A relationship-focused view. *Journal of hospitality & Tourism Research*, 29(4), 484–507.

Oliver, R. L. (1997). *Satisfaction: A behavioural perspective on the consumer.* New York: McGraw-Hill.

Oliver, R. L. (1993). Cognitive, affective, and attribute bases of the satisfaction response. *Journal of Consumer Research*, 20(3), 418–430.

Oliver, R.L. (1981). Measurement and evaluation of satisfaction process in retail settings. *Journal of Retailing*, 57(3), 25–46. Oliver, R. L. (1980). A cognitive model of the antecedents and consequences of satisfaction decisions. *Journal of Marketing*, 17, 460–469.

OMT. (2012). Global report on food tourism. *Unwto*, 66. https://doi.org/ISSN 1728-9246.

Othman, Z., Zahari, M. S. M., & Radzi, S. M. (2013). Customer behavioural intention: Influence of service delivery failures and service recovery in Malay restaurants. *Procedia – Social and Behavioural Sciences*, 105, 115–21.

Parasuraman, A., Zeithaml, V., & Berry, L. (1994). Reassessment of expectations as a comparison standard in measuring service quality: Implications for further research. *Journal of Marketing*, 58(1), 111–124. doi: 10.2307/1252255.

Parasuraman, A., Zeithaml, V. A. & Berry, L. L. (1988). SERVQUAL: A multiple-item scale for measuring consumer perceptions of service quality. *Journal of Retailing*, 64(1), 12–37.

Patterson, P. G., & Spreng, R. A. (1997). Modelling the relationship between perceived value, satisfaction and repurchase intentions in a business-to-business, services context: An empirical examination. *International Journal of Service Industry Management*, 8(5), 414–434. http://doi.org/10.1108/09564239710189835.

Peter, J. P., & Olson, J. C. (2003). Consumer *behavior and marketing strategy* (6th ed.). Singapore: McGraw Hill.

Prendergast, G., & Man, H. (2002). The influence of store image on store loyalty in Hong Kong's quick service restaurant industry. *Journal of Food Service Business Research*, 5(1), 45–59.

Qin, H., & Prybutok, V. R. (2009). Service quality, customer satisfaction, and behavioural intentions in fast-food restaurants. *International Journal of Quality and Service Sciences*, 1(1), 78–95. https://doi.org/10.1108/17566690910945886.

Raajpoot, N. (2002). TANGSERV: A multiple item scale for measuring tangible quality in foodservice industry. *Journal of Foodservice Business Research*, 40(3), 109–127.

Reichheld, F. (1996). *The loyalty effect*. Boston, MA: Harvard Business School Press.

Reichheld, F., & Sasser, W. E. (1990). Zero defections: Quality comes to service. *Harvard Business Review*, 68(5), 105–111.

Rhee, H. T., Yang, S.-B., & Kim, K. (2016). Exploring the comparative salience of restaurant attributes: A conjoint analysis approach. *International Journal of Information Management*, 36(6), 1360–1370. https://doi.org/10.1016/j.ijinfo mgt.2016.03.001.

Robson, A. (1999). Turning the tables: The psychology of design for high-volume restaurants. *Cornell Hotel and Restaurant Administration Quarterly*, 40(3), 56–63.

Ryu, K. & Han, H. (2010). Influence of the quality of food, service, and physical environment on customer satisfaction in quick-casual restaurants: moderating role of perceived price. *Journal of Hospitality & Tourism Research*, 34(3), 310–329.

Ryu, K., & Han, H. (2011). The influence of physical environments on disconfirmation, customer satisfaction, and customer loyalty for first-time and repeat customers in upscale restaurants. *International Journal of Hospitality Management*, 30, 599–611.

Ryu, K., & Jang, S. (2008). DINESCAPE: A scale for customers' perception of dining environments. *Journal of Foodservice Business Research*, 11(1), 2–22.

Ryu, K., Han, H., & Kim, T.H. (2008). The relationships among overall quick-casual restaurant image, perceived value, customer satisfaction, and behavioral intentions. *International Journal of Hospitality Management*, 27(3), 459–469.

Ryu, K., Han, H., & Jang, S. (2010). Relationships among hedonic and utilitarian values, satisfaction and behavioural intentions in the fast-casual restaurant industry. *Journal of Contemporary Hospitality Management*, 22(3), 416–432.

Ryu, K., Lee, H., & Gon Kim, W. (2012). The influence of the quality of the physical environment, food, and service on restaurant image, customer perceived value, customer satisfaction, and behavioural intentions. *International Journal of Contemporary Hospitality Management*, 24(2), 200–223. https://doi.org/10.1108/09596111211206141.

Scarpato, R. (2000). *New Global Cuisine: The perspective of postmodern Gastronomy Studies*. Unpublished Master's thesis, Royal Melbourne Institute of Technology.

Soriano, D. (2003). Customers' expectations factors in restaurants: The situation in Spain. *The International Journal of Quality & Reliability*, 19(8), 1055–1068.

Sparks, B., Bowen, J., & Klag, S. (2003). Restaurants and the tourist market. *International Journal of Contemporary Hospitality Management, 15*(1), 6–13.

Spreng, R., & Mackoy, R. (1996). An empirical examination of a model of perceived service quality and satisfaction. *Journal of Retailing, 72*(2), 201–214.

Stevens, P., Knutson, B., & Patton, M. (1995). Dineserv: A tool for measuring service quality in restaurants. *Cornell Hotel and Restaurant Administration Quarterly, 36*(2), 56–60. https://doi.org/10.1177/001088049503600226.

Sulek, M. J., & Hensley, L. R. (2004). The relative importance of food, atmosphere and fairness of wait. *Cornell Hotel and Restaurant Administration Quarterly, 45*(3), 235–247.

Sunghyup S. H. (2010). Predictors of relationship quality and loyalty in the chain restaurant industry. *Cornell Hospitality Quarterly, 51*(2), 251–267. https://doi.org/10.1177/1938965510363264.

Susskind, A. M., Kacmar, K. M., & Borchgrevink, C. P. (2007). How organizational standards and coworker support improve restaurant service? *Cornell Hotel and Restaurant Administration Quarterly, 48*(4), 370–379. https://doi.org/10.1177/0010880407300158.

Swan, J. E. (1981). Disconfirmation of expectations and satisfaction with a retail service. *Journal of Retailing, 57*(3), 49–96.

Tan, Q., Oriade, A., & Fallon, P. (2014). Service quality and customer satisfaction in Chinese fast food sector: A proposal for CFFRSERV. *Advances in Hospitality and Tourism Research, 2*(1), 30–53. http://www.ahtrjournal.org/admin/dosyalar/6/30_53.pdf.

Tannahill, R (1988). *Food in history*. New York: Three Rivers Press.

Teng, C.-C., & Chang, J.-H. (2013). Mechanism of customer value in restaurant consumption: Employee hospitality and entertainment cues as boundary conditions. *International Journal of Hospitality Management, 32*, 169–178. https://doi.org/10.1016/j.ijhm.2012.05.008.

Visser, M. (1991). *The rituals of dinner: The origins, evolution, eccentricities and meaning of table manners*. New York: Penguin Group.

Wakefield, K. L., & Blodgett, J. G. (1996). The effect of the servicescape on customers' behavioural intentions in leisure service setting. *Journal of Services Marketing, 10*(6), 45–61.

Wall, E. A., & Berry, L. L. (2007). The combined effects of the physical environment and employee behavior on customer perception of restaurant service quality. *Cornell Hotel and Restaurant Administration Quarterly, 48*(1), 59–69. https://doi.org/10.1177/0010880406297246.

Wansink, B., & van Ittersum, K. (2012). Fast food restaurant lighting and music can reduce calorie intake and increase satisfaction. *Psychological Reports*, 111(1), 228–232. https://doi.org/10.2466/01.PR0.111.4.228-232.

Wood, R. C. (1995). *The sociology of the meal*. Edinburgh: Edinburgh University Press.

Yi, Y. (1990). A critical review of consumer satisfaction. In: V. A. Zeithaml (Ed.), *Review of Marketing*. Chicago, IL: American Marketing Association, pp. 68–123.

Yuskel, A., & Rimmington, M. (1998). Customer satisfaction measurement. *Cornell Hotel and Restaurant Administration Quarterly*, 39(6), 60–70.

Zeithaml, V. A., Berry, L. L., & Parasuraman, A. (1996). The behavioural consequences of service quality. *Journal of Marketing*, 60(2), 31–46.

Jarmo Ritalahti

From High Street to Digital Environments: Changing Landscapes in Travel Intermediation

1 Introduction

Traditional travel intermediaries continue to grapple with the reason for their existence in an environment where an overwhelming amount of information is available online, and transactions can be conducted directly between buyers and sellers on the Internet (Novak & Schwabe, 2009). Despite different authors identifying the need for these travel intermediaries to reposition themselves in the marketplace by adding value to the services they offer clients and by acting as more than just mere ticket reservation offices (Dilts & Prough, 2002; Alamdari, 2002; Cheyne, Downes, & Legg, 2005), little research has been conducted recently to identify these value-added services desired in the market, and the skills and competencies that traditional intermediaries require to deliver these services. While a number of studies have tried to predict the future of traditional travel intermediaries (see, for example, Castillo-Manzano, & López-Valpuesta, 2010) careful consideration must also be given to the actual skills and competencies that intermediaries will need in the future to remain viable and competitive.

The development and adoption of information and communication technologies (ICTs) have generated the growth of online purchasing on the Internet. Online shopping allows 24/7 sales which makes both selling and purchasing independent of physical spaces. The evolution of consumer behaviour on the Internet undergoes similar stages to those on more traditional channels. It begins with the adaption or the first purchase, continues with the acceptance of the channel through the first re-purchases, and ends when online purchases become an everyday routine. Once the consumer has made at least one purchase online, the acceptance of the new channel is stronger. From the seller's side, it is important to understand the different consumer and purchasing behaviour between consumer groups. In the competition between online and high-street travel agencies, consumers sometimes prefer to purchase air tickets in traditional travel agencies. This preference is based especially on security concerns when purchasing online, reliability and user-friendliness by travel agents. Online purchasing provides consumers with round-the-clock availability, rapid response time, and easiness of use. This article discusses the challenges traditional high-street travel agencies and tour operators continue to face in a fast changing operational environment. This will provide a deeper understanding of the depth of these changes that has already shaken the intermediation of the travel and tourism industry for over a decade.

2 Traditional Travel Intermediation

The term intermediary can be defined as any dealer who acts as a link in the chain of distribution between the company and its customers (Lubbe, 2000). In the tourism industry, travel agents and tour operators are considered as intermediaries or distributors. Though, the line between a travel agency and tour operator is very thin or invisible today, traditionally a travel agency can be regarded as a retailer and tour operator as a wholesaler. According to Lominé & Edmunds (2007, pp. 194–195) a tour operator pre-arranges and distributes/sells holidays to the public. Originally, they were packages, but now it can be more such as customised or tailor-made packages. A travel agent offers for sale, products and services created by tour operators, cruise lines, airlines, trains and ferry operators. Travel intermediaries' main task is to bring buyers and sellers in the field together and reduce transaction and supply/ownership costs between buyer and seller, instead of completely eliminating an intermediary (such as a distributor). Possible benefits of travel intermediaries for suppliers are that they are able to sell in bulk and might also be able to take a certain risk instead of suppliers when selling travel services to end users. Tour operators can be tied to contracts with suppliers. Furthermore, intermediaries also take part in the promotion of services. Consumers or end-users benefit by avoiding search and transaction costs, especially when purchasing inclusive or package tours, and gaining from specialist knowledge of a tour operator. When buying a package, consumers might also often gain from lower prices. Today, the benefits of traditional travel intermediaries are not that obvious any more.

The use of travel intermediaries by suppliers, such as hotels, will result in the loss of margins and in the loss of influence in the distribution process. According to Scaglione & Schegg (2016) the online intermediaries have also huge market knowledge, as they are able to collect insight in customer behaviour, like the service suppliers visited, length of stays on individual pages, services purchased and the amount of money used. For the consumer, choice may be reduced and increased prices, especially with further concentration and consolidation of travel intermediaries.

Traditionally, independent travellers often put their own itinerary together. They could do so by purchasing accommodation or transport directly from suppliers, from their own outlets or via a travel agent. It was common for domestic travellers to purchase their trip directly because they usually had good product knowledge and ready access to phone or the internet to make reservations (Cooper, Fletcher, Fyall, Gilbert & Wanhill, 2005). It was common for airlines, bus and shipping companies to have their own outlets in large cities where the public could purchase their travel products directly. Furthermore, call centres became very popular amongst airlines to handle customer requests. Retailers such as travel agents sold individual components of a trip, transport tickets, accommodation, excursions, but they might also put their own brand of tours together. The most common way of distributing foreign holiday travel in Europe was through inclusive tours packaged by tour operators and sold by travel agents. Some holiday packages were sold directly by tour operators. This will not continue, especially due to the technology revolution and new alliances with different actors and stakeholders in travel intermediation.

According to Zeljko Trezner (2012), a member of Incoming Tourism Working Group of The European Travel Agents' and Tour Operators' Associations (ECTAA) travel intermediaries are not just intermediaries; they act as an interface between supply and different segments of demand. They are able to create a new demand or to expand the present demand. Furthermore, consumers tend to make greater use of travel agents and tour operators when purchasing complex products or travelling to remote destinations. He defines a complex product as package travels, package holidays and package tours, as well as excursions and events. Remote destinations are overseas markets and also distant European markets. Modern travel intermediaries have many different forms and very complex relationships. In tourist destinations, they cooperate with handling agents, ground operators, consolidators, wholesalers, inbound tour operators, and destination management companies. In outbound markets, their partners can be travel management companies, consolidators, wholesalers, outbound tour operators, travel agents, retail chains, on-line travel agents, and home-based travel agents to name a few (Trezner, 2012). According to Rossini (2015), emerging players in the online travel intermediation are technology companies like Google and TripAdvisor.

Distribution is one of the most crucial factors for the competitiveness of tourism organisations. It serves as a link between various tourism suppliers and customers, individual tourists and organisations. In tourism, the distribution system is complex and multi-faceted, as often multiple distribution channels are used by tourism businesses. Tourism distribution channels vary according to the type of products and countries (Buhalis, 2001 in Buhalis & Laws, 2008, p. 7). Most distribution channels, though, share the functions of providing information to prospective customers and making travel arrangements. Pearce & Taniguchi (2008) state that distribution is recognised as a critical source of competitive advantage in the marketing mix. Multichannel distribution systems involving a mix of direct and indirect channels are frequently used by tourism businesses to extend coverage, respond to preferences of different market segments, reduce costs, and take advantage of technological change (Pavlides, 2006).

3 Changing Consumer Behaviour

Consumer behaviour has been researched for decades. It consists of psychology, economics, sociology, anthropology and neuroscience. It has always been a marketing landscape mostly with business-to-consumer (B2C) ways of thinking. However, this has changed with the internet and social media to more consumer-to-consumer (C2C) controlled marketing. Consumers are participating, taking active roles in various marketing functions. Marketing and influencing by recommendations, word-of-mouth, mobile, or so-called connected marketing is more powerful than ever (Kimmel, 2010). Furthermore, these networks can form a communication platform of importance. The networks can grow into communities where participants share common interests. The natural tendency among humans is to take into account others' or peers' opinions and decisions. Thus, the online networks or communities can be sources to get deeper insight of consumer preferences, for example service and product development (Kaple, Kulkarni, & Potika, 2017).

The market environment of today where travel services are bought and sold has undergone tremendous changes. These changes are mostly based on megatrends like ageing population, globalisation and sustainability, to name a few. Vejlgaard (2008) describes megatrends as cultural, economic, political, or technological changes or shifts that are just about to happen. The implication of these megatrends will affect all or almost all society. According to him, megatrends last longer, they have impacts on many different aspects of society, and they involve a complex process that often includes politics, economy, and technology. Trends can be differentiated based on the time frame and their impacts. Factors to consider include: globalisation, demographic change, information society and individualism; societal trends (awareness, aging societies, tolerance and equality and other); and consumer and lifestyle trends (ethical consumption, youth invasion, metrosexuals, soft hedonism) (Veikkola, 2004).

Megatrends and trends have their impacts on consumer behaviour, and also on purchasing behaviour. Generally, consumers or individuals act in their own interest. They buy or purchase for personal consumption or to meet the needs of the family or household unit. Consumer behaviour scholars have tried to build a model for consumer decision-making and consumer choice by emphasising that the behaviour is preceded by information processing. So, the stages in purchasing process are, according to Satyanarayana (2013), follow brand recognition; attitude to that brand; confidence in the brand; intention to purchase; and purchase itself.

According to Quinton & Harridge-March (2008) consumers develop an impression about the seller from their whole experience both in a real or virtual retail environment. They also state that when purchasing offline the important factors are people working at retailers, impression and reputation of the brand, added value given, and possibility to use multiple channels. Furthermore, when purchasing online, the important factors are purchasing process, people, and impression and reputation. So, consumers are influenced by different factors or elements when purchasing, in this case wine, in real and virtual environments.

In retail and travel business, loyalty programmes have impacts on purchasing behaviour. A loyalty programme is an integrated system of marketing actions that aims to make customers more loyal by developing personalised relationships with them. The principle purpose of loyalty programmes is to select, identify and segment heavy users who are sensitive to targeted promotions or certain product categories and thereby provide an improved allocation of resources (Meyer-Waarden, 2008). According to Reichheld (1996), loyalty programmes have two effects on purchasing behaviour: differentiation loyalty and purchase loyalty. Differentiation loyalty decreases the degree of sensitivity customers have towards competing offers or prices and thereby prompts customers to pay higher average process for goods they usually purchase, buy them in higher quantity or choose better quality products and/or more expensive brands. To summarise, loyalty programmes help to take consumers' minds off the price. According to Meyer-Waarden (2008), loyalty programmes have impacts in purchasing behaviour among programme members. Programme members have much higher purchasing intensities, share of purchases, purchasing frequencies and inter-purchasing times than non-members.

4 Information and Communication Technologies (ICTs) and Travel Intermediation

ICTs has revolutionised distribution channels in tourism. With the information function being to a larger extent transferred over the Internet, and the travel arrangements being performed by the automatised computer systems, travel agencies have faced the challenge of positioning themselves in the tourism distribution system and competing with the tourism suppliers over the customers. Already a decade ago many authors pointed out the need for travel agencies to re-asses their core competencies and concentrate on value-added services that go beyond bookings and ticketing (Buhalis & Laws, 2008; Cheyne, Downes & Legg, 2005).

Hérnandez-Ortega, Jiménez-Martínez & Martín-DeHoyos (2008) have defined three various categories for e-customers that are potential shoppers, new shoppers and experienced shoppers. The results of their study show that there are significant differences in the purchasing behaviour of the different groups when consuming online. For example, the first and inexperienced group emphasises the importance to the Internet use and satisfaction as well as the easy use of the online shop. The individual who makes his/her first purchase wants the process to be simple. From the seller's side, it is important to understand the different consumer and purchasing behaviour between the three consumer groups based on their experiences in online buying.

Over 10 years ago, Athiyaman (2002) studied the competition between online and high street travel agencies and found out that consumers preferred to purchase air tickets in traditional travel agencies. Law, Leung, & Wong (2004) summarise that travellers perceive services provided by high street travel agencies important. Furthermore, they go on that travel agents should be aware and positive towards the fast-changing distribution environment. Lastly they see that travel agencies should not see Internet as a threat, but as an opportunity to offer added-value services that could not be done earlier. The very fast growth of online shopping has also changed attitudes to purchase travel products online, so that the results of studies from the beginning of this millennium are perhaps not any more so valid.

The virtual market space is still new to many consumers and the knowledge of collective consumer experience is missing. The growth of e-tailing or purchasing online has not been as fast as forecasted due to the missing trust by consumers who can still be suspicious of online retailers (Durkan, Durkin, & Gillen, 2003). It seems that trust is more important in the virtual world than in the physical (McCole, 2002). According to Nicholson, Clarke, & Blakemore (2002) inter-personal liking is essential in the development of trust in long-term channel relationships. They go on that inter-personal liking is impossible in the virtual business environments due to the lack of physical proximity, visual contact and social interaction. Furthermore, the international nature of the Internet makes the consumer protection issues confusing. Trust is of critical importance for Internet retailers (Einwiller, Geissler, & Weill, 2000).

Decision-making processes and the factors that can have an effect on whether or not a customer makes a purchase is complex. Understanding what motivates consumers to buy a product or a service is crucial in ensuring that those features and benefits they wish to have, are found in the product or service. The fundamental factors that influence a consumer's purchase behaviour can be divided into two categories: psychological and sociological. Psychological factors are those like needs, drive, motivation and goals. Maslow's hierarchy of needs (physiological, safety, social, egoistic and self-actualisation) can be explained in short that before one is able to fulfill higher-level needs, the lower-levels must be satisfied. When a lower-level need is satisfied it works as a motivator to reach for the next level. According to Blythe (2013), fulfillment of needs motivates us to change. He also argues that as in the wealthier countries as the basic survival needs have been already met, consumers tend to concentrate to more in pleasing (hedonism) and fun things that satisfy them. Drive is the basis of motivation and acts like the force that stimulates our need to close the gap between an actual state and desired state of being. For example being thirsty would be the actual state and desired stated would be not thirsty, so one is motivated to drink to fulfill the need (Blythe, 2013; Schiffman &Wisenblit, 2015).

Motivation is what drives consumers to buy as a motive is the reason for carrying out a particular behaviour. Motives can be classified in different dimensions that affect the end result. Primary motives are reasons leading to, for example buying a new car due to the old one being unreliable. Primary motives include rational motives (reasoning and logical thinking which car to buy) and conscious motives (awareness of needing a new car). Secondary motives are attached to buying a certain brand. Emotional motives would be feelings about a certain car brand. Dormant motives are below conscious level, for example a wish to buy a sports car can be subconsciously linked to middle-ageing (Blythe, 2013; Schiffman & Wisenblit, 2015).

The Engel, Kollat, & Blackwell consumer decision process (CDP) referred to by Blythe (2013) consists of seven stages that drive the consumers' decision. Before the process an individual is affected by drives, desires and situational factors and they start to guide behaviour. The first stage is when a need is recognised. In the second stage a consumer is searching for information, either from their own memory or experiences (internal) or from external sources such as the internet. The pre-purchase evaluation stage is when the alternatives are considered. The final purchase is happening on the fourth stage. Consumption is the fifth stage in which a consumer is fulfilling the original need that started the process. Post-consumption evaluation is where an individual is considering was the need satisfied or not. Last, seventh stage is divestment in which the product is disposed or anything that was left from the consumption (Blythe, 2013).

Schiffman & Wisenblit (2015) have divided the decision-making process into three levels; input, process and output. In the input level, the factors that influence the consumer's decisions are based on the company's marketing regarding product, its price and promotion, and where it is sold. Sociocultural influences such as family and friends, social class and cultural entities also have an effect in the input level. The method by which information is received from a company or sociocultural sources are present as well at the input level (Schiffman & Wisenblit, 2015).

The process level is about how consumers make decisions. The psychological factors affect how the marketing efforts and sociocultural aspects influence the recognition of a need, pre-purchase search for information and evaluation of alternatives. The evaluation creates an experience, which is influenced by the consumer's psychological factors by the process of learning. The output level is when a consumer decides whether the purchase was right and possibly makes a new purchase (Schiffman & Wisenblit, 2015).

The virtual market space is still new to many consumers. The growth of e-tailing or purchasing online was not as fast as forecasted over a decade ago due to, for example the lack of trust by consumers who are suspicious of online retailers (Durkan, Durkin, & Gillen, 2003). It seems that trust was more important in the virtual world than in the physical (McCole, 2002). According to Nicholson, Clarke, & Blakemore (2002), the inter-personal liking was essential in the development of trust in long-term channel relationships. They further state that inter-personal liking was impossible in the virtual business environments due to the lack of physical proximity, visual contact and social interaction. Moreover, the international nature of the Internet made and makes the consumer protection issues confusing. When the Internet has become the most important sales medium for the majority of tourism and hospitality companies (Starkov, 2010), traditional intermediaries have been facing huge challenges trying to survive in the fast-changing operating environment. How can their business stay sustainable? Is it possible to talk about economic responsibility in traditional intermediaries business activities? When consumers need to book accommodation, the Internet provides a convenient platform to assess value offered, without interacting with a hotel or intermediary representative (Varini, Scaglione, & Schegg, 2011). One can say that the Internet generated not only a paradigm shift, but an actual change in the operational practices in the tourism and hospitality industry (Buhalis & Laws, 2008; Ip, Leung & Law, 2011).

Already in 2002, O'Conner & Frew stated that online distribution was seen as a shift away from traditional sales channels. Even though technology-mediated reservation represented already in 2002 a large part of, that is, hotel reservations (O'Conner & Frew, 2002), has no evidence that travel agency-mediated reservations would be declining (Grönflaten, 2009; Hong-Bumm, Seonok, & Hye-Young,

2012). The growth of travel agency-mediated bookings is based on the growth of online travel agencies, which started their operations already in the 1990s. Kracht & Wang (2010) point out that development in ICT have not reduced the number of intermediaries, but have resulted in a more complex network of intermediaries. Online intermediaries are now more powerful and also relevant to tourism suppliers (Morosan & Jeong, 2008).

Egger (2005) stated that when travel distribution increases more on the Internet, the number of high street or location-based travel agencies is decreasing. Intermediation is moving towards disintermediation, which means the elimination of the intermediary or middlemen is performed by using the Internet. Even though Internet enhances disintermediation, it also gives travel agencies the opportunity to re-intermediation, the use of internet to survive in the more competitive environment (Bennet & Lai, 2005). According to Zehrer & Möschl (2008), there was still much debate and speculation on how the Internet and its use had impacted the established intermediation industry. They went on saying that high street agencies see themselves confronted with strategic challenges. They must rethink their business models and distribution channels, because the modern ICTs enable the majority of travellers to gather information and book services independently and on their own. Cheung & Lam (2009) state that traditional intermediaries can sustain their positions in the market by re-intermediating and reinvigorating their business strategies in the emerging marketplace. Apart from securing the ownership of necessary co-specialised assets, traditional travel agencies have to acquire new technologies to reconfigure themselves as electronic commerceable intermediaries to preserve the advantages that they have built.

5 Conclusions

According to the literature review of travel intermediation and consumer behaviour in this chapter, the challenges of the traditional travel agencies and tour operators face are several. It is not only about supposed added-value that a high street travel agency might be able to supply to the customers. The main challenges are more linked to the megatrends and trends that have impacts on all of us as well as industries. The world is getting older, more urbanised and middle class, and the technology is developing faster than ever. These megatrends steer the consumer and purchasing behaviour of customers. When the service supply is available 24/7 on the Internet that is manageable to most of us, where do we need face-to-face contacts. Online shopping is easier and safer than before, and consumers' trust of online shopping has increased. It is very normal, almost a daily activity to many of us. Another challenge facing traditional travel intermediaries is the decreasing customer loyalty. Customers, and especially their purchasing behaviour is more polarised than ever. One day they prefer five-star services, and the other day their preferences switch to two-star services. Travelling has become banal that one does not need to show off anymore. Furthermore, travelling is so frequent that a consumer does not need to do purchases only at one service supplier.

References

Alamdari, F. (2002). Regional development in airlines and travel agents relationship. *Journal of Air Transport Management*, 8(5), 339–348.

Athiyaman, A. (2002). Internet users' intention to purchase air travel online: An empirical investigation. *Marketing Intelligence & Planning*, 4, 234–242.

Bennet, M., & Lai, C. (2005). The impact of the internet on travel agencies in Taiwan. *Journal of Tourism and Hospitality Research*, 6(1), 1–17.

Blythe, J. (2013). *Consumer behavior*. London: Sage.

Buhalis, D. (2001). Tourism distribution channels: practices and processes. In D. Buhalis & E. Laws (Eds.), *Tourism distribution channels: patterns, practices and challenges*, 7–32. London: Thompson.

Buhalis, D., & Laws, R. (2008). Progress in information technology and tourism management: 20 years on and 10 years after the Internet: The state of eTourism research. *Tourism Management*, 29(4), 609–623.

Castillo-Manzano, J. I., & López-Valpuesta, L. (2010). The decline of the traditional travel agent model. *Transportation Research Part E: Logistics and Transportation Review*, 46(5), 639–649.

Cheung, R., & Lam, P. (2009). How travel agencies survive in e-business world. *Communications of the IBIMA*, 10, 85–92.

Cheyne, J., Downes, M., & Legg, S. (2005). Travel agent vs. internet: What influences travel consumer choices? *Journal of Vacation Marketing*, 12(1), 41–57.

Cooper, C., Fletcher, J., Fyall, A., Gilbert, D., & Wanhill, S. (2005). *Tourism: Principles and Practice*. Harlow: Pearson Education Limited.

Dilts, J., & Prough, G. (2002). Travel agencies: A service industry in transition in the networked economy. *The Marketing Management Journal*, 13(2), 96–106.

Durkan, P., Durkin, M., & Gillen, J. (2003). Exploring efforts to engender online trust. *International Journal of Entrepreneurial Behaviour and Research*, 9(3), 93–110.

Egger, R. (2005). *Grundlagen des eTourismus – Informations- und Kommunikationstechnologien in Tourismus*. Shaker Verlag: Aachen.

Einwiller, S. Geissler, U., & Weill, M. (2000). Engendering trust in Internet business using elements of corporate branding. The Net Academy, hosted by University of St. Gallen, Switzerland.

Grönflaten, Ö. (2009). Predicting travelers' choice of information sources and information channels. *Journal of Travel Research*, 48(2), 230–244.

Herdandéz-Ortega, B., Jiménez-Martínez, J., & Martín-DeHoyos, M. J. (2008). Differences between potential, new and experienced e-customers. *Internet Research*, 18(3), 248–265.

Hong-bumm, K., Seonok, H., & Hye-young, M. (2012). The impact of hotel property size in determining the importance of electronic distribution channels. *Journal of Hospitality and Tourism Technology*, 3(3), 226–236.

Ip, C., Leung, R., & Law, R. (2011). Progress and development of information and communication technologies in hospitality. *International Journal of Contemporary Hospitality Management*, 23, 533–551.

Kaple, M., Kulkarni, K., & Potika, K. (2017). Virtual Marketing for Smart Cities: Influencers in Social Network Communities. In *Proceedings of 2017 IEEE Third International Conference on Big Data Computing Service and Applications*. Retrieved from http://ieeexplore.ieee.org/document/7944926/.

Kimmel, A. J. (2010). *Connecting with consumers: marketing for a new marketplace realities.* Oxford: Oxford University Press.

Kracht, J., & Wang, Y. (2010). Examining the tourism distribution channel: evolution and transformation. *International Journal of Contemporary Hospitality Management*, 2(5), 736–757.

Law, R., Leung, K., & Wong, J. (2004). The impact of the Internet on travel agencies. *International Journal of Contemporary Hospitality Management*, 16(2), 100–107.

Lominé, L., & Edmunds, J. (2007). *Key concepts in tourism.* New York: Palgrave.

Lubbe, B. (2000). *Tourism distribution: Managing the travel intermediary.* Kenwyn: Jutta and Co.

McCole, P. (2002). The role of trust for electronic commerce in services. *International Journal of Contemporary Hospitality Management*, 14(2), 81–87.

Meyer-Waarden, L. (2008). The influence of loyalty programme membership on customer purchase behaviour. *European Journal of Marketing*, 42(1/2), 87–114.

Morosan, C., & Jeong, M. (2008). Users' perceptions of two types of hotel reservations Web sites. *International Journal of Hospitality Management*, 27(2), 284–292.

Nicholson, M., Clarke, I., & Blakemore, M. (2002). One brand, three ways to shop: Situational variables and multichannel consumer behaviour. *The International Review of Retail Distribution and Consumer Research*, 12(2), 1131–1148.

Novak, J., & Schwabe, G. (2009). Designing for reintermediation in the brick-and-mortar world: Towards the travel agency of the future. *Electronic Markets*, 19, 15–29.

O'Connor, P., & Frew, A. (2002). The future of hotel electronic distribution: Expert and industry perspectives. *Cornell Hotel and Restaurant Administration Quarterly*, 43(3), 33–45.

Pavlides, M. (2006). Distributing through multiple channels and still making money. Paper presented at the Travel Distribution Summit Asia, Singapore.

Pearce, D. G., & Taniguchi, M. (2008). Channel Performance in multichannel tourism distribution systems. *Journal of Travel Research*, 46(3), 256–267.

Quinton, S., & Harridge-March, S. (2008). Trust and online wine purchasing: Insights into UK consumer behavior. *International Journal of Wine Business Research*, 20(1), 68–85.

Reichheld, F. (1996). The *loyalty effect: the hidden force behind growth, profits and lasting value*. Cambridge, MA: Harvard Business School Press.

Rossini, A. (2015). OTA sector between increasing consolidation and the possible rise of new key players. Retrieved from http://blog.euromonitor.com/2015/06/ota-sector-between- increasing-consolidation-andthe-possible-rise-of-new-key-players.html.

Satyanarayana, P. V. V. (2013). A study on customer buying perception on home appliances with reference to LG products. *International Journal of Applied Services Marketing Perspectives*, 2(3), 468–474.

Scaglione, M., & Schegg, R. (2016). Forecasting the final penetration rate of online Travel Agencies in different hotel segments. In R. Schegg & B. Stangl (Eds.), *Information and Communication Technologies in Tourism 2016*, 709–721. Switzerland: Springer-Verlag.

Schiffman, L. G., & Wisenblit, J. (2015). *Consumer behavior*. Boston: Pearson.

Starkov, M. (2010). In hospitality, not all internet bookings are created equal. Retrieved from http://www.hospitalitybusiness.com/blog/not-all-internet-bookings-are-created-egual/. Accessed on 15 April 2011.

Trezner, Z. (2012). The role of travel agents and tour operators in extending the tourist season. A presentation for European Tourism Day 2012. Retrieved from https://ec.europa.eu/docsroom/documents/7022/attachments/1/translations/en/renditions/pdf. Accessed on 29 May 2014.

Varini, K., Scaglione, M., & Schegg, R. (2011). Distribution channel and efficiency: An Analytic Hierarchy Process approach. In R. Law, M. Fuchs & F. Ricci (Eds.), *Information and Communication Technologies in Tourism 2011*, 547–558. Wien: Springer-Verlag.

Vejlgaard, H. (2008). *Anatomy of a trend*. Denmark: Confetti Publishing.

Veikkola, T. (2004). Consumer trends as an element in user centric design (unpublished presentation).

Zehrer, A., & Möschl, P. (2008). New distribution Channels and Business Strategies for Location-based Travel Agencies. In P. O'Connor, W. Höpken & U. Gretzel (Eds.), *Information and Communication Technologies, in Tourism 2008.* 359–370. Wien: Springer-Verlag.

Lars Rettig, Eric Horster

Student Satisfaction with the Student Counselling Service[1] and Its Influence on Course Enrollments

1 Introduction

The Student Counselling service is usually the first point of contact for university students and thus the 'face' of the university. It can be assumed that the satisfaction with the quality of service received in this first contact has an influence on the decision to enroll. The service quality is also an important antecedent for the subsequent loyalty of the students to the university (Helgesen & Nesset, 2007).[2] This article deals with the question of which concepts could be used to foster course enrollment. It specifically concerns student counselling regarding the offers developed in 73 funded projects across Germany as part of the federal and state competition 'Advancement through Education: Open Universities'[3] over the past six years (2011–2017).

Three thematic constellations were examined by means of an online survey that was sent to all of the supported projects: (1) The importance of and satisfaction with various counselling channels; (2) The importance of and satisfaction with the central themes of the counselling; as well as (3) the desired consultation

---

1 The 'Student Counselling Services' is understood as a holistic approach towards the dispensing of academic advice. Therefore, it incorporates more than the administrative task of sharing information about the admission process (Student Admissions) or giving advice about the courses to take (Academic Advice). The 'Student Counselling Services' is there for prospective and present students to mutually find solutions to successfully deal with the challenges of combining study, work and family.

2 Helgesen & Nesset (2007) presented a model that shows the interdependancy of service quality, image and facilities with the satisfaction and loyalty of the students. Service quality and the facilities were regarded as antecedents. Thus, the authors were able to illustrate that the variables of student satisfaction, image of the university and the image of the course of study were direct drivers of the loyalty of students at a Norwegian University College.

3 'Open University' is the abbreviation for all of the funded project universities supported by the federal and state competition 'Advancement through Education: Open Universities' (www.wettbewerb-offene-hochschulen-bmbf.de).

times for the surveyed target group. Thus, an image of the central services of Student Counselling is generated and areas that can be improved upon are thereby depicted. However, before the results are presented, the theoretical framework on which the investigation is based will be specified. The methodical design, which forms the basis for the final explanation of the investigations, will subsequently be presented.

2 Theoretical Framework

Satisfaction with services is the subject of various theoretical models. These include, inter alia, the Kano Model of Customer Satisfaction, the Confirmation-Disconfirmation Paradigm, the Frequency-Relevance Analysis for Problems (FRAP) as well as the importance satisfaction matrix, Tri:M Grid. These are explained in the following, as they are essential for understanding the evaluation of this empirical investigation.

2.1 Confirmation-Disconfirmation Paradigm (C/D) Paradigm

The C/D Paradigm deals with the comparison between the expected target state of a service and its actual state as depicted in Figure 1 (Homburg, 2008; Oliver, 1980). The comparison can generate three possible results: (1) If the expected state and the actual state correspond, the satisfaction level is at the confirmation level. This means that the customer is neither satisfied nor dissatisfied. His or her expectations were fulfilled exactly. (2) If the actual state is below the confirmation level, dissatisfaction results. (3) If it is above, the customer is satisfied. The confirmation level is thereby not a fixed value, but rather depends strongly on the expectation that the customer had placed on the supply of services in advance (Hofbauer & Dürr, 2007). The expectation itself is not only influenced by the customer's own experience, but also by the scope of the customer's search activities and the information generated in this way (Kotler & Schellhase, 2011).

During contact with Student Counselling, various universities are initially perceived and key information[4] is compared (Hofbauer & Dürr, 2007). Should the interested party then decide on participating in a consultation session, the result of his or her personal target/actual comparison with regard to this conversation

---

4   According to Kroeber-Riel, Weinberg, & Gröppel-Klein (2009), key information is the information which can contain many different bits of information bundled together. It serves the customer before purchasing by reducing the testing process to specific parameters. Typical examples of key information are quality certificates, the price or the brand of a service.

is strongly dependent on the expectations, which have been generated in advance by the search process. Based on this finding, service processes can be designed in such a way that, on the one hand, expectations are at a realistic level and, on the other hand, in the end, if possible, the benefits are better than promised. However, since services are difficult to standardise, the result is generally heterogeneous (Horster, 2013). The Kano Model of Customer Satisfaction, on the other hand, helps to divide the service into various categories, each having different effects on the customer's perception of the service.

Figure 1: C/D Paradigm[5]

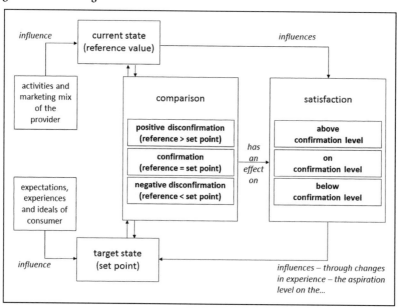

2.2 Kano Model

The Kano Model of Customer Satisfaction has three key characteristics for products and services (Kano, Seraku, Takahashi, & Tsuji, 1984). These are known as the basic characteristics, performance characteristics, and the excitement characteristics. All three have an effect on customer satisfaction, but in different ways.

---

5   Source: Authors' depiction in accordance with Homburg, 2008, p. 21.

According to the model, the **basic characteristics** are the features of the service, which must be fulfilled in order for the service not to be experienced as incomplete. The availability of the contact person in the Student Counselling office would be, for example, in line with expectations, but this alone does not contribute to satisfaction. If, on the other hand, the Student Counselling service were to be outsourced to the secretariats of the responsible departments, which are only available for half of the day, this would be abnormal or unusual and could easily lead to dissatisfaction among those seeking consultation.

Performance characteristics are the characteristics of the services, which can both positively and negatively, affect satisfaction. In the context of the Student Counselling service, this could be, for example, how well-versed the advisors are in the matter being discussed. The better the counselling on the content and topics of the course, the more positive the value of this performance characteristic as seen in Figure 2.

Figure 2: Kano Model of Customer Satisfaction[6]

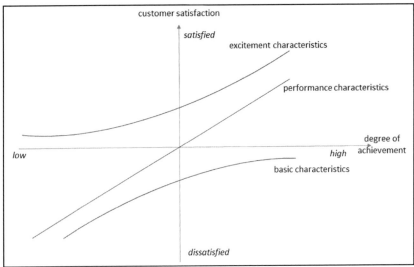

A service offering can ultimately be enhanced by the **excitement characteristics**. These are characteristics of the service that the customer usually doesn't expect. Thus, they have the potential to trigger excitement (so-called 'Wow effect'). For

---

6   Source: Authors' depiction in accordance with Matzler, Stahl & Hinterhuber (2009, p. 20).

the Student Counselling service, these would be services, which go beyond the usual consultation. If, for example, consultation times were offered outside of office hours, a 'Wow effect' could be triggered. Or, if the Student Counselling service were to offer to check the documents of a professionally engaged potential student in the university's database free of charge to see if externally acquired competences could count towards credit in a planned course of studies, this could trigger excitement.

Should one now wish to discuss which service elements are relevant to the customer and how often problems with the service can arise, this can be illustrated in a pragmatic diagramme: the FRAP, which is explained in the following.

2.3 Frequency-Relevance Analysis for Problems

The FRAP is based on the idea that customers are more satisfied with a service when the problems, which they experience during their contact with the company, are solved well.[7] The frequency with which the customer's problems occur (*Frequency*) and the importance of the individual problem for the customer (*Relevance*) give this analysis method its name (Stauss & Seidel, 2014). For the company, this means that it is all the more urgent to address the problems that arise with their customers as the more **frequently** the problem arises, the more **importance** the customer places on it (Bruhn, 2013). Transferring this to the Student Counselling service leads us to the question of which topics/problems are the Student Counselling confronted with frequently and to what extent are the contact seekers satisfied with the answers/solutions they are offered.

In order to prioritise which of the problems should be eliminated first, a concentration diagramme (Pareto diagramme) can be used after the problems have been identified and classified in a two-dimensional matrix (Frequency and Relevance) (Kaiser, 2006) as depicted in Figure 3. To do this, the frequency of each problem is first multiplied by the ascertained average relevance of the problem. The resulting problem value provides the prioritisation for the resolution of the problems. In order to make them comparable, the results can be represented as an index. To create this index, the calculated value of each problem is then divided by the sum of all of the problem values calculated in this manner and the result is the so called Problem Value Index (*PWI*). The highest index value is ranked first and thus has the highest urgency when eliminating the problems (Stauss & Seidel, 2014).

---

7   It is therefore applied in various sectors (see, for example, Thurm, 2010; Zinzow, 2001).

Figure 3: Frequency-Relevance Analysis for Problems[8]

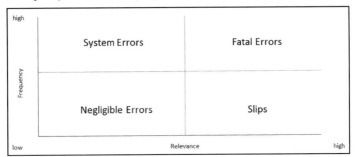

The analysis reaches a critical limit when service elements are used only once or infrequently, as frequency values for the occurrence of the problems can then only be meaningfully observed over a longer period of time (Bruhn, 2013).

A solid database is required to achieve categorisation of the service elements in accordance with the Kano Model and then subsequently analyse them by means of a FRAP. The so-called Tri:M Grid was used for this purpose within the scope of the present study.

2.4 Tri:M Grid

The abbreviation Tri:M Grid was coined in the nineties by the market research institute Infratest Burke (today known as TNS Infratest). Tri:M stands for three 'M's (*measuring, managing, monitoring*). It describes the three phases of the data-based consulting process. In the measuring phase (*measuring*), the data is collected and its influence on the satisfaction of the customer is determined. In the managing phase, concepts and activities are developed to reduce weaknesses and expand strengths. The monitoring phase closes the circle by recording the changes achieved. This method was adapted for the present study. The first 'M' was of particular interest for the measuring of *Importance* and *Satisfaction* with regard to the consulting service (see Section 3.4).

The results of the survey have been broken down so that basic characteristics of the service (according to Kano) or hygiene factors (Tri:M Grid) can be described, as well as making it possible to identify hidden opportunities (Tri:M Grid) that could trigger excitement (Kano). The stretched grid also makes it possible to recognise where good service has already been achieved and where there is room for

---

8   Source: Authors' depiction based on Kaiser, 2006, pp. 112–113.

improvement, from which specific recommendations for action can be derived (as defined by a FRAP).

3 Methodological Approach

The study is divided into the following successive steps: Firstly, by means of two expert interviews with the central Student Counselling service of the West Coast University of Applied Sciences, as well as an interview with the course advisor for a postgraduate master's programme at the same university, an approximation to the question 'Which consulting concepts support course enrollment?' was achieved. In the next step, the fields of topics, which the Student Counselling is most often confronted with, were then derived from the interviews (see also Section 2.3 for the FRAP). Three core themes were identified, which were then evaluated within the framework of the online survey.

3.1 Objects of Investigation

The first topic that could be identified in the expert interviews was that of the **consultation channels**. This deals with the general question of whether information on how to establish contact could be found quickly and easily. Moreover, it is interesting to know through which channels the Student Counselling service should be available. The second topic was the **consultation hours** of the Student Counselling service. For this, the desired consultation times were included as part of the online survey to obtain the opinions of the target group. The third topic deals with the **content of the consultation**. The aim here was to find out which topics are relevant for the prospective students and how satisfied they are with the consultation.

The importance of the topics was then placed into context with the question of individual satisfaction as well as overall satisfaction. Finally, the question was asked as to whether the participant chose a degree programme or a certificate course.

At the end of the survey, demographic data, such as gender, marital status, number of children and employment information, was recorded. The survey was sent to all universities with funded projects within the framework of the federal and state competition 'Advancement Through Education: Open Universities' with the request that it will be disseminated to all their participants and students. The survey ran from 22 June until 31 July 2016.

3.2 Sample

The obtained sample contained 324 responses. Of these, 130 participants answered the final questions concerning the demographic data. Among them, 73 were female and 57 were male. The remaining 194 did not provide any information regarding their gender. Of the 130 people that provided demographic data, 68 were single, 54 were married, 2 were divorced and 6 did not provide any marital status.

3.3 Response Scales

The aim of the survey was to assess the importance and satisfaction, or their counterparts, non-importance and dissatisfaction, with the Student Counselling service. The variables of importance and satisfaction were recorded on a five-level, end point named Likert scale from 1 (very important) to 5 (unimportant) and respectively 1 (very satisfied) to 5 (dissatisfied). Due to the uneven scale levels, it was also hereby possible for the subjects to give indifferent responses by selecting the middle of the scale.

For the consultation periods, a matrix with multiple response possibilities was stretched out, in which the desired consultation periods could be activated by a click. The consultation channels that were offered as a response were: in-person consultation, web conference, by email, by telephone, via chat (text only) and via Facebook, as well as an empty text field 'Other' for the participants to enter their own input.

To determine the consultation topics, it seemed best to offer multiple answers with selection from the following subjects: course contents, time expenditure, financing of studies, formal prerequisites, credits/recognition of achievements, attendance dates, compatibility between study and work as well as compatibility between study and family. This selection was supplemented with an open question about missing consultation topics.

The participant was then guided through the survey with filter questions. For example, the question 'Have you been informed by the Student Counselling service?' ensured that the satisfaction with the consulting could only be answered by those that had actually received consultation.

3.4 Evaluation Methods

As outlined at the outset, the Tri:M Grid method (see Section 2.4) was used for the thematic constellations of *accessibility* and *consultation topics*. Both the importance as well as the satisfaction was surveyed. In addition, the overall satisfaction with the consultation was collected. Using these values, the *grid* could then be stretched (see Figures 4 to 6). By way of example, the evaluation process will be explained using the first theme block *accessibility*. The method not only reveals the drivers of the overall satisfaction, but also makes it possible to identify hidden opportunities and potential savings, thereby offering approaches for action planning to increase satisfaction in relation to importance.

Figure 4: Evaluation of the Consultation Channels[9]

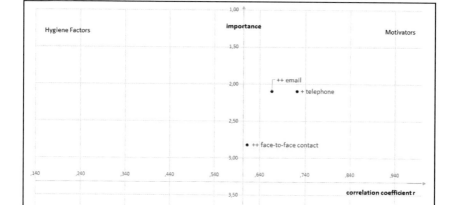

9   Source: Own depiction (n = 61). Basis: All respondents who have used counselling, i.e. all of those who responded in the affirmative to Question 3 (Have you used the Student Counselling service for a consultation?).

Figure 5: Preferred Consultation Times[10]

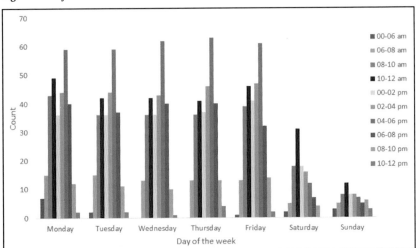

Figure 6: Evaluation of the Consultation Topics[11]

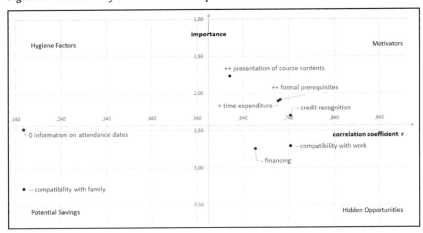

---

10 Source: Own depiction (n = 138).

11 Own depiction (n = 51). Basis: All respondents who have used counselling, i.e. all of those who responded in the affirmative to Question 3 (*Have you used the Student Counselling service for a consultation?*).

In the evaluation, at first the individual *aspects of importance* of the accessibility of the Student Counselling service through various consultation channels were determined and the respective mean values were plotted on the **y-axis**.

In the second step, the mean values of the individual *aspects of satisfaction* with the accessibility of these consultation channels were determined. Each individual aspect of satisfaction with the Student Counselling service was then correlated with the overall satisfaction, i.e. put into context. The correlation coefficient *r* (Pearson correlation) provides information about the relationship between individual aspects of satisfaction and overall satisfaction. It can accept values between −1 (completely negative context) and +1 (completely positive context) and is plotted here on the **x-axis** (Bortz & Döring, 2006). In this manner, each item is represented by a point in the coordinate system with x and y values.

By stretching out the cross-formed by the axes, four fields of a grid are created, in which the results are divided into individual sections and thereby show possibilities for action. These are classified by the terms 'Motivators' (I. quadrant), 'Hygiene Factors' (II. quadrant), 'Potential Savings' (III. quadrant) and 'Hidden Opportunities' (IV. quadrant) (Janßen, 2016).

Motivators: The first quadrant shows the motivators. They have a great impact on overall satisfaction and were, to a certain extent, important to the survey takers. Improvements in this segment should be reflected in increased overall satisfaction.

Hygiene Factors: The second quadrant describes the Hygiene Factors. These have little influence on the overall satisfaction, but are important nevertheless. Characteristics of the Student Counselling service, which can be found in this quadrant, belong to the Basic Factors in the Kano Model. They are therefore those services, which make the customer very dissatisfied if they are absent, but do not make a large contribution to the overall satisfaction if they are present, as they are expected anyway.

Potential Savings: The third quadrant shows potential savings. They are, therefore, unimportant components of the Student Counselling service, which did not have a great deal of importance attached to them by those surveyed and had little influence on the overall satisfaction.

Hidden Opportunities: The fourth quadrant is of great importance for the overall satisfaction, without the survey participants being aware of this, as they have placed little importance on the characteristics in this quadrant. This points to hidden opportunities. The awareness and importance of these characteristics can be increased through the use of communication measures directed at the prospective students (Regarding the four quadrants, Stahl, Binder & Cosler, 1998).

In the third step of the data evaluation, the potentials of the individual aspects of satisfaction were then calculated, by determining the deviation of the respective mean value from the mean value of the cumulative average values of the individual aspects of satisfaction. In order to visualise the potentials thus identified, the deviations were divided into five groups ranging from ++ (upper fifth) to 0 (middle fifth) down to – (lower fifth) (see Figure 4). These identifiers were added to the coordinates as a supplement to the item labels. This showed at a glance the areas in which the offering was already good and where there was potential for improvement.

The same approach was also chosen for the depiction of the importance and satisfaction with the *consultation topics*.

4 Results of the Investigation

The evaluation of the importance and satisfaction with the consultation channels showed that among those surveyed, accessibility by *telephone, email* and *face-to-face contact* is important. Here, the universities are already well-established, showing the potential for satisfaction with the three items being located in the first quadrant. Their positive potentials are represented by ++ and +. They show the positive deviation from the mean of the six mean values of the individual aspects of satisfaction.

Hidden opportunities can be found in the online, synchronous consultation channels *web conferences* and *chat*. They are currently not regarded as important by the participants of the survey, but nevertheless contribute to the satisfaction with the consultation.

The social network *Facebook*, on the other hand, was identified by the respondents as being an unimportant consultation channel, which does not contribute to the overall satisfaction (Potential –0.849 and thus shown as – (lower fifth) in Figure 4).

The grid for the evaluation of the consultation topics also revealingly visualises the results of the survey. For those that have taken advantage of a consultation session, the topics of *Credit Recognition* and *Compatibility with Work* contributed the most to overall satisfaction. However, these topics still have negative potential values (Credit Recognition –0.303; Compatibility with Work –0.367), i.e. there is a need for action in the quality of consulting for these topics.

The universities are already good at Presentation of Course Contents, the Formal Prerequisites and in consulting concerning Time Expenditure. The topics of Financing and Compatibility with Work should, on the other hand, be given greater consideration as they influence the overall satisfaction without the respondent being aware of this (hidden opportunities).

Within the framework of the consultation Information on Attendance Dates does not contribute to overall satisfaction. It is likely that this information should already be on the website for a further education course and thus does not have to be part of the consultation.

Why Compatibility with the Family was not seen as important and not decisive for the overall satisfaction cannot be determined from the available data, as neither a clear dependence on family status nor the number of children could be proven by t-tests.

5 Discussion

5.1 Explanation of the Results

Regardless of the location of the offers, this study examines the satisfaction with and importance of the consultation channels of the Student Counselling service as well as the consultation topics. It also provides an overview of the desired consultancy times of the target group.

Concerning the consultation channels, it is clear that *email, telephone* and *face-to-face contact* are the main consultation channels. Opportunities exist in online, synchronous consultation channels. As Facebook is located in the area of potential savings, it can be assumed that social networks are not preferred as consultation channels. This, paired with the preference for classical means of communication like telephone or face-to-face contact, is understandable insofar as a further education course or a certificate course is a product or a service, which means considerable financial and time expenditure. It seems as if students are interested in a bilateral and synchronised form of communication, which allows direct inquiries, in order to obtain a personal consultation which is tailored to their needs. It is, however, also possible that the channel *Facebook* gains relevance in the information process at a later stage once the prospective students have solidified their plans and are also willing to inform themselves in a (partially) public forum (such as a comment on a Facebook page).

The topics of *Course Contents, Formal Prerequisites* and *Time Expenditure* are already well evaluated in the consultation. There are opportunities for the topics *Financing* and *Compatibility with Work*. These topics are obviously relevant as the resources most spent on further education are time and money. The consultation can therefore be targeted directly at these topics. There is therefore, with a clear and coherent concept, the possibility of increasing the satisfaction with the Student Counselling service.

With regard to *Credit Recognition*, there are also great opportunities for a satisfactory consultation concept, aimed at the target group addressed by the competition 'Advancement through Education: Open Universities'. The importance of the topic is also recognised by the respondents and its influence on overall satisfaction is high (Quadrant I). However, it must be noted that, on the one hand, this topic is currently subject to constant change in the political framework and, on the other hand, further research is still necessary. It is therefore obvious that in most cases an ad hoc response to any inquiry about credit recognition of achievements is not possible, which in turn makes it much more difficult to increase the quality of consultation on this topic. Nevertheless, approaches to system-assisted, flat-rate and thus transparent recognition of extra-curricular activities are available (see, for example, Rettig, 2016; Seger & Waldeyer, 2014; Hanft, Brinkmann, Gierke & Müskens, 2014).

Following the Kano Model although *Credit Recognition* is on the way to becoming a performance characteristic, good consultation services in the fields of *Financing* and *Compatibility with Work* are the characteristics which the Student Counselling services can use to excite people (see Section 2.2). A FRAP at the location of the respective university would consequently be the next step, in order to offer more and more satisfactory solutions for detailed questions in these consultation topics.

5.2 Methodological Criticism and Recommendations for Further Research

Despite a good response rate to the survey request (324 respondents), only 124 participants filled out the survey completely. As the demographic data was collected at the end of the survey, it is correspondingly only available for this smaller group. In order to be able to carry out more analyses with the control variables (age, gender, etc.), it would have been helpful to have collected this data at the beginning of the survey. Nevertheless, the main goal of the survey could be achieved, and central elements for a consultation concept for the Student Counselling service could be elicited. The sub-goal, deriving possible courses of action for individual locations, was not possible as only a few respondents (n = 37) indicated in which university they were assessing the offer (voluntary information). However, the information gathered shows which universities of the OH-Project Universities[12] were reached with the survey. Further studies could build on the results presented here and expand on them.

---

12 OH stands for 'Open University' and is the abbreviation for all of the funded project universities supported by the federal and state competition 'Advancement through Education: Open Universities' (www.wettbewerb-offene-hochschulen-bmbf.de).

5.3 Recommendations for the Practice

In addition to research and teaching, further education is anchored as the third pillar of the universities. The present study has shown that this task has not fallen by the wayside and core elements for consultation concepts have been developed.

Concepts for course enrolments for target group of professionally active people, should not only take into account the preferred evening and Saturday morning consultation times, but should also focus on other topics. Credit recognition of past achievements/performance, financing and the question of compatibility with work are important topics for professionally active prospective students in a consultation and they have a large effect on the perceived satisfaction with the consultation. According to the results of this study, these potentials have not yet been exhausted.

It could also be worthwhile to test new consultation channels, like an open web chat session on Saturday morning or the availability of the Student Counselling service outside of normal office hours via chat sessions. The flexibility of the consultation desired by the target group, requires, as it were, flexibility in the working hours of the consultants. Not only in terms of time, but also in terms of content, complexity is increased by a higher level of consultancy, with the simultaneous expectation of short feedback periods. The time and effort for the credit recognition of extra-curricular activities is also increasing as a result of the individual checks that need to be carried out. However, this can be reduced again through the introduction of a quality-assured, flat-rate credit system (requiring the establishment of a database of achievements which can be credited).

In summary, the present study broadens the understanding of prospective students in this new target group of the universities and provides a first indication of the potential for improvement in the Student Counselling service for further education measures.

Acknowledgements

The project 'Open Universities in Schleswig-Holstein: Learning in the Net, Advancement on Site (LINAVO)' was funded by the Federal Ministry of Education and Research. It was funded at the West Coast University of Applied Science under the funding code FKZ 16OH12030. The authors hold the sole responsibility for the content of this publication.

GEFÖRDERT VOM

References

Bortz, J., & Döring, N. (2006). *Forschungsmethoden und Evaluation für Human- und Sozialwissenschaftler*, 4th revised edition. Berlin, Heidelberg, New York: Springer.

Bruhn, M. (2013). *Qualitätsmanagement für Dienstleistungen: Handbuch für ein erfolgreiches Qualitätsmanagement. Grundlagen – Konzepte – Methoden.* 9th completely revised and extended ed. Berlin, Heidelberg: Springer Gabler.

Hanft, A., Brinkmann, K., Gierke, W. B., & Müskens, W. (2014). Anrechnung außerhochschulischer Kompetenzen in Studiengängen. Studie: AnHoSt „Anrechnungspraxis in Hochschulstudiengängen". *Oldenburg.* Carl von Ossietzky Universität Oldenburg, Arbeitsbereich Weiterbildung und Bildungsmanagement (web) [online]. Available from https://www.uni-oldenburg.de/fileadmin/user_upload/anrechnungsprojekte/Anhost.pdf [2015-09-15].

Helgesen, Ø., & Nesset, E. (2007). Images, satisfaction and antecedents: Drivers of student loyalty? A case study of a Norwegian University College. *Corporate Reputation Review*, 10(1), 38–59. doi: 10.1057/palgrave.crr.1550037.

Hofbauer, G., & Dürr, K. (2007). *Der Kunde – das unbekannte Wesen. Psychologische und soziologische Einflüsse auf die Kaufentscheidung.* Berlin: Uni-Ed.

Homburg, C. (2008). *Kundenzufriedenheit. Konzepte, Methoden, Erfahrungen.* 7th revised ed. Wiesbaden: Gabler Verlag.

Horster, E. (2013). *Reputation und Reiseentscheidung im Internet.* Grundlagen, Messung und Praxis, Wiesbaden: Springer Gabler.

Janßen, O. (2016). Abbildung: TRI*M Analyse-Tools zum Management der Kundenbeziehungen. *Kundenbeziehungsmanagement.* Ed. by T. N. S. Kantar. [online]. Available from https://www.tns-infratest.com/Branchen-und-Maerkte/industriemarkt_b2b-kunden.asp [2016-12-13].

Kaiser, M. (2006). *Kundenzufriedenheit kompakt. Leitfaden für dauerhafte Wettbewerbsvorteile.* Berlin: Schmidt.

Kano, N., Seraku, N., Takahashi, F., & Tsuji, S. (1984). Attractive quality and must-be quality. *Journal of the Japanese Society for Quality Control*, 14(2), pp. 147–156.

Kroeber-Riel, W., Weinberg, P., & Gröppel-Klein, A. (2009). *Konsumentenverhalten.* 9th ed., München: Vahlen.

Kotler, P., & Schellhase, R. (2011). *Grundlagen des Marketing.* 5th revised ed. München: Pearson Studium.

Matzler, K., Stahl, H. K., & Hinterhuber, H. H. (2009). Die Customer-based View der Unternehmung. In: H. H. Hinterhuber und K. Matzler (eds.): *Kundenorientierte Unternehmensführung. Kundenorientierung – Kundenzufriedenheit - Kundenbindung.* 6th revised ed. Wiesbaden: Gabler, pp. 3–32.

Oliver, R. L. (1980). A cognitive model of the antecedents and consequences of satisfaction decisions. *Journal of Marketing Research,* 17(4), 460–469.

Rettig, L. (2016). Offene Hochschule – Anrechnung von beruflichen Kompetenzen, Master ohne Bachelor? Wie kann lebenslanges Lernen im Tourismus umgesetzt werden? *Zeitschrift für Tourismuswissenschaft,* 8(1), Ausbildung im Tourismus, DeGruyter Oldenbourg, pp. 23–48. doi: 10.1515/tw-2016-0003.

Seger, M. S., & Waldeyer, C. (2014). *Qualitätssicherung im Kontext der Anrechnung und Anerkennung von Lernergebnissen an Hochschulen. Standards für transparente und nachvollziehbare Analyseverfahren und Anrechnungsprozesse.* Aachen: Shaker Verlag.

Stauss, B., & Seidel, W. (2014). *Beschwerdemanagement. Unzufriedene Kunden als profitable Zielgruppe.* 5th completely revised ed. München: Hanser.

Stahl, M., Binder, G., & Cosler, D. (1998). TRI:M-Studie zur Kundenzufriedenheit (Mehrfachkunden). Unter Mitarbeit von Joachim Scharioth. Ed. by Informationszentrum Sozialwissenschaften der Arbeitsgemeinschaft Sozialwissenschaftlicher Institute e.V. (ASI). Bonn (IZ-Arbeitsbericht, #13): Gesellschaft Sozialwissenschaftlicher Infrastruktureinrichtungen e.V. (GESIS), einer Einrichtung der Wissenschaftsgemeinschaft Gottfried Wilhelm Leibniz (WGL) [online]. Available from http://www.gesis.org/fileadmin/upload/forschung/publikationen/gesis_reihen/iz_arbeitsberichte/ab13.pdf [2016-12-13].

Thurm, M. (2010). Hochschulabschluss für Hoteldirektoren. *Allgemeine Hotel- und Gastronomie-Zeitung* (50), p. A002 [online]. Available from https://www.wiso-net.de/document/AHGZ__121011148%7CAHGA__121011148/hitlist/0?all= [2016-12-13].

Zinzow, S. (2001). Die Frequenz-Relevanz-Analyse für Probleme unterstützt Qualitätsmanager wirkungsvoll. *Betriebswirtschaftliche Blätter* (11), p. 538. [online]. Available from https://www.wiso-net.de/document/BBL__20011100011/hitlist/0?all= [2016-12-13].

Tomas Pernecky, Jill Poulston

Cultural Creatives' Accommodation Preferences and the Honeybee Leadership Philosophy

1 Introduction

The term 'Cultural Creatives' was coined by Ray & Anderson (2000), who spent 22 years surveying over 100,000 Americans, conducting 60 in-depth interviews and approximately 500 focus groups, trying to make sense of a new emerging subculture with distinct beliefs and values. As they explain, the underlying themes express serious ecological and planetary perspectives, emphasis on relationships and women's point of view, commitment to spirituality and psychological development, disaffection with the large institutions of modern life, including both left and right wing politics, and rejection of materialism and status display. Cultural Creatives are concerned with ecology, relationships, peace and social justice, and are interested in self-actualisation, spirituality, and self-expression. They are apprehensive about the 'problems of the global environment' (p. 4), such as global warming, rainforest destruction, species destruction, and the loss of the ozone layer, and come from all walks of life and education levels, ranging from working class to the elite.

This article examines the accommodation preferences of Cultural Creatives when they travel for business and leisure, to determine how their values translate into accommodation preferences, and the importance of these on accommodation providers. The article also examines leadership approaches suited to businesses likely to be favoured by this group, because of its strong interest in social justice and ethics. The links between sustainable leadership and environmentally aware consumers have been rarely examined in the literature, so the aim of this study is to determine if there are explicit links between Cultural Creatives' accommodation preferences, and the Honeybee Approach to sustainable leadership (Avery, 2004; 2005; Avery & Bergsteiner, 2011a; 2011b). Cultural Creatives are not particularly interested in highly ranked hotels that are managed with great efficiency, but rather, they support businesses that take care of their people, are ethical, nurturing, and supportive. They are therefore posited to desire a sustainable or 'Honeybee Approach' to hotel leadership.

2 Literature Review

2.1 Cultural Creatives

Cultural Creatives can be divided into two main groups: the Core group and the Green Cultural Creatives. Ray & Anderson (2000) describe those belonging to the Core group as 'leading edge thinkers' (p. 14), including writers, artists, musicians, environmentalists, feminists, alternative health care providers, and other professionals. Strong advocates of sustainable practices – including those in hospitality and tourism businesses – fall into this category. Although all Cultural Creatives have 'green' values, the Core Group is more 'intense and activist' about ecology and sustainability (Ray & Anderson, 2000, p. 14). Consider, for example, accommodation in which all decisions are underpinned by sustainable principles: the design of the building and room layout, management, organisational core values, day-to-day operations, the use of organic and fair-trade produce, supplier contracts, and additional services (e.g., green transport).

Figure 1: Cultural Creatives in the USA[1]

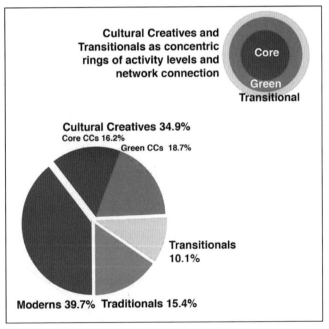

Green Cultural Creatives are no less passionate about the environment, social issues and relationships, but tend to be less intense, more pragmatic, less activist, and also less educated than those in the Core group. If one were to imagine Cultural Creatives as comprising inner and outer rings – depicted in Figure 1 – the most ardent core members would form the centre, with the Green Cultural Creatives surrounding them.

In 2000, Ray & Anderson estimated that the Core group consisted of about 24 million people (less than half the Cultural Creatives). Based on more recent data, Ray (2015) now estimates that Cultural Creatives overall increased in proportion to the general population from an initial 23.6% of American (USA) adults in 1995 (approximately 44 million adults), to 26% in 1999 (approximately 50 million), to 34.9% in 2008 (approximately 80 million). The latest comparisons are shown in Figure 1, in which Cultural Creatives are contrasted with Moderns (a label used to describe people who focus more on personal gains and success) and Traditionalists (those who are religiously conservative, adhere to 19th-century worldviews, and live mostly in rural areas and small towns). An additional 10% of the population is in transition and, as shown in Figure 1, this group forms the outer ring of the subculture. This segment has been labelled the 'working class Transitional group', and is concerned about the climate crisis while still holding to traditional values (Ray, 2015, p. 10). However, despite the fact that Cultural Creatives can be identified and conceptualised as a distinct subculture, it would be misleading to think of them in terms of an organised structure with a hierarchy and membership as in (for example) most political parties and religions. Cultural Creatives are scattered across society, but 'missing self-awareness as a whole people' (Ray & Anderson, 2000, p. 39). Hence, individually, they may be unaware of the vast number of like-minded people, but considered as a group, they represent a powerful influence and worthy of examination in the context of hospitality and tourism.

2.2 Sustainability and Leadership

Sustainability sits at the very heart of Cultural Creatives' beliefs, and hospitality and tourism organisations are labour intensive, requiring complex leadership skills. This section therefore overviews relevant literature on hospitality leadership and sustainable leadership. There is both a conceptual and a research gap in the way hospitality leadership is approached and understood. Although the focus of this paper does not extend to a detailed analysis of leadership in this field, suffice it to say that sustainable leadership has notably little presence in the hospitality literature, where the focus is mostly around customer needs and leadership in the traditional sense of the term (i.e., establishing collective norms and motivating employees to work towards set goals). Sustainable leadership as discussed in this paper, is a broader philosophy that goes beyond customer service and employee management, and is more concerned with holistic leadership than management per se. Sustainable leadership considers not only the organisation and customers; it concentrates on building a long-term partnership with employees, the local community, suppliers, and other stakeholders, and reviews its practices, policies, and the impact these have on the environment.

Commercial hospitality incorporates services in which production and consumption are contemporaneous (Brotherton, 1999), placing time pressures on staff (Susskind, Borchgrevink, Kacmar, & Brymer, 2000). This requirement for speed, against a background of hierarchical organisation and traditional modes of operation, lends itself to transactional leadership (Whitelaw, 2013), and the associated tendency for high staff turnover. However, and as Whitelaw notes, although the pressure of achieving specific standards lends itself to transactional leadership styles, transformational styles are more highly valued (Cichy & Schmidgall, 1996; Greger & Peterson, 2000). Whereas transactional leadership relies on explicit transactions between leaders and followers (e.g., contingent rewards), transformational leadership is inspirational, encouraging followers to subscribe to a shared vision (Bass, 1990). Transformational leadership is necessarily ethical leadership because it inspires and motivates followers in a way that unethical leadership is unlikely to achieve. Transformational leadership develops better moral codes in followers (Mulla & Krishnan, 2011; Tang et al., 2015), enhances employee well-being (Gill, Flaschner, & Shachar, 2006; Kara, Uysal, Sirgy, & Lee, 2013), and reduces staff turnover (Gill et al., 2006; Tang et al., 2015).

Although a range of sustainable environmental practices has been common in hospitality for some time, sustainability research in hospitality is still at an early stage (Boley & Uysal, 2013; Melissen, 2012), and relatively few hospitality organisations employ sustainable labour practices that successfully address the problem of staff turnover (Davidson & Wang, 2011). Research linking sustainability and leadership in hospitality is therefore timely, as sustainable leadership practices are both ethical and transformational, and therefore well placed to solve not just the industry's labour problems, but also to inspire staff to follow sustainable practices.

2.3 The Honeybee Philosophy

The literature on sustainable leadership includes the Honeybee philosophy (Avery, 2004; 2005; Avery & Bergsteiner, 2011a; 2011b), which focuses on stakeholder-oriented approaches to leadership, considering stakeholders as including employees, local community, suppliers, and clients. In this approach to leadership, employees are highly valued and perceived as valuable assets that need to be looked after, nurtured and developed. Sustainable leaders are socially and environmentally responsible, focus on long-term goals and outcomes, and are passionate about ethical business practices. In their view, the environment in which we live and work is not one to be exploited but utilised with respect – hence the metaphor of the honeybee.

It is helpful to clarify the links between Cultural Creatives and the values espoused in the Honeybee philosophy. Apart from caring for the environment, additional commonalities become particularly clear when the focus is turned towards what Cultural Creatives are opposed to. This includes materialism, greed, status display, social inequalities of race and class, failure to care adequately for elders, women, and children, hedonism, and apprehension of and distrust in large institutions (Ray & Anderson, 2000, p. 17). All are related to a dislike of unethical practices.

The Honeybee Approach is an ethical leadership model, identifying 23 principles for sustainable leadership and practice (Avery & Bergsteiner, 2011a). Figure 2 summarises these in a pyramid, showing 14 foundational practices, six higher-level practices, three key performance drivers, and several performance outcomes. The foundational practices, as the authors (Avery & Bergsteiner, 2011a) explain, include staff training and development, valuing people, promoting ethical behaviour, and so forth. The higher-level practices derive from these, and include

> devolved and consensual decision-making, creating self-managing employees, harnessing the power of teams, developing a trusting atmosphere, forming an organisational culture that enables sustainable leadership, and sharing and retaining the firm's knowledge (p. 8).

The key performance drivers in the third layer reveal what customer experience is or ought to be, and are therefore customer-focused, emerging from the previous two tiers. Finally, the top of the pyramid lists five performance outcomes that contribute to the organisation's sustainability.

This study therefore examines the accommodation preferences of Cultural Creatives, who favour ethical and sustainable practices. The aim was to discover if the interests of Cultural Creatives extended to issues relating to sustainable human resources practices such as those espoused in the foundational level of the Honeybee philosophy. Alternatively, Cultural Creatives might just consider what appears to be environmentally friendly accommodation, and have little interest in the labour and policies behind this. 'Green washing' (claiming to be environmentally friendly for marketing purposes while having no real commitment to sustainable practices) has long been an issue in hotels (e.g., Tufts & Milne, 2014), whose practice of reducing towel laundry (ostensibly not only to save the planet, but also save considerable labour and laundry costs) was the original inspiration for the term (e.g., Orange, 2010).

Figure 2: Sustainable Leadership Pyramid[2]

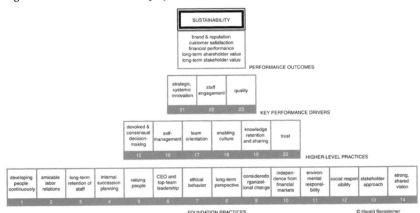

3 Research Approach

The aim of the study was to identify any explicit links between the accommodation preferences of Cultural Creatives, and the Honeybee leadership philosophy. This was achieved through two objectives:

1. determine the accommodation preferences of Cultural Creatives; and
2. identify preferences related to sustainable leadership approaches (e.g., ethical labour practices).

Data were collected using an online survey. The survey consisted of a combination of 35 open and closed-ended questions designed to probe perceptions of hospitality and identify accommodation preferences. Of the 176 prospective respondents that started the survey, just 61 completed it, as most did not fit the profile of a Cultural Creative; filter questions are used to ensure that respondents meet this profile are presented in Table 1. This reduction to 61 participants from an initial pool of 176 corresponds with the estimates produced by Ray & Anderson (2013) is such that Cultural Creatives comprise around 35% of the total population. Questions were adopted from Ray & Anderson's seminal text (2000), and employed ten or more statements to identify a Cultural Creative; the more statements respondents agreed with, the stronger the affiliation they had with this group. Although potential respondents were asked to tick any number of statements they believed

---

2   Source: Avery & Bergsteiner, 2011a, p. 8.

reflected their personal beliefs, philosophy, and practices, only those who ticked ten or more statements were allowed to continue the survey.

Table 1: Cultural Creatives' Identifiers used as Filter Questions

1   I love nature and am deeply concerned about its destruction.

2   I am strongly aware of the problems of the whole planet (global warming, destruction of the rainforests, overpopulation, lack of ecological sustainability, exploitation of people in poorer countries) and want to see more action on them, such as limiting economic growth.

3   I would pay more taxes or pay more for consumer goods if I could know the money would go to clean up the environment and to stop global warming.

4   I place a great deal of importance on developing and maintaining my relationships.

5   I place a lot of value on helping other people and bringing out their unique gifts.

6   I do volunteering for one or more good causes.

7   I care intensely about both psychological and spiritual development.

8   I see spirituality or religion as important in my life, but am concerned about the role of the religious right in politics.

9   I want more equality for women at work and more women leaders in business and politics.

10 I am concerned about violence and abuse of women and children around the world.

11 I want our politics and government spending to put more emphasis on children's education and well-being, on rebuilding our neighbourhoods and communities, and on creating an ecologically sustainable future.

12 I am unhappy with both the Left and the Right in politics, and want to find a new way that is not in the mushy middle.

13 I tend to be somewhat optimistic about our future, and distrust the cynical and pessimistic view that is given by the media.

14 I want to be involved in creating a new and better way of life in my country.

15 I am concerned about what the big corporations are doing in the name of making more profits: downsizing, creating environmental problems, and exploiting poorer countries.

16 I have my finances and spending under control, and am not concerned about overspending.

17 I dislike all the emphasis in modern culture on success and 'making it', on getting and spending, and on wealth and luxury goods.

18 I like people and places that are exotic and foreign, and like experiencing and learning about other ways of life.

The survey was promoted to the general public online using Google AdWords, which displays advertisements on Google, as well as selected shops such as organic stores, and hospitality businesses identified as appealing to those interested in sustainability, spirituality, and holistic health. Advertisements were also placed on newagetravel.com and spiritlibrary.com. These sites were chosen in light of Ray & Anderson's (2000, p. 29) description of Cultural Creatives as being interested in alternative health care and natural foods, seeing nature as sacred (over 90%), believing in religious mysteries (approximately 52%), and invested in self-actualisation (approximately 49%). Given the overall strategy of targeting the desired respondents, the study utilised purposive sampling, in which participants are limited to those with specific characteristics sought by the researchers to ensure data are appropriate and relevant (Oliver, 2006).

This article discusses data obtained through the open-ended questions, and not the pre-determined closed-ended questions (e.g., demographic information, average expenditure, etc.). Although the survey included 35 hospitality-related questions, the following sections concentrate on data that particularly add new insights to the relationship between sustainability and sustainable leadership. Findings consist of key themes extracted by the NVivo software, and are based on word frequency analysis. Aside from revealing the values and attitudes of this segment of customers, there was evidence that Cultural Creatives are not only aware of sustainable leadership principles – albeit not in an academic sense – but actively look for these when making accommodation choices.

4 Findings

Respondents were asked about their accommodation preferences when travelling, particularly as influenced by their beliefs, philosophies and practices. Two main categories were created to distinguish between different purposes for travel: (1) business and (2) leisure. The study sought to identify any significant variations in responses based on respondents' preferences and needs when accommodated away from home.

4.1 Travelling for Business

There are five themes that emerged when travelling for business. As detailed below, respondents sought: (1) ethical employment and practices; (2) positive environment and stimulating location; and (3) green and sustainable practices.

4.1.1 Ethical Employment Practices

The need to treat employees fairly in a just and respectful manner was a prevalent theme. Cultural Creatives prefer establishments that provide equal employment opportunities for all, offer reasonable wages, and value their employees. They believe that a happy workforce translates into positive experiences for guests, as indicated by the comment:

> If the staff are happy, it is a good place and I will be happy.

They also expressed the view that accommodation should be:

> ideally locally owned so that profits go back to the local community.

They considered it important to pay fair wages, and where necessary, provide reasonable accommodation to employees. Key phrases used by respondents included:

> right use of power with employees, reflecting the cultural diversity of the place, employing both men and women, employing people of ethnic background and hotels that have non-discriminatory policies.

4.1.2 Positive Environment and Stimulating Location

Cultural Creatives seek accommodation in close proximity to nature, and located near areas where they can learn about the local culture, its people and visit any interesting sites. They also like accommodation providers to source food locally. Some respondents indicated that they seek a 'relaxed ambience' and prefer accommodation where 'positive energy is felt from happy individuals'. Having personal space for religious or spiritual practices was also mentioned.

4.1.3 Green and Sustainable Practices

Respondents emphasised their preference for environmentally friendly features and practices in their accommodation when travelling for business. For example, one commented:

> Great if [the hotel] follows sound environmental practices, e.g. modest electricity (long life bulbs/automatic switch off) and water consumption (have showers), recycle food/ waste, don't just say it but actually don't wash bed sheets/towels each day.

Some like environmentally friendly products, such as low allergenic soaps, and eco-friendly detergents and cleaning products. When asked what kind of features respondents avoided when travelling on business, two key themes stood out.

4.1.4 Avoid Poor Location and Maintenance Problems

Respondents tended to avoid accommodation near power lines, busy roads, and noisy entertainment districts. They also stay away from polluted areas. Furthermore, when they travel for business, they avoid establishments too far from where their main work-related activities are carried out. With regard to specific accommodation features, items such as 'poor sanitation and wall insulations', 'places that are run down', and 'shared facilities (e.g. bathrooms)' were all listed as undesirable.

4.1.5 Avoid Unethical Operational Practices

This theme pertains to the extreme opposites of the looked-for themes Green and Sustainable Practices and Ethical Employment Practices. Respondents reported that they avoid accommodation with inefficient use of resources (e.g., water) and processes (e.g., washing linen every day and wasting food). Furthermore, they stayed away from establishments that do not treat employees fairly and equally. For example, they did not like establishments that only employ men or 'young staff whom they can pay less', and were not prepared to support (by staying in the hotel) poor conditions for local workers. Highly priced accommodation and hotels that charge 'for every service provided' were also disliked.

4.2 Travelling for Leisure

Seven themes emerged under the category of travelling for leisure. As detailed below, the features respondents sought comprised four major themes: (1) natural environment and design; (2) sustainable leadership and practices; (3) all things local; and (4) peaceful ambience.

4.2.1 Natural Environment and Design

Natural beauty, natural environment, and natural surroundings were important considerations when travelling for leisure, with respondents particularly emphasising natural settings and peaceful surroundings. In particular, the term 'good feng shui' was noted numerous times. 'Feng shui' originated in China approximately 3,000 years ago and denotes a philosophy of creating harmony and energetic balance in one's environment (Lai, 1974). Respondents used this term in connection with a wide variety of aspects of accommodation: the design of the building, interior décor, customer service, the proximity of the accommodation to natural surroundings, materials, cleanliness, and 'green practices by owners'. The use of the concept of 'harmony' by Cultural Creatives points to a more holistic meaning than just a physical environment, but extends to subconscious and spiritual responses to the environment.

4.2.2 Sustainable Leadership Practices

This broader theme pertains to operational and employment practices. Respondents preferred to stay in lodgings that follow, implement, and promote green practices. Examples included recycling, following sustainable protocols, having sustainable transport options, using locally made products, and abiding by 'green/eco guidelines'. Cultural Creatives feel strongly about the just and ethical treatment of a workforce. Key statements indicative of a strong sense of their commitment to treating people well included: 'right human relations', 'adding value rather than exploiting the local area/community', and 'respect for staff'. Respondents generally preferred providers to form partnerships with their stakeholders, such as local community and staff, rather than treating them as resources to exploit. An important comment that warrants discussion under this theme was 'personal contact with operators', indicating that for some Cultural Creatives it is important to be able to communicate with business owners and have more personal encounters and experiences. The website www.airbnb.com was given as an example where travellers can exchange emails and messages directly with the lodging providers.

4.2.3 All Things Local

Utilising local resources is intrinsic to sustainable leadership practices (see above), so there was also a strong emphasis on the keyword 'local' and for this reason it is considered separately. Respondents felt strongly about accommodation providers serving local produce, providing local newspapers, utilising local indigenous materials, and offering employment to local people. It was also considered important that hotels and accommodation providers demonstrated 'cultural and social commitment to local community'.

4.2.4 Peaceful Ambience

Ambience was strongly linked to location. When travelling for leisure, Cultural Creatives, tend to prefer places that are 'peaceful' and with 'positive energy' and solemnity. This extends to design, staff, and the hotel's operations. The following comments illustrate the key features of this theme:

> I look for accommodation that reflects peacefulness, quiet and a sense of whimsy while paying attention to the practical side of life such as how much noise rises

> It's just the people they are the key for me. I know straight away whether I want to stay and will just drive away if the people are 'wrong'

When asked what kind of features respondents avoided when travelling for leisure, three themes emerged:

4.2.5 Avoid Poor Location and Environment

Consistent with the category of business travel, when travelling for leisure, Cultural Creatives avoid accommodation near high tensile power lines, industrial and noisy areas, and in polluted and unsafe locations. Noise, high traffic, and pollution were all high on their lists of undesirable features. In particular, respondents avoided accommodation on busy streets, tourism 'hot-spots', and places too close to mainstream tourism attractions. One comment particularly captured the kind of experience some Cultural Creatives avoid:

> synthetic fabrics, small pokey rooms, rooms with small windows and poor ventilation, rooms where the décor is loud and noisy, deep pile carpets, big television, drinks cabinet, shared bathroom.

4.2.6 Avoid Unethical Operational Practices

As with business travel, Cultural Creatives tend to avoid establishments that show little respect for the environment and local people. They avoid lodgings with 'unjust' or 'poor employment practices' and where locals 'are exploited' and 'don't benefit'. This theme is consistent with the preferred Sustainable Leadership Practices (see 4.2.2), underscoring the importance of operating lodging businesses according to sustainable principles.

4.2.7 Lack of Hospitality

Respondents revealed that they try to avoid accommodation with unfriendly staff and service, illustrated by the comment:

> Uncaring attitudes on behalf of management, which includes those who are too unctuous in their service, as it isn't REAL.

Although some indicated that they avoided 'luxury hotels with fawning staff', they liked hotels that have been carefully built, are well maintained, and that have the 'appropriate' amount of service. This last point was illustrated by the comment

> [I don't want to be] bothered by lots of questions! These days it takes 6 to get a coffee, and 12 to get a sandwich!

4.3 Summary

Accommodation preferences for Cultural Creatives can be considered under the two major headings of business practices and environment. Preferred business practices included ethical employment practices such as recruitment policies that protect the rights of local workers and do not discriminate on the basis of gender or ethnicity. Other favoured practices mostly related to environmental practices such as energy conservation and the avoidance of toxins, but also included the allocation of resources to ensure accommodation was clean and well maintained. Preferred physical environments were relaxed and peaceful with natural features, away from air and noise pollution. However, preferred environments also reflected a desire to be cared for by employees who are friendly and helpful because they are happy in their work, rather than because they are obliged to be.

5 Discussion and Conclusions

The core focus of this paper was the accommodation preferences of Cultural Creatives and the relationship of these to sustainable leadership practices. The study also contributes to the body of literature on sustainable leadership by providing a lens through which we begin to see that there is a demand by customers for practices aligned with sustainability and the Honeybee Approach to leadership.

There are, at a minimum, three interconnected points that warrant discussion. Firstly, the domain of sustainable leadership is not merely a theoretical exercise or management tool, but is better conceived of as a fundamental philosophy that resonates with a certain type of customer (Cultural Creatives) that supports ethical accommodation following sustainable principles, and avoids accommodation that does not. Secondly, the findings are relevant to the role of movements and grassroots organisations committed to creating change.

Grassroots leaders, in the context of customers, can be defined as travellers who 'vote with their wallets', and as travellers who demand and co-create change for the better of organisations and society generally. In this respect, Cultural Creatives can be understood as actors at a grassroots level. They represent a segment of customers who, despite having little power individually, can be very powerful as a group. According to Kezar and Lester (2011, p. 9), grassroots leaders are interested in pursuing

> organisational changes that often challenge the status quo of the institution and are seldom in positions of authority.

Furthermore, they create 'their own structure, network, and support systems' (p. 8).' Informal exchanges of ideas and ideals among Cultural Creatives can occur in online community groups and forums, and through platforms that enable customers to communicate with businesses (e.g., www.airbnb.com). This study shows that Cultural Creatives will use their financial power to influence the survival of businesses with whom their beliefs and values resonate, while at the same time, penalising those who ignore ethical and sustainable imperatives, by avoiding their accommodation. In this way, Cultural Creatives demonstrate and seek the leadership qualities valued by the Honeybee Approach to leadership.

Thirdly, if Ray & Anderson's (2000) predictions are accurate, approximately 35% of the population in the USA and Western Europe can be identified as Cultural Creatives. Although the findings in this paper are not representative of this group at large, they highlight the tendencies and views that exist in this influential pool of customers. More studies into Cultural Creatives may be a promising area of research in tourism and hospitality studies.

The findings from this study offer a rare insight into the values and attitudes of this segment of travellers. They also support prior research that the green image of a hotel is an important influence on consumers' lodging preferences (see Yusof, Liu, & Poulston, 2016), and suggest that Cultural Creatives are unlikely to be fooled by greenwashing tactics, showing considerable interest in how labour and products are sourced. Yusof et al. note that many hotel customers are sceptical of green products, and suspicious that economic and litigious imperatives are prioritised over environmental concerns (see D'Souza, Taghian, Lamb, & Peretiatkos, 2006). This study confirms this, showing that consumers interested in sustainability are also likely to be interested in how this is achieved.

In relation to the findings of this paper, themes reveal that Cultural Creatives pay attention to sustainable practices, and seek accommodation that conducts business fairly and ethically. Cultural Creatives want employees to be respected and supported, and prefer to be surrounded by staff of various ethnic backgrounds, and a balance of gender. In their opinion, hotels and lodgings should add value to the local community by employing local people and utilising locally made goods and produce. Whether they travel on business or for leisure, Cultural Creatives are conscious of the environment and do not like resources to be wasted. They will avoid establishments that are noisy, located in busy and polluted areas, and that lack authentic hospitality. Most importantly, Cultural Creatives will try to avoid businesses that are unethical – whether this be a lack of care for the environment or people, or by overcharging for services provided. On the other hand, their ideal accommodation (when not constrained by business) is a harmonious place, as suggested by the repeated use of the term 'feng shui', and in close proximity to natural surroundings. Their preferred accommodation will be an inspiring and peaceful site, designed with a view to operating sustainably. Overall, findings suggest that sustainable leadership principles are deeply ingrained in Cultural Creatives, who expect to see these implemented when looking for somewhere to stay. Given that this represents about a third of the adult population, this is one of the most important findings in terms of hospitality and tourism practice. Hospitality leadership practices that recognise and take account of this finding are ultimately those that will be truly sustainable.

References

Avery, G. C. (2004). *Understanding leadership: Paradigms and cases.* London, UK: SAGE.

Avery, G. C. (2005). *Leadership for sustainable futures: Achieving success in a competitive world.* Cheltenham, UK: Edward Elgar Publishing.

Avery, G. C., & Bergsteiner, H. (2011a). Sustainable leadership practices for enhancing business resilience and performance. *Strategy & Leadership, 39*(3), 5–15. doi: 10.1108/10878571111128766.

Avery, G. C., & Bergsteiner, H. (2011b). *Sustainable leadership: Honeybee and locust approaches.* New York, NY: Routledge.

Bass, B. M. (1990). *Bass & Stogdill's handbook of leadership: Theory, research, and managerial applications* (3rd ed.). New York, NY: Collier MacMillan.

Boley, B. B., & Uysal, M. (2013). Competitive synergy through practicing triple bottom line sustainability: Evidence from three hospitality case studies. *Tourism & Hospitality Research, 13*(4), 226–238.

Brotherton, B. (1999). Towards a definitive view of the nature of hospitality and hospitality management. *International Journal of Contemporary Hospitality Management, 11*(4), 165–173.

Cichy, R. F., & Schmidgall, R. S. (1996). Leadership qualities of financial executives. *Cornell Hotel & Restaurant Administration Quarterly, 37*(2), 56–62.

Davidson, M. C. G., & Wang, Y. (2011). Sustainable labor practices? Hotel human resource managers' views on turnover and skill shortages. *Journal of Human Resources in Hospitality & Tourism, 10*(3), 235–253. doi: 10.1080/15332845.2011.555731.

D'Souza, C., Taghian, M., Lamb, P., & Peretiatkos, R. (2006). Green products and corporate strategy: An empirical investigation. *Society and Business Review, 1*(2), 144–157. doi: 10.1108/17465680610669825.

Gill, A., Flaschner, A., & Shachar, M. (2006). Mitigating stress and burnout by implementing transformational-leadership. *International Journal of Contemporary Hospitality Management, 18*(6), 469–481. doi: 10.1108/09596110610681511.

Greger, K. R., & Peterson, J. S. (2000). Leadership profiles for the new millennium. *Cornell Hotel & Restaurant Administration Quarterly*, 41(1), 16–29.

Kara, D., Uysal, M., Sirgy, M. J., & Lee, G. (2013). The effects of leadership style on employee well-being in hospitality. *International Journal of Hospitality Management*, 34, 9–18. doi: 10.1016/j.ijhm.2013.02.001.

Kezar, A., & Lester, J. (2011). *Enhancing campus capacity for leadership: An examination of grassroots leaders in higher education.* Stanford, CA: Stanford University Press.

Lai, C.-Y. D. (1974). A feng shui model as a location index. *Annals of the Association of American Geographers*, 64(4), 506–513.

Melissen, F. (2012). Sustainable hospitality: A meaningful notion? *Journal of Sustainable Tourism*, 21(6), 810–824. doi: 10.1080/09669582.2012.737797.

Mulla, Z. R., & Krishnan, V. R. (2011). Transformational leadership: Do the leader's morals matter and do the follower's morals change? *Journal of Human Values*, 17(2), 129–143. doi: 10.1177/097168581101700203.

Oliver, P. (2006). Purposive Sampling. In V. Jupp (Ed.), *The Sage dictionary of social research methods.* London, UK: SAGE.

Orange, E. (2010). From eco-friendly to eco-intelligent. *Futurist*, 44(5), 28–42.

Ray, P. H. (2015). The potential for a new, emerging culture in the U.S.: Report on the 2008 American Values Survey. In S. Dinan (Ed.), *Sacred America, sacred world: Fulfilling our mission in service to all.* Charlottesville, VA: Hampton Roads. Retrieved from http://www.wisdomuniversity.org/CCsReport2008SurveyV3.pdf.

Ray, P. H., & Anderson, S. R. (2000). *The Cultural Creatives: How 50 million people are changing the world.* New York, NY: Harmony Books.

Ray, P. H., & Anderson, S. R. (2013). Cultural Creatives: The leading edge of cultural change. Retrieved 5 February, 2015, from http://culturalcreatives.org/cultural-creatives/.

Susskind, A. M., Borchgrevink, C. P., Kacmar, K. M., & Brymer, R. A. (2000). Customer service employees' behavioural intentions and attitudes: An examination of construct validity and a path model. *International Journal of Hospitality Management*, 19, 53–77. doi: 10.1016/S0278-4319(99)00030-4.

Tang, G., Cai, Z., Liu, Z., Zhu, H., Yang, X., & Li, J. (2015). The importance of ethical leadership in employees' value congruence and turnover. *Cornell Hospitality Quarterly*, 56(4), 397–410. doi: 10.1177/1938965514563159.

Tufts, S., & Milne, S. (2014). Greening, green-washing, and union activism in hospitality. *Women & Environments International Magazine*, 94(95), 41–43.

Whitelaw, P. (2013). Leadership up the ladder: The construction of leadership styles in the hospitality industry. *The Journal of Contemporary Issues in Business and Government*, 19(1), 65–79.

Yusof, N. A., Liu, C., & Poulston, J. (2016). Customers' expectations of hotel green marketing: A New Zealand case study. In A. C. C. Lu, Y. Rao, & D. Dursoy (eds.), *Proceedings of the 6th Advances in Hospitality and Tourism Marketing and Management Conference*. July 14–17. Guangzhou, China: AHTMM.

Sabrina Seeler, Ellen Böhling, Bernd Eisenstein

Global Destination Brand: An International Comparative Study

1 Internationalisation of Travel

The travel industry is experiencing continuous growth and is one of the most important and fastest growing business sectors in the world. In 2015, 1.2 billion guest arrivals were registered, growth of 4.6 percent compared to the previous year (UNWTO, 2016). By 2030, 1.8 billion international guest arrivals are projected and this growth is expected to be generated by the Asian markets as well as the Middle East (UNWTO, 2016).

Besides the traditional destinations in Europe and North America, there is an increasing number of new countries that are opening their doors to tourism – both for incoming and outgoing tourism. As a result, the number of available destinations is growing and the potential guest is faced with the challenge of choosing from a multitude of similar and partly interchangeable tourist destinations. At the same time, tourists are increasingly international and the needs and requirements differ between source markets and cultures. In order to anchor the destination in the minds of potential guests and to remain competitive in an increasingly competitive environment, destination marketing organisations (DMOs) need to develop strategies that not only meet the needs of the demand, but surpass the expectations of the guests. Against the backdrop of the increasingly international and multicultural guest structure, as well as the constantly and dynamically changing demand, this has become a significant challenge for DMOs and other tourism providers (Bornhorst, Brent Ritchie, & Sheehan, 2010; Ritchie & Crouch, 2003).

Even though the Western industrialised nations (esp. Europe and North America) are still the strongest international source markets for tourism in terms of sheer volume, new markets from developing and emerging countries are coming out as future growth engines. Demographic change, which is particularly noticeable in the Western industrialised nations, with shrinking populations as well as a stagnant 'old middle-class', and the concurrent economic growth in developing and emerging countries, is leading to a 'new global middle-class' (Popp, 2014). The developmental politician Guarín (2012) described this as a silent revolution which progressively encourages the poorer parts of the world's population to participate in the global prosperity. This new emerging middle class is a result of income growth, which is characterised by increasing purchasing power as well as rising and changing consumer needs. From an economic point of view, emerging countries in Asia and Latin America have mainly been the focus of global economic activity (Guarín, 2012; Popp, 2014) and particular attention is given to the BRIC (Brazil, Russia, India and China) countries (Ouyang, 2016; Schrooten, 2011). It is not yet possible to answer the question of how the consumption behaviour of the new middle class will have a concrete effect (economically, politically, and ecologically), but the growing middle class will certainly be of great relevance for the tourism industry in the future. In addition to the economically positive development, the political framework conditions, including the entry and exit formalities, have in some cases been considerably eased. International air traffic from countries where freedom of travel had previously been restricted experienced a positive development as well. For example, Chinese citizens can only travel to countries that have the legal status of being an approved destination. After a long period of Chinese population not being able to travel abroad for leisure purposes, China's outgoing tourism was gradually liberalised with the visa politics that were introduced in 1990. In 2004, an Approved Destination Status (ADS) memorandum was finally adopted between the China National Tourism Administration (CNTA) and the European Union. The effects of this memorandum and the freedom to leisurely travel to Europe are clearly reflected in the tourist arrivals from mainland Chinese (Arita, Edmonds, La Croix, & Mak, 2011; Dai, Jiang, Yang, & Ma, 2016).

Despite having to wait out the current climactic political situation to see how these framework conditions will continue to develop, the past few years have clearly shown that the travel industry is becoming increasingly global. Travel source markets, such as China and India, are not only showing significant growth rates, but are also seen as futuristic markets due to the size of the population as well as the monetary situation. These 'new' guests are also showing divergent travel behaviour (Arlt, 2006; Li, Lai, Harrill, Kline, & Wang, 2011). These changes are creating new challenges for the strategic management of tourist destinations worldwide as well as the development of appealing travel products. Due to the multitude of international source markets and the target areas, as well as the heterogeneity of demand and the limited availability of resources, it is necessary to address potential guests more precisely and according to their specific demands. Official statistics and general forecasts identify general developmental tendencies of these markets. What DMOs are missing at this stage is a clear understanding of the necessary marketing steps for specific international markets. In order to become anchored in the mental maps of the international guests, DMOs need to know whether it is more about creating awareness, increasing likeability or generating visitor appeal. These are fundamental questions that tourism stakeholders and especially DMOs have to face in order to make the best possible use of available resources to exploit potential international markets. The study 'Global Destination Brand' is aimed at contributing to filling existing research gaps, both in empirical and applied sciences. The methodology of this pilot study and some key findings are discussed in this chapter.

2 Methodology and Objective of the Study

The pilot study of the Global Destination Brand study series examined the customer-oriented brand value of international tourist destinations from the perspective of selected tourism source markets. The study design was based on the existing and successfully implemented research project 'Destination Brand'. In 2009, the Institute for Management and Tourism (IMT) of the West Coast University of Applied Sciences firstly measured the customer-oriented brand value of German tourist destinations from the perspective of the Germans. Since then, the study has been annually repeated which changing research focus. With 'Global Destination Brand', the tested research design was aimed to be transferred to an international level. In close cooperation and with the academic support of the IMT, the TIRC Network GmbH[1] implemented a quantitative case study design to conduct the international comparative research. The literature suggests that the incorporation of multiple case studies allows more robust findings and results in analytical benefits compared to single case study designs. According to Yin (2014), a multiple case study design encourages deep and rich country-specific findings and enables cross-national comparisons. Hence, international comparative studies are of great importance in the fields of social sciences and political sciences as they allow and encourage comparisons and benchmarking (Hantrais, 2007).

The overall aim of this study was the establishment of the widest possible benchmarking and therewith the enablement of comparison and encouragement of breadth of knowledge (Patton, 2002). More precisely, the aim was to evaluate the brand value of international tourist destinations from an international tourist perspective and establish a database that enables comparison on different levels. The survey design was based on a four-dimensional model. This so-called brand funnel consists of brand awareness (aided), brand likeability, willingness to visit and past usage. A web survey design and deductive approach with a high degree

---

1   For more information visit http://tirc-network.com.

of standardisation was identified as the most appropriate method to collect data (Patton, 2002). Collecting empirical data through standardised survey questionnaires provides systematic and structured information that enable comparison of information from a larger sample population in a short time period and therewith contributes to the desired breadth of knowledge (de Vaus, 2014; Nardi, 2014).

The selection of the case studies for this research was based on a multilevel criteria catalogue. This criteria catalogue included indicators measuring the importance of tourism in the respective country (e.g. top incoming markets, value added tourism), as well as key figures for foreign travel volumes and behaviour of the respective markets (e.g. international travel intensity, top foreign travel destinations, average expenditure for international travel). The criteria catalogue also acknowledged general variables related to the economic and social developments of the markets (e.g. population growth, GDP development). On the basis of the list of criteria, a pre-selection of ten countries was made. The pre-selection of case studies encompassed the world's most important source markets (Germany France, Italy, Spain, UK, and USA) as well as several fast-growing emerging markets (Brazil, China, India, and Russia). Due to existing demand,[2] the Netherlands, Switzerland and Austria were also included in the study. Conclusively, data were collected in 13 case studies. In each case study, the four dimensions of the previously introduced brand funnel framework were examined in relation to 20 international tourist destinations (national level). The integration of 20 tourist destinations per case study allowed a comprehensive comparison matrix for the analysis of findings. An overview of the case studies and examined tourist destinations as well as the evaluation possibilities are illustrated in Figure 1.

A quota sample design was followed and a sample size of 1,000 respondents per case study was aimed for. Across the 13 case studies, a total of 13,000 people participated in this international comparative research. For the construction of the sample in this research an interlocked quota based on socio-demographic variables was adopted. This allowed a population proportionate sample that is representative of the respective (urban[3]) population living in private households, being at least 18 years of age and with at least one overnight vacation trip to a foreign country in the past.

---

2   Global Destination Brand is a contracted study. In order to ensure a comparative basis, a basic framework was set for destinations to be included in the research. Further destinations were only taken into account when the contract was awarded. The same applied to additional modules, such as the investigation of spontaneous associations.

3   In the cases of Brazil, Russia, India and China, the sample was based on the urban population for sampling and methodology reasons.

Figure 1: Comparison Matrix: Case Studies (Horizontal) and Examined Tourist Destinations (Vertical)[4]

		CASE STUDIES												
		BR	RU	IN	CN	UK	IT	FR	ESP	DE	AT	CH	NL	USA
Set tourist destinations	Brazil	-												
	China				-									
	UK					-								
	Italy						-							
	France							-						
	Spain								-					
	Germany									-				
	Austria										-			
	Switzerland											-		
	The Netherlands												-	
	USA													-
Additional tourist destinations	Luxembourg													
	Belgium													
	Greece													
	Denmark													
	Norway													
	Sweden													
	Finland													
	Ireland													
	Mexico													

The survey questionnaire was designed relatively short and focussed on the four key dimensions of the brand funnel. All questions were closed-ended, and response alternatives were either categorical (dichotomous or rating scales) or interval-scaled (Likert-type scales). The question for brand awareness, for example, was designed a dichotomous yes-no question while the degree of the likeability of a specific tourist destination was tested on a discrete four scale (e.g. very likeable, rather likeable, less likeable, not at all likeable). Besides the key dimensions of the brand funnel, respondents were asked several questions related to their socio-demographic profiles. The incorporation of socio-demographic criteria was not only necessary to ensure the proportionate sample, but also to allow differentiated analysis to be carried out based on sub-groups. An identical questionnaire was introduced in the 13 case studies, yet translated to the respective national language. Besides limitations related to linguistic equivalences that need to be acknowledged in multicultural and multinational studies (see critical reflection),

---

4   Source: IMT/TIRC Network GmbH (2015).

the high standardisation of the data collection instrument and survey questionnaire enabled several opportunities of comparative analysis and benchmarking.

3 Multidimensional Evaluation and Comparisons

Foremost, this study aimed to examine the customer-oriented and destination-related brand value of international tourist destinations. In addition to country-specific and one-dimensional analysis of the findings, the research's aim was to enable comparative analyses on various levels thus providing a multidimensional and comprehensive overview of the brand value of international tourist destinations from a worldwide perspective. In the following sections, the different evaluation and comparison possibilities are theoretically introduced and exemplified using exclusive research findings. All findings are based on the original dataset of the study 'Global Destination Brand' and internal, unpublished documentation of the IMT/TIRC Network GmbH.

3.1 One-dimensional Analysis of Research Findings

A one-dimensional analysis concentrates on findings from one case study and one single examined tourist destination. In the following example of a one-dimensional analysis, Germany's brand strength is evaluated from the perspective of the Indian population. With a steadily growing middle class and rising economic power, India is one of the fastest growing and emerging economies in the world (Guarín, 2012; Popp, 2014). Although the intensity of foreign travel is very low due to the high population, especially the Indian middle class is becoming more and more relevant to global incoming tourism and is described as one of the fastest growing travelling nations. After the UK, Germany is the most visited tourist destination of Indians in Europe with a market share of 20% (DZT, 2015). The findings derived from the study 'Global Destination Brand', and the statistical data, make it possible to assess the potential of India's outgoing tourism in general and the role of Germany in particular. The study provides insights into the degree of familiarity, likeability and willingness to visit Germany from the perspective of the urban Indian population, 18 years old and up, living in private households.

Findings show that Germany is known as a travel destination for 92.6 percent of the Indian respondents. In addition, 82.1 percent rated Germany as a rather likeable or very likeable holiday destination. Thus, more than two-thirds of the respondents who know Germany as a tourist destination (brand experts) were transferred to the level of brand sympathisers. This transfer from brand experts to brand sympathisers is expressed as transfer rate 1 (TR1) in this study. When asked to what extent

Germany is being considered for a holiday trip with at least one overnight stay in the next 12 months, a total of 70.9 percent of the Indian respondents indicated that Germany is definitely or most likely being considered. Thus, the clear majority of brand sympathisers can also be taken to the next level of visit willingness, which is computed in transfer rate 2 (TR2). The uni-dimensional results are represented in the form of the so-called brand funnel (Figure 2). While the height of the bars presents the process step values, the arrows between bars show the transfer rates from one to the next level.

Figure 2: Brand Funnel for Germany from the Perspective of the Urban Indian Population[5]

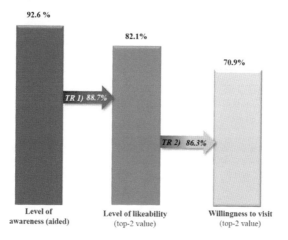

3.2 Vertical Analysis of Research Findings

In a vertical comparison, the data from one case study are used and findings from all surveyed tourist destinations or a selection of tourist destinations are compared. In this section, the brand strengths of Germany, Italy, France, Spain, the UK and the USA are evaluated from the perspective of the urban Russian population.

All of the destinations considered in this vertical analysis were known as travel destinations by more than nine out of ten respondents. This means that Germany, Spain, Italy, France, the UK and the USA each experienced a very high level of (aided) awareness as a tourist destination among the urban Russian population. Comparing the likeability claim, in contrast, demonstrates clear differences between

---

5   Source: IMT/TIRC Network GmbH (2015).

the surveyed tourist destinations. For example, the USA was known as a travel destination by 92.4 percent of the respondents, but only 55.2 percent of the representative Russian population rated the country as a rather likeable or very likeable tourist destination. This means that less than two-thirds of the brand experts were transferred to the level of sympathisers (TR1). Spain, Italy and France also experienced a very high level of (aided) awareness (each 98% of respondents) and at least nine out of ten brand experts were transferred to the level of brand sympathisers. Findings related to the future willingness to visit the examined destination indicate lower potentials as the transfer rates were comparably weak. However, several differences between examined tourist destinations were identified. Whereas 65.1 percent of the Russians could imagine having a holiday in Italy within the next 12 months, thus making it possible to transfer more than two-thirds of the sympathisers to the visit willingness level, France was only being considered as a travel destination by a little more than half of the respondents (53%). Germany was also known as a travel destination to the vast majority of Russians and was classified as rather likeable or very likeable by 83 percent, but Germany was only being considered as a holiday destination by 44.2 percent of the Russians in the coming 12 months. The results of this vertical are illustrated in Figure 3.

Figure 3: Brand Strength of International Destinations from the Perspective of the Urban Russian Population[6]

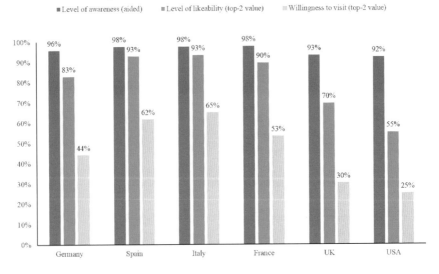

6   Source: IMT/TIRC Network GmbH (2015).

The findings illustrate the relevance of vertical comparisons in international studies and support the overall research aim to allow broader benchmarking and comprehensive understanding of specific emerging source markets for international tourism.

3.3 Horizontal Analysis of Research Findings

In a horizontal comparison, one tourist destination is analysed more precisely and the results of brand awareness, brand likeability and willingness to visit are compared from different case studies (survey countries). In this example, the brand strength of the USA as a tourist destination is evaluated from the perspective of the BRIC countries' participants.

As a tourist destination, the USA experienced a high level of aided awareness. The degree of familiarity was 92.4 percent among Russian respondents and 97.8 percent among Chinese participants. With regard to brand likeability, however, findings revealed clear differences. The relatively low number of Russian respondents that regarded the USA as rather likeable or very likeable was striking. The highest TR1 (brand experts to brand sympathisers) here was from the source market of India. In total, 89.5 percent considered the USA to be a likeable or very likeable tourist destination. Concussively, 92 percent of brand experts were transferred to the level of brand sympathisers. For the vast majority of Indians surveyed, the USA also came into consideration as a future travel destination. At the same time, only a quarter of the Russian population could imagine visiting the USA for a holiday trip in the coming 12 months. The key results of this horizontal analysis are illustrated in Figure 4.

The relevance and value of a horizontal comparison can be underpinned by the example of the Chinese source market. Even though the USA experienced the highest degree of familiarity as a tourist destination by the Chinese population, more Brazilian and Indian brand experts were transferred to the level of brand sympathisers (TR1), as well as to the level of willingness to visit (TR2). Only a horizontal comparison makes these kinds of analysis possible, which can be of decisive relevance for the management of destinations in the increasingly competitive business environment.

Figure 4: USA's Brand Strength from the Perspective of the BRIC Countries' Participants[7]

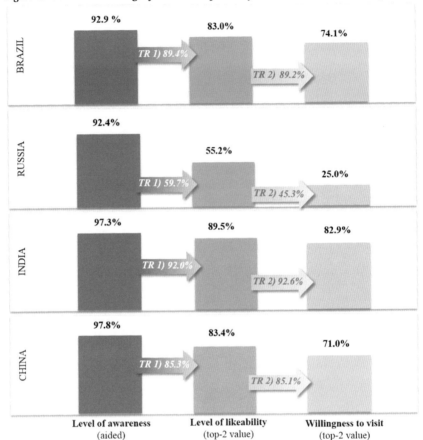

| | Level of awareness (aided) | Level of likeability (top-2 value) | Willingness to visit (top-2 value) |

3.4 Multidimensional Analysis of Research Findings

In addition to uni-dimensional analyses, horizontal as well as vertical comparisons, the data structure allows to evaluate and analyse individual key figures in a
multidimensional manner. In this section, the brand likeability values of selected
European tourist destination (France, Italy, Spain, and UK) are evaluated from the
BRIC countries' participants establishing a 4 × 4 comparison matrix.

---

7   Source: IMT/TIRC Network GmbH (2015).

Findings show that 93.4 percent of the Russian population rated Italy as a rather likeable or very likeable tourist destination (uni-dimensional analysis). Comparing the likeability values of Italy to the other examined European destinations (horizontal analysis) further signalises Italy's high likeability among the Russian population as the likeability values for France, Spain and the UK are each lower than the value for Italy. When assessing a vertical analysis and comparing the brand likeability for Italy by participants from the other BRIC nations, Russia was identified as the source market with the highest brand likeability claim. Although Italy was rated the most attractive European holiday destination by the Brazilians, the overall likeability level is comparatively low, both Russia and China regarded Italy as much more likeable as a tourist destination. Table 1 provides a summary of the multidimensional comparison, shows the top-2 values as well as the achieved ranks in a horizontal and vertical analysis.

Table 1: *Likeability Values of the Main European Tourist Countries from the Perspective of the BRIC Countries' Participants*[8]

CASE STUDY	BRAZIL			RUSSIA			INDIA			CHINA		
TOURIST DESTINA-TION	Like-ability (top-2)	Rank (horiz.)	Rank (verti.)	Like-ability (top-2)	Rank (horiz.)	Rank (verti.)	Like-ability (top-2)	Rank (horiz.)	Rank (verti.)	Like-ability (top-2)	Rank (horiz.)	Rank (verti.)
Spain	78.1%	4	3	92.8%	1	2	79.2%	3	2	83.7%	2	4
Italy	82.3%	3	1	93.4%	1	1	78.9%	4	3	88.3%	2	2
France	79.9%	4	2	89.5%	2	3	85.1%	3	1	90.9%	1	1
UK	64.6%	4	4	69.5%	3	4	78.9%	2	3	86.5%	1	3

This example of a multidimensional comparison clearly illustrates that the interpretation of the findings from different case studies need to be cultural specific. For example, the likeability values of the Brazilians were generally somewhat lower, while the Chinese classified the selected European destinations as above-average likeable or very likeable. Furthermore, the cross-national comparison of findings demonstrates that there are relatively small variations in both the Indian and Chinese levels of approval (difference of 6.2 percentage points; China: difference of 7.2 percentage points), whereas considerably larger differences were present in the case of Russia (difference 23.9 percentage points).

---

8   Source: IMT/TIRC Network GmbH (2015).

3.5 Analysis by Sub-groups Using the Example of the Chinese Market

Particularly in large, heterogeneous source markets with regional disparities and fluctuating purchasing power parity, a differentiated approach based on the origin of the respondents is recommended. In the following, the Chinese willingness to visit European tourist destinations differentiated by the respondents' origins is compared. In the People's Republic of China, cities are grouped together into so-called 'tiers'. A distinction is made between overall average of three factors: the population size, the economic power and GDP, the political administration of a city (South China Morning Post, 2016). Although uniform segmentation is not available, the cities are usually clustered together as follows in Table 2:

Table 2: Sub-groups by the Origin of the Respondents[9]

Sub-region	Number of cases[10]	Cities
Tier 1	n = 458	Beijing, Shanghai, Guangzhou
Tier 2	n = 333	Qingdao, Nanjing, Hangzhou, Wenzhou, Fuzhou, Xiamen, Shenzhen, Wuhan, Chengdu, Chongqing, Ningbo, Dalian
Hong Kong	n = 150	Hong Kong

The findings by sub-groups show that for all the European destinations considered, the highest willingness to visit was identified by the respondents from the metropolises Beijing, Shanghai and Guangzhou (Tier 1). Within the next 12 months, more than 7 out of 10 Chinese from Tier 1 stated that they could imagine travelling to Germany, France, Spain, Italy, France or the UK. The respective willingness to visit was somewhat lower for the Tier 2 population. The lowest future willingness to visit was determined to be present in the Hong Kong Chinese population. Here, the values fluctuated between 57 percent, with regard to a visit to Spain, to 66 percent who claimed that they could imagine a holiday trip to Germany within the next 12 months. However, when considering the top value only (definitely willing to visit in the next 12 months), findings reveal that the approval values of the Hong Kong Chinese are mostly higher than those of

---

9   Shenzhen and Chongqing are sometimes assigned to Tier 1, however, within the framework of this study and the consideration of the foreign travel behaviour, it was more appropriate to classify these cities as being in the Tier 2 cluster. Source: IMT/TIRC Network GmbH (2015).

10 59 respondents did not give any information about their origin.

the Tier 2 Chinese and partly above the approval values of the Tier 1 Chinese. The differentiated findings by sub-groups for the five European tourist destinations are illustrated in Figure 5.

Figure 5: Willingness to Visit (top-2) by Sub-Groups[11]

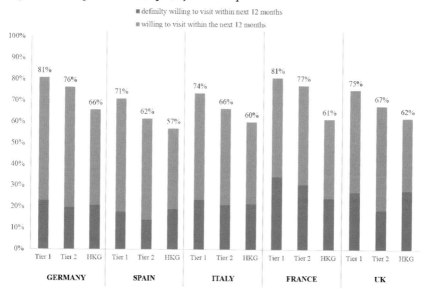

The findings clearly encourage the necessary consideration of differentiated analyses and interpretation of findings when source markets are large and heterogeneous.

4 Critical Reflection

Applying a case study research design to measure the customer-oriented brand value of international tourist destinations from different perspectives enables a comprehensive and multidimensional comparison that was missing to date. Hence, the study 'Global Destination Brand', conducted by the Germany-based research institute TIRC Network GmbH is the first of its kind and delivers information that was missing, yet of critical importance for strategic destination management. In the previous sections of this chapter, the different evaluation and complex comparison possibilities were described underpinning the value of the

---

11 Source: IMT/TIRC Network GmbH (2015).

study, both theoretical and practical value. The multidimensional comparability is enabled by the methodological choices and the utilisation of a uniform study design and a fully standardised questionnaire. Although the study series has been successfully established at the German national level since 2009 and is based on a reliable and tested study design, a conceptual revision was necessary for an international orientation and implementation in different case studies. One major adjustment was required in terms of the definition of the sample. In the national study, a population representative sample was encouraged. For methodological reasons, population representative samples are less feasible in emerging markets such as the BRIC countries. Conclusively, the target sample was defined as a representative sample of the urban population only.

The study was conducted exclusively online, so only the respective online population was reached. As in all web surveys, the representativeness also depends on the Internet availability and online affinity of the respective population and is associated with reduced generalisability of research findings (Nardi, 2014). In studies that focus on Western industrialised countries with an online population of more than 80 percent (The World Bank Group, 2016), the online availability is no longer a constraint for web survey designs. In developing and newly industrialised countries with a smaller share of Internet users (e.g. India with about 18% of the population), this limitation needs to be taken into account when interpreting the results. However, in the case of this study, this restriction was considered to be less relevant as it was assumed that population stratums that were unable to be reached through web surveys are also less likely to represent the current potential for international travel.

The added value of international and multicultural comparative studies is invaluable. Factors such as linguistic and conceptual equivalence increasingly raise at least partially legitimate criticism of international comparative studies in general (Dimanche & Uysal, 1994; Mangen, 2007). Ethnocentrism and the equivalence of measurement methods and times are also often referred to as being insurmountable obstacles to international comparative studies. These factors were taken into account in the development and implementation of the 'Global Destination Brand' study. In order to ensure feasibility and ultimately comparability and validity, the study was put together in collaboration with experts in the respective case studies. The equivalence of the survey terms, as well as question types and scales remain challenges and risks which cannot completely circumvented in comparative studies carried out in such different cultures and language areas.

With the current study design, 'Global Destination Brand' provides quantitative data on the brand strength of international tourist destinations, so that the results are based on hard facts. Qualitative factors have not yet been taken into account, but are likely to have a strong influence on the holistic interpretation of the survey findings. The literature discusses cultural differences as a major barrier for the execution of international and intercultural comparative studies (Dimanche & Uysal, 1994). In this context, a lot of references are made to the cultural dimensions implemented by Geert Hofstede. For example, Johnson, Kulesa, Cho, & Shavitt (2005) found that extremes of a scale are primarily used by respondents from cultural areas with a high degree of expression on the cultural dimensions of *Masculinity* or *Power distance*. This is partly reflected in the findings of the 'Global Destination Brand' study. Russia has a high index in the cultural dimensions of power distance (93) and uncertainty avoidance (95) (Hofstede, n.d.) and the response behaviour of the urban Russian population shows that on the one hand the extremes were used, and on the other hand the approval values were often comparatively low. Furthermore, differences can be identified in relation to the socially desired response behaviour, which is often closely related to self-presentation and impression management. This effect is particularly noticeable in collectivistic countries, for example in China (Fang, Prybutok, & Wen, 2016; Riemer & Shavitt, 2011). With regard to the question of future willingness to travel, political and economic factors such as visa requirements or purchasing power parity must also be taken into account for a holistic assessment of the future potential.

The inhibitions mentioned and the challenges to overcome not only apply to the study presented in this chapter, but are also generally applicable to international comparative studies. Nevertheless, destinations have to increasingly adapt to international guests and the demand for international market-research based data is steadily growing. With regard to this, the issue of destination branding is being given ever-increasing importance, so that various approaches to measuring brand awareness and strength have already been implemented. The 'Global Destination Brand' study provides comparative data on the customer-oriented brand value, which was previously not available in this scale. The study delivers valuable insights into the brand awareness, brand likeability and willingness to visit a destination from the perspective of potential international guests and makes it possible to carry out an initial potential assessment for future strategic decisions related to the international orientation of tourist destinations. In particular, the possibilities given by the vertical as well as the horizontal comparison offer clear added value compared to one-dimensional surveys which had been implemented in the past.

5 Future Research

As previously mentioned, the increasingly international tourism landscapes require more in-depth market research and information. In addition to successfully established, quantitatively-oriented modules for brand strength of international tourist destinations, subject competency and characteristic assessments are recommendable in the future. When taking qualitative factors into account, the depth of knowledge can supplement the now targeted and presented breadth of knowledge. Open response questions and unsupported queries can aid to achieve more depth of knowledge and add additional value to research results. Within the framework of the 'Global Destination Brand' study series, an additional subjectively oriented query has been enabled. Here, the prompted spontaneous associations to a specific tourist destination are examined to deliver unsupported responses in addition to the supported query on the destination's brand strength. This add-on module can be used to assure more individual depth of the results as well as the primarily targeted breadth of knowledge.

Based on the pilot study presented in this chapter as well as previous research on the national ground, the Germany-based research institute TIRC Network GmbH recently investigates further research areas and possibilities to be implemented in the future. A close cooperation between the founding research institute of the study series, namely the IMT of the West Coast University of Applied Sciences, the research and consultancy firm inspektour GmbH, who has been realising the German national study since 2014 and the TIRC Network GmbH is established to enable scientifically sound and applied research in the field of international destination branding. As is already the case in the nationally successful established study series Destination Brand, further thematic individual studies might be implemented in varying rhythm, which might also allow time comparisons in addition to spatial comparisons.

References

Arita, S., Edmonds, C., La Croix, S., & Mak, J. (2011). Impact of approved destination status on Chinese travel abroad: An economic analysis. *Tourism Economics, 17*(5), 983–996.

Arlt, W. G. (2006). *China's outbound tourism*. New York, NY: Routledge.

Bornhorst, T., Brent Ritchie, J. R., & Sheehan, L. (2010). Determinants of tourism success for DMOs & destinations: An empirical examination of stakeholders' perspectives. *Tourism Management, 31*(5), 572–589. doi: 10.1016/j.tourman.2009.06.008.

Dai, B., Jiang, Y., Yang, L., & Ma, Y. (2016). China's outbound tourism – stages, policies and choices. *Tourism Management*. doi: 10.1016/j.tourman.2016.03.009.

de Vaus, D. (2014). *Surveys in social research* (Vol. 6). Sydney, Australia: Allen & Inwin.

Deutsche Zentrale für Tourismus e.V. (DZT). (2015). *Marktinformation: Incoming-Tourismus Deutschland 2016 – Indien*. Frankfurt am Main, Germany: Deutsche Zentrale für Tourismus e.V. (DZT).

Dimanche, F., & Uysal, M. (1994). Cross-cultural tourism marketing research: An assessment and recommendations for future studies. *Global Tourist Behavior*, 6(3/4), 123–134.

Fang, J., Prybutok, V., & Wen, C. (2016). Shirking behavior and socially desirable responding in online surveys: A cross-cultural study comparing Chinese and American samples. *Computers in Human Behavior*, 54, 310–317. doi: 10.1016/j.chb.2015.08.019.

Guarín, A. (2012). *Ein Blick auf die neue globale Mittelschicht*. Bonn, Germany: Deutsches Institut für Entwicklungshilfe (DIE). Retrieved from https://www.die-gdi.de/uploads/media/Kolumne_Guarin.27.02.2012.pdf.

Hantrais, L. (2007). Contxtualization in cross-national comparative research. In L. Hantrais & S. P. Mangen (Eds.), *Cross-national research methodology & practice* (pp. 3–18). London, UK: Routledge.

Hofstede, G. H. (n.d.). *What about Russia?* Retrieved from https://geert-hofstede.com/russia.html.

Institut für Management und Tourismus (IMT), & TIRC Network GmbH. (2015). *Global Destination Brand 2015* (unpublished data). Hamburg/Heide, Germany.

Johnson, T., Kulesa, P., Cho, Y. I., & Shavitt, S. (2005). The relation between culture and response styles. *Journal of Cross-Cultural Psychology*, 36(2), 264–277. doi: 10.1177/0022022104272905.

Li, X., Lai, C., Harrill, R., Kline, S., & Wang, L. (2011). When East meets West: An exploratory study on Chinese outbound tourists' travel expectations. *Tourism Management*, 32, 741–749. doi: 10.1016/j.tourman.2010.06.009.

Mangen, S. P. (2007). Qualitative research methods in cross-national settings. In L. Hantrais & S. P. Mangen (Eds.), *Cross-national research methodology & practice* (pp. 19–34). London, UK: Routledge.

Nardi, P. M. (2014). *Doing survey research: A guide to quantitative methods* (Vol. 3). London, UK: Paradigm Publishers.

Ouyang, Y. (2016). *The development of BRIC and the large country advantage*. Singapore: Truth and Wisdom Press: Springer Science + Business Media.

Patton, M. Q. (2002). *Qualitative research and evaluation methods.* Thousand Oaks, CA: SAGE.

Popp, S. (2014). Die neue globale Mittelschicht. *Aus Politik und Zeitgeschichte (APuZ), 64*(49), 30–37.

Riemer, H., & Shavitt, S. (2011). Impression management in survey responding: Easier for collectivists or individualists? *Journal of consumer psychology: the official journal of the Society for Consumer Psychology, 21*(2), 157–168. doi: 10.1016/j.jcps.2010.10.001.

Ritchie, J. R. B., & Crouch, G. I. (2003). *The competitive destination: A sustainable tourism perspective.* Oxon, UK: CABI.

Schrooten, M. (2011). Brazil, Russia, India, China and South Africa – strong economic growth – major challenges. *DIW Economic Bulletin 4.2011.* Retrieved from https://www.diw.de/documents/publikationen/73/diw_01.c.386693.de/diw_econ_bull_2011-04-4.pdf.

South China Morning Post. (2016). China's tired city system explained. Retrieved from http://multimedia.scmp.com/2016/cities/.

The World Bank Group. (2016). Internet Users. Retrieved on 31.08.2016 from http://data.worldbank.org/indicator/IT.NET.USER.P2.

World Tourism Organization (UNWTO). (2016). UNWTO Tourism highlights, 2016 edition. Madrid, Spain: World Tourism Organization (UNWTO). Retrieved from http://www.e-unwto.org/doi/pdf/10.18111/9789284418145.

Yin, R. K. (2014). *Case study research: Design and methods.* Los Angeles, CA: SAGE.

Sabrina Seeler, Michael Lück, Heike Schänzel

The Concept of Experience in Tourism Research: A Review of the Literature

1 Introduction

The concept of experience is widely applied in academic, professional, and everyday language and has attracted researchers from different disciplines and fields. The topic is not new, but changes in society and in consumer needs and behaviour have triggered the need for a more comprehensive understanding of what 'experience' and 'experiencing' actually means. As experiences are essential for value creation and are the drivers of destination competitiveness, research has intensified within recent decades, as well as their academic interest in the creation of experiences has gained centre stage in the delivery of tourism products and services. The important role of experience creation in tourism has resulted in a plethora of research on the topic and a large increase in publications. Existing research mainly follows Pine and Gilmore's (1999) concept of the Experience Economy. In their most influential work, these authors adopted a management/marketing perspective towards the consumption of experience, which has resulted in the dominance of an objective approach in current research on the topic. The importance of subjective approaches from a social science perspective is acknowledged in the literature, but limited. While tourism marketers sell once in a lifetime experiences and address the increasingly experienced tourists, conceptual questions remain unanswered.

The overarching purpose of this chapter is to deliver a summary of the literature on the concept of experience within tourism research, and to provide an analytical synthesis of information gathered from secondary data sources. Major contributors, advances and discoveries, ongoing debates and existing gaps in the literature are addressed. The literature review is concept-centric, thematically organised and structured in three parts:

- The terminology of experience
- Creating experiences in tourism
- Consuming experiences in tourism

It is hoped that this structure will enable a better general understanding of the term 'experience' and provide a holistic overview of the meanings of experience from both supply side (the tourism providers) and demand side (the tourists) perspectives. Besides tourism research, other disciplines, such as behavioural sciences, psychology and social sciences, are taken into consideration to avoid becoming a prisoner within a single discipline and to allow the inclusion of relevant theories and concepts from other scientific fields. The review is followed by a critical evaluation and the identification of research gaps. Lastly, a conclusion and recommendations for future research are presented.

2 Experience in Tourism Research

2.1 Terminology of Experience

In the tourism context, experiences are considered the locus of value creation and the drivers of destination competitiveness (Jensen, Lindberg, & Østergaard, 2015; Pine & Gilmore, 2011). As the experience concept occupies an important role in tourism value creation, it has attracted academics from different disciplines and research traditions for more than 50 years. Over these years, limited attempts have been undertaken to bridge the gaps between research disciplines to provide a more holistic picture incorporating different scientific fields (Jensen et al., 2015). Major difficulties in clearly demarcating tourist experiences are the semantic differences and linguistic subtleties related to the term 'experience'. A review of lexical definitions reveals not only the different meanings of the term, but it also demonstrates the diverse interpretations as well as the necessary distinction between experience as a noun and experience as a verb (Table 1).

Table 1: Definitions of 'Experience' in Selected Online Dictionaries

Source	Definition	
Oxford Dictionary (2017)	(1) a. Practical contact with and observation of facts or events. b. The knowledge or skill acquired by a period of practical experience of something, especially that gained in a particular profession.	noun
	(2) An event or occurrence which leaves an impression on someone.	noun
	(3) a. Encounter or undergo. b. Feel (an emotion or sensation).	verb

Source	Definition	
Merriam-Webster Online Dictionary (2016)	(1) a. Direct observation of or participation in events as a basis of knowledge. b. The fact or state of having been affected by or gained knowledge through direct observation or participation.	noun
	(2) a. Practical knowledge, skill, or practice derived from direct observation of or participation in events or in a particular activity. b. The length of such participation.	noun
	(3) a. The conscious events that make up an individual life. b. The events that make up the conscious past of a community or nation or humankind generally.	noun
	(4) Something personally encountered, undergone, or lived through.	noun
	(5) The act or process of directly perceiving events or reality.	noun
Cambridge Dictionary (2017)	(1) (The process of getting) Knowledge or skill from doing, seeing, or feeling things.	noun
	(2) Something that happens to you that affects how you feel.	noun
	(3) If you experience something, it happens to you, or you feel it.	verb
The American Heritage Dictionary (2017)	(1) The apprehension of an object, thought, or emotion through the senses or mind.	noun
	(2) a. Active participation in events or activities, leading to the accumulation of knowledge or skill. b. The knowledge or skill so derived.	noun
	(3) a. An event or a series of events participated in or lived through. b. The totality of such events in the past of an individual or group.	noun
	(4) To participate in personally; undergo.	verb

Some definitions provided are countable (i.e., the direct participation in events), others are uncountable (i.e., the accumulation of skills and knowledge). The interdependence between these two elements is clearly discussed in the definition provided by *The American Heritage Dictionary*. The definitions (2) and (3) are broken down into two parts. The first (a) represents the countable, immediate experience, which reflects a moment-by-moment lived experience. The second (b) represents the uncountable element of experience, which is accumulated over time and subjectively reflected and evaluated. Scholars frequently apply the German terms *Erlebnis* and *Erfahrung* to overcome the ambiguities and difficulties in discriminating the term satisfactorily. Applying these terms allows the drawing of boundaries, eliminating misunderstandings, and enabling the differentiation of countable (*Erlebnis*) and uncountable (*Erfahrung*).

Similarly, Volo (2009) discussed an experience as essence and an offering, and referred to the customers' and marketers' roles and relationships. LaSalle and Britton (2003) also emphasised the necessary interaction between customers and products/markets when discussing 'the power of experience' (p. 28). They further pointed to the customer's individual Experience Engagement Process when experiencing a service or good. The interconnectedness and different roles were also addressed by Smed (2012) who claimed that Erlebnisse is an essential component and precondition for a tourist to accumulate experiences, yet Erfahrungen is the direct result when tourists engage in an Erlebnis making the two elements inseparable. Jantzen (2013) provided a similar conclusion arguing that

> Erlebnis is the origin of Erfahrung [… and] Erfahrungen are also the sources of new Erlebnisse. (p. 153)

Table 2 summarises some of the most dominant keywords used in the academic literature in association with the two terms.

Table 2: Keywords Associated with 'Erlebnis' and 'Erfahrung'

Erlebnis	Erfahrung
Moment-by-moment/moment in time/ immediate lived experience	Period of time/over lifetime
On the spot experience	Process view of experience/accumulation of experiences/encounters
Online experience/on-site experience	Memory-work/recollection/post hoc
Partaking experience	Reminiscing experience
Undergoing event/observing/sensing/ encountering/participating	Evaluating/reconstructing
Objective experience	Subjective to reflection and prescribed meaning
Before/during trip (expectations/events)	Post-trip (memory)
Countable	Not countable

Beside semantic analyses and lexical meanings, several attempts were undertaken to deliver an intelligible and unifying definition of the term 'experience' and the concept of experience. To date, no generally accepted conceptualisation has been derived, but several commonalities are identified:

- Experiences consist of tangible and intangible assets
- Experiences cannot be bought, sold, or stored
- Experiences are subjective, individual, and unique
- Experiences are dynamic, emergent, and multiphasic

Whereas the first two points refer to the objective meaning of experience and reflect an Erlebnis, the latter two points emphasise the role of the individual, the subjectivity of experiencing, the element of time, and therefore Erfahrung. Selected examples of definitions are provided in Table 3.

Table 3: Attempts to Define the Term 'Experience' (Selected Examples)

Author	Definition of 'experience'
Selstad (2007, p. 20)	'Experiences are imaginative and seemingly without bounds.'
O'Dell (2007, p. 38)	'Experiences are highly personal, subjectively perceived, intangible, ever fleeting and continuously on-going.'
Boswijk (2013, p. 173)	'Experiences determine who we are: they form our characteristics, shape our personality and determine what we believe in, what makes us happy and how satisfied we manage to be about ourselves in relation to others and our environment.'
Fox (2008, p. 41)	'Experience is a multilayered phenomenon; individuals make sense of experience through cultural, cognitive, subconscious, and personal interpretive layers, by negotiating norms and dominant values, attending to immediate human relationships, and through an individual's context within larger societal and historical positioning.'
Cutler & Carmichael (2010, p. 3)	'Experiences are argued to be subjective, intangible, continuous and highly personal phenomena.'
Pine & Gilmore (2011, p. 17)	'No two people can have the same experience – period. Each experience derives from the interaction between the staged event and the individual's prior state of mind and being.'
Stephenson & Papadopoulos (2006, p. 7)	'Experience takes on an authenticating function; it is the grounds from which knowledge is developed and the yardstick against which it can be evaluated.'

In most of the conceptualisations presented here, experiences are set in a humanistic and social science perspective, putting the individual into focus and emphasising that experiences are not staged snapshots, but complex individual processes that develop over time, involve multiple stakeholders, and possess long-term value. However, in tourism research most studies that relate to the concept of experiences follow a marketing/management approach and focus on Pine and Gilmore's (1999, 2011) *Experience Economy*. From this perspective, tourist experiences equate to consumer experiences, which means that the creation of (staged) experiences as business offerings are central to a tourism organisation's success (Björk, 2014; Selstad, 2007). Consequently, experiences in tourism research have mostly been studied from a marketer's perspective, and experiences are considered as *Erlebnisse*. Ek, Larsen, Hornskov, & Mansfeldt (2008) supported this perception, arguing that

> [...] writings about and studies of 'the experience economy' have privileged the supply-side over the demand-side, the performance of the industry over consumers and tourists. (p. 123)

Referring to the tourist experience value hierarchy, Björk (2014) provided a similar conclusion, stating that

> [...] there is scant research focusing on how situation-specific experiences are embedded in experience-of-life and are linked to perceived value and values. (p. 23)

Despite the predominance of managerial perspectives and general linguistic ambiguities, the contextually different, yet interconnected concepts of tourism experience, touristic experiences and tourist experiences have been adopted interchangeably and this has impeded a comprehensive understanding. Whereas the first two relate to the supply-side dimensions of tourism (macro perspective) and are regarded from a marketer's perspective, the latter addresses the demand side of tourism consumption and the tourists themselves (microperspective). Several scholars have stressed that the micro and macro perspectives, and consequently the sociological/psychological and marketing/management approaches, are not homogenous but interconnected and need to be understood holistically in order to gain an overall comprehension of the concept of experiences in tourism (Aho, 2001; Jensen et al., 2015; Quan & Wang, 2004).

2.2 Creating Experiences in Tourism

Tourism providers are facing an increasingly segmented and fragmented market in which consumer behaviours and attitudes towards travelling change rapidly. The creation of memorable and unique experiences has become one of the major aims of the industry as it is a key driver to remaining competitive and perpetuating market shares in the ever-increasingly competitive environment (Ritchie & Crouch, 2003). Destinations and tourism suppliers become the stagers and facilitators of experiences within today's Experience Economy, which has been globally described as 'the fourth economic offering' (after commodities, goods and services; Pine & Gilmore, 2011, p. 3) and is believed to be essential for long-term economic success. In their influential work, Pine & Gilmore (2011) discussed the characteristics of experiences and categorised four realms of experience – entertainment, educational, esthetic, and escapist – across two dimensions (Figure 1).

Figure 1: Four Realms of an Experience[1]

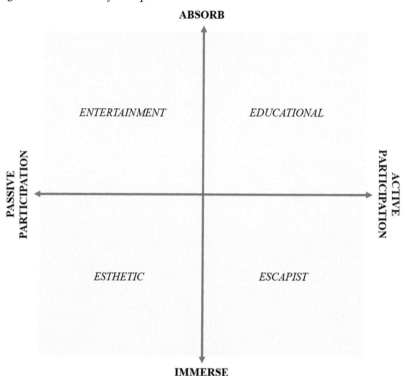

Pine & Gilmore (2011) provided a profound discussion of the creation of an experience in a specific place. As the authors adopted a managerial/marketing perspective, antecedents and consequences of the experience were subordinate; yet, the necessary differentiation between the moment-by-moment lived experience and the recollection and memory of experiences was conceded. The authors also emphasised that experiences are mostly a means to an end as what customers are really aspiring to is transformation. Ultimately, the experiences provided are just as memorable as their ability to guide these transformations.

---

1   Source: based on: Pine & Gilmore, 2011, p. 46.

When Pine & Gilmore (1999) introduced the concept of the *Experience Economy*, the tourism industry was not specifically acknowledged. However, due to the tourism product's distinctive character of staging experiences, the concept has been adopted widely in both tourism academia and practice.

Another model concerning the moment-by-moment lived experience and considering the locus of experience sensing was introduced by Quan & Wang (2004). Three interlinked components of an experience have been distinguished: (1) peak/ primary experience; (2) supporting/secondary experience; and (3) daily routine experience (Figure 2). The peak experience comprises the major touristic, highly influential, and formally paid element of the experience, which occurs during the trip and stands in sharp contrast to daily life. The supporting experience is often related to the informal economy, reflects basic consumer needs, and corresponds to an extension, integration, or intensification of daily routines.

Figure 2: Conceptual Model of Tourism Experiences[2]

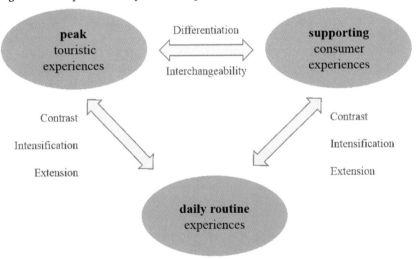

The peak experiences in Quan & Wang's (2004) model are strongly related to the creation and staging of memorable experiences. Earlier, Tung & Ritchie (2011) suggested four dimensions of memorable experiences: affect, expectations, consequentiality, and recollection. Thus, the authors referred to dimensions that go

---

2   Source: based on Quan & Wang, 2004, p. 300.

beyond the on-site experience and stressed the need to encompass all trip elements (prior, during, and post) in the creation of memorable experiences.

With regard to the spatial and temporal dynamic nature of experiencing and acknowledging the performance turn in tourism studies, Ek et al. (2008) derived a conceptual model they termed the Experience Design Wheel (Figure 3). The metaphysical dimensions time and space, which had been neglected in earlier models, were firstly acknowledged, and the dynamic and static forms of design and experience, as well as the macro-micro perspectives of experiencing were considered.

Figure 3: Experience Design Wheel[3]

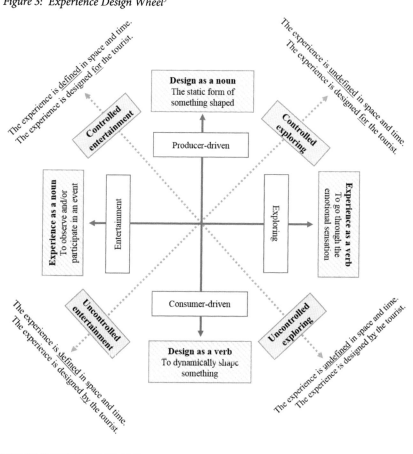

---

3   Source: based on Ek et al., 2008, p. 135.

Although Ek et al. (2008) made it clear that places of tourism creation and eventually consumption need to be seen as relational in terms of time, space, and co-creation, they assumed that experiences during the trip and, most importantly, at the tourist destination are the most intense and significant. Conclusively, the tourist destination takes centre stage in the tourism industry's experience economy.

2.3 Tourist Destinations as 'Experiencescapes'

Tourists are continuously searching for new experiences that meet their unsatisfied needs and are asking for spaces outside their everyday routines as places in which to consume the desired experiences. In this regard, Volo (2009) concluded that real tourist experiences require non-usual environments, which were summarised as unique *experiencescapes* (Mossberg, 2007) and environments for the tourist's global consumption. Tourist destinations of any size or character can portray these *experiencescapes*, become experiences in themselves, and have the potential to create and deliver tourism offerings that satisfy unmet needs. From the tourist's perspective, a tourist destination is a holistic entity and geographical location that encompasses a bundle of offerings that cannot be found in the everyday environment, but have the potential to satisfy unmet needs. The tourist destination comprises an amalgam of different stakeholders, who individually and uniquely contribute to the value creation of the destination's offerings, experiences, and subsequently overall success. Peters, Weiermair, & Katawandee (2006) encapsulated the composition of a destination as '[…] a tapestry of multiple identities' (p. 79).

From a process-oriented perspective, a tourist destination replicates a service chain with the overall requirement of creating a seamless experience (Fischer, 2009). Despite the competitive nature of tourism suppliers within a destination, cooperativeness in delivering this seamless sequence of experiences is inevitable. This presents the destination with a balancing act and stresses the need for a network-oriented approach. The tourist destination corresponds to a strategic network that consists of interconnected, co-producing, and at the same time independent, competitive providers within a defined physical space (Fischer, 2009; Snepenger, Snepenger, Dalbey, & Wessol, 2007). Experiencing takes place not only within the destination, but it also constitutes a cyclical model in different phases encompassing different stages of pre-trip anticipation, on-site travel and activity, and post-trip recollection. The competitiveness of the destination largely depends on the delivered on-site experiences. Entering all stages of experiencing, and acknowledging that tourists are not merely experiencing but also co-designing the space, are vital success factors for tourism providers and destinations. It is of critical importance for the destination to close the object-subject gap and to understand the global consumption of experiences in space and time. While creating global memorability is constrained by the subjective consumption, it should be the destination's aim to enable flexible and dynamic experience networks that improve the probability of delivering memorable experiences and provoking emotional reactions (Ek et al., 2008; Tung & Ritchie, 2011).

Paradoxically, although a tourism destination's success is highly dependent on the creation of memorable inputs, providing these inputs – the stage and the space – is insufficient. A physical body to translate the experience into practice is required. However, the consumption and translation are processual in terms of time and space, and the process is strongly impacted by the individual's prior state of being. Ek et al. (2008) used a marathon runner to exemplify the dynamic nature of these performing individuals with regard to space, time, and interaction with others within a controlled environment:

> Experiences are not created in space, experiences are space, constantly reproduced and designed through performances and the bodily practices by the runner, the other runners, the material surroundings, spectators and other people that participate in some way in the event. (pp. 131–132).

The authors convey that the spaces of experiencing are relational and emphasise that while tourist experiences are shaped within the individual's mind, they are also influenced by others and not totally unscripted and uncontrolled. However, despite the destination's central role in tourism consumption and the industry's efforts to deliver memorable experiences, destinations only provide the input; the tourists themselves translate these inputs into experiences.

2.4 Consuming Experiences in Tourism

A more subjective social science approach needs to be adopted when tourist experiences and the tourists themselves – their anticipation, perception and memories – are at the forefront of the research. In past tourism research, the tourists were mainly reduced to passive spectators and gazers on the experience (Ek et al., 2008). With the critical turn in tourism research, tourists are now acknowledged as active performers, co-creators, and producers within tourism consumption and have been upgraded from receivers to experiencers (Mossberg, 2007; O'Dell, 2007; Uriely, 2005). Not only are tourists put into a 'self-directed, self-expressive [...] driving seat' (Bosangit, Hibbert, & McCabe, 2015, p. 2), there is now a need to consider and deliver multisensory experiences. The shift from an objective to a more subjective perspective expresses a move from a functional to a phenomenological point of view in which tourist experiences are understood as psychological phenomena deeply rooted in an individual's mind and a form of self-expressive consumption (Bosangit et al., 2015). In this regard, Chen, Prebensen, & Uysal (2014) summarised tourist experiences as

> [...] an amalgam of cognitive and affective marks, caused by the bricolage of encounters occurring before, during and after the trip, reflecting in a passive or active state of mind. (p. 14)

In their definition, Chen et al. (2014) considered some of the most dominant characteristics of tourist experiences: the subjectivity, the conscious and unconscious filters, the inner processes and the role of the individual, as well as the interaction and sequential process of experience consumption. Tourists are no longer passive elements; they represent a mix of producer and consumer (prosumer), who provide the physical body and mental place in which the experience can be performed and eventually accumulated. Through the accumulation of individual experiences and meaningful moments, personal identity is constructed over an ongoing period of time, and transformation of the self is reinforced (Bosangit et al., 2015; Noy, 2004). Tourism suppliers provide the spaces and input to stimulate the experience accumulation; however, the processes are mental and subjective and only to a limited extent controllable by the supply side (Andersson & Andersson, 2013; Mossberg, 2007).

These dynamic interactions and relationships have been studied from different perspectives and by various scholars, but it remains undecided which components of an experience are constitutive, meaning-making, and influential for the individual's accumulation of experience and respective experience level. Due to the touristification of the individual's everyday life, the distinction between tourist experiences and everyday life experiences is diminishing. This further challenges the unambiguous identification of determinants. Questions around the actual accumulation of experiences and how memory-work eventually enables transformation and changes behaviour are still unanswered (Bosangit et al., 2015; Noy, 2008; Urry & Larsen, 2011; Volo, 2009).

2.5 Drivers of Tourist Experiences

In modelling the process of tourist experiences, Aho (2001) distinguished four core components of experiencing: getting emotionally effected; getting informed; getting practiced; and getting transformed. By differentiating these aspects, he demonstrated the interactional and sequential elements of experiencing, as well as the accumulative process that is not only influenced by the tourist's storing of experiences, but also by others within the tourist's individual reference group.

Although Aho (2001) concentrated on the individual's process of experiencing in different stages, he also emphasised the interconnectedness between macro and micro perspectives when discussing the scope of experiences. Here, he distinguished the on the spot experience from the process view of experience. The former equates to the moment-by-moment lived experience, hence the experience created and provided by the supply side; the latter corresponds to the accumulation process over a lifetime, the individual's subjective experience storage and thus the demand side of tourism consumption.

As discussed earlier, Quan & Wang (2004) described the different components of experiences that can be translated as on the spot experiences consumed in either the daily, mundane or non-daily, unique environment. The unique environments comprise real tourist experiences, are space-bound, and enable tourists to undergo peak experiences in contrast to their daily life and to further intensify and extend their daily routine experiences through additional supporting experiences (Prebensen, Chen, & Uysal, 2014; Ryan, 2002). In addition to the physical space, the time dimension of experience consumption in tourism is described outside the contracted time (Volo, 2009). The sequence of experiencing is contextual and situational, yet, space and time correspond to the metaphysical variables. Besides external stimuli from the physical environment, interactive drivers (e.g., Chen et al., 2014) and personal resources, including mental and emotional memories (e.g., Aho, 2001; Andersson, 2007), influence the individual's process of experiencing. This emphasises the interconnectedness between partaking experiences that are predominantly consumed and encoded on-site during the trip, and reminiscing experiences which are post-trip reconstructions and recollections that are lived through outside the actual experiencescape. These reminiscing experiences support the notion that experiencing is a mental and memory process and reinforce the relationship of experience with cognitive and personality processes.

When aiming to understand the reasoning behind tourist behaviour and destination choice, the subjective and sensitive information stored in the individual's memory needs to be addressed and accessed. Memories are complex and highly subjective filtering mechanisms, which can be classified as either implicit (unconscious) or explicit (conscious). Explicit memories can be categorised further as either semantic or episodic. Semantic memories encompass general knowledge and facts, while episodic memories imply an individual's storage of personal experiences that were impressionable enough to enter their long-term memory (Larsen, 2007). These consciously remembered memories are of great interest to the tourism industry as especially the autobiographical elements of episodic memories, which are recollections of the individual's own life, are the best predictors for the tourist's future behaviour (Tung & Ritchie, 2011; Wirtz, Kruger, Scollon, & Diener, 2003).

Earlier research showed that the degree of remembering is strongly dependent on the memorability of the partaking experience (on-site experience during the trip) itself. This emphasises the suppliers' imperative to provide memorable experiences in order that the destination will be remembered. Despite the awareness of the importance of the topic, accessing individuals' memories has been proven to be difficult. Several scholars challenge the ability to exhaustively understand individuals' memories as they can only be accessed by the individuals themselves (Cutler & Carmichael, 2010; Larsen, 2007; Csikszentmihalyi, 1988). These memory processes involve affective and cognitive readiness to be retrieved and are partly processed in the unconscious. Hence, not even the individuals themselves are entirely aware of their filtered experiences and cannot fully control, recall, and reconstruct them (Andersson, 2007; Chen et al., 2014). In addition, memories and thus the reflection of past experiences, are not actual experiences: they are stories that individuals tell themselves and share with others within their reference groups. These reported stories can be consciously or unconsciously altered, which makes the process of fully accessing the actual lived experience even more complex. The central role of memories in the process of experience accumulation is undisputed; however, the challenge of accessing and retrieving those memories impeded the measurement of past experiences.

There have been attempts to measure individuals' past experiences and the influence of different levels of past experiences on future travel behaviour. In an earlier study, Mazursky (1989) emphasised the importance of accumulated experiences and knowledge on an individual's decision-making process and integrated past experiences in the expectation-disconfirmation paradigm, which had previously neglected this aspect. Despite the acknowledgement of past experiences in the decision-making process, the process of experience accumulation and the factors that influence it have not been addressed in previous research on the topic (e.g., Mazursky, 1989; Pearce & Lee, 2005; Pearce & Moscardo, 1985).

In existing studies, indicators for the measurement of past experiences were pre-defined and limited to variables such as age, trip duration or quantity of trips. Despite the fact that prior knowledge is believed to be multidimensional, past research focussed on single, quantifiable criteria. Impacts of past experiences on destination loyalty, repeat visitation, destination choice, or satisfaction and expectations were addressed and their influence on the supply side examined (Lehto, O'Leary, & Morrison, 2004; Pearce & Kang, 2009). The accumulated experiences were given centre stage and were presumed. It remained unclear how the individuals themselves are influenced over their lifetimes. What is missing, is a comprehensive understanding of the factors that influence the individuals' processes of experience accumulation and the drivers of transformation and self-identity. A more psychological perspective is needed to understand the factors that drive the intentional and unintentional processes of experience accumulation over time and to implement an unambiguous measurement tool.

2.6 Experiences as Guide for Transformation

Cognitive aspects of their tourism experiences encourage tourists to consciously and subconsciously acquire knowledge, learn, and become educated while travelling. Li (2000, p. 872) summarised tourism as possessing the 'potential for cathartic experiences', including being entertained and being educated as realms of experiencing. Tourism experiences have the potential to challenge the status quo and are much more than merely experiencing a place. Experiences comprise developmental qualities, enable transformational moments, allow individuals to experiment with identities in a specific place and can replicate personal milestones, and, thus, can contribute to self-identity and personal transformation (Jantzen, 2013; Noy, 2004; Selstad, 2007). Although factors such as relaxation and enjoyment are commonly understood to be major drivers behind tourist behaviour and motivation, individuals also try to escape their personal and interpersonal daily life and consciously or unconsciously seek transformational moments that last beyond the actual lived experience and contribute to self-identity. Ryan (1997) linked the individual's escapism to dreams and hopes while Cohen (2010) delivered a similar conclusion, claiming that

> [...] travel is romanticised as an exercise of 'self-directed idealism', for which striving to fulfil imaginative ideals is an integral part of the experience. (p. 29)

Travelling is not necessarily life-changing, but the transitional elements of tourist experiences have the potential to positively contribute to personal change, development, growth and self-realisation, and eventually affect the individual's everyday life. Scholars have further investigated the close relationship and dependence on others in the transformation of selves (Li, 2000), examined the self-perception of tourists' transformations, and distinguished between proactively pursued changes and changes in the individuals' unawareness (Jensen et al., 2015; Noy, 2004). In addition, the role of tourism within these personal changes has been investigated (Cohen, 2010; Desforges, 2000; Ryan, 1997) as well as the destination's role in creating memorable and unique experiences that enter individuals' episodic memories to contribute to identity constructions (Smed, 2012). It is the destination's and tourism supplier's responsibility and task to set the stage for these experiences. The overall aim is beyond merely satisfying tourists' demands. Exploiting the potential to be remembered becomes a key component of experience creation and the major goal for tourism suppliers. However, the fact that tourists are not only gazers but active participants in the realisation of an experience challenges the extent of the influence that tourism providers possess. Whether transformations were sought purposefully or occurred in unawareness, development of the self requires individual's stream of consciousness to be fully perceived and acquired. Hence, only when individuals pay attention and are fully aware of their thoughts, feelings, and sensations can lived experiences enter the episodic memories and contribute to personal changes and transformations. When experiences are memorable, transformation, construction, and development of self-identity can be major outcomes in an individual's consciousness. This highlights the dependencies between partaking and reminiscing experiences, the relationship between the supply and demand sides of tourism, and finally the importance of consciousness in the process of experiencing.

Conclusively, memorable experiences are pivotal in transformation of self, and at the same time the key to a destination's competitiveness. The challenges of creating and staging these experiences are provided and accelerated by destination marketers. Delivering memorable and extraordinary experiences contributes to tourists' transformations, but, as tourists' needs change and the extraordinary becomes ordinary, the industry is provoked to develop ever new and unique experiences which will be remembered (LaSalle & Britton, 2003). As transformative processes and identity construction are everlasting, experiencing evokes a dialectical tension. This dialectical tension has been compared with the Shirley Valentine Syndrome which implies that an experience that was memorable once must be substituted by another in order to enable continuous personal change (Ryan, 1997). In this regard, Csikszentmihalyi (1988) introduced the concept of 'flow' and referred to the conscious control over an experience. The author posited that the complexity of activities must be continuously increased in order to engage in optimal experience and finally encourage transformation:

> To remain in flow, one must increase the complexity of the activity by developing new skills and taking on new challenges. [...] this inner dynamics of the optimal experience is what drives the self to higher and higher levels of complexity. Flow forces people to stretch themselves, to always take on another challenge, to improve on their abilities. (p. 30)

The connectedness between creating, offering, consuming, reminiscing, and accumulating experiences needs to be understood as mutually dependent and the micro and macro perspectives of tourism equally considered in the process of experiencing. Comprehending the drivers and processes of experience accumulation is just as imperative for creating memorable experiences as apprehending how the destinations themselves are impacted by the individual's transformation and changes in behaviour.

3 Critical Evaluation and Research Gaps

The ongoing academic discussion across fields and disciplines accentuates the multifacetedness and multidisciplinarity of the concept of experience and is evidence for the relevance and significance of the topic. One might argue that the different approaches to the concept of experience (objective and subjective) each metaphorically provide a brick to complete the structure; yet, what is lacking, is the mortar to create the holistic building. The interdependencies between experience creation and consumption, as well as the impacts on tourist behaviour and destination choice have been addressed widely, and several models proposed to describe and understand experiencing in tourism. From the early stages of research in the field and from different perspectives, it has been concluded that accumulated knowledge and experiences change consumer needs and consumption behaviour and eventually contribute to identity formation. A close relationship between the object (staged experiences provided by the supply side) and subject (tourists consuming, collecting, and reminiscing about experiences) has also been highlighted. Emphasis, however, has been given to the creation of (memorable) experiences. The introduced models focussed on outside forces, single trips, on-site engagement, and eventually the impacts on the tourism suppliers and hosts. In the past, little research attention has been given to the impacts of experiences on the tourists themselves over their lifetimes, and how their transformations actually accelerate changes in a wider environment, particularly at the tourist destination. While several scholars referred to the increase in past experiences and the impact of accumulated experiences on future behaviour, the drivers behind past experiences were presupposed and limited to pre-defined and countable factors. It remains unanswered what accumulated actually means, which factors eventually influence the processes of experience accumulation, and what prior experiences consist of. An empirically sound comprehension of the variables and factors influencing the process of experience accumulation will contribute to a holistic understanding of what experienced means and how destination marketers can reach these increasingly experienced tourists.

A conceptual framework as a roadmap and graphical representations of the main concepts and relationships of the phenomenon under study has been developed to summarise the findings from existing literature, and to support the propositions and assumptions for future research (Figure 4).

Figure 4: Conceptual Framework of the Concept of Experiences in Tourism (Own Illustration)

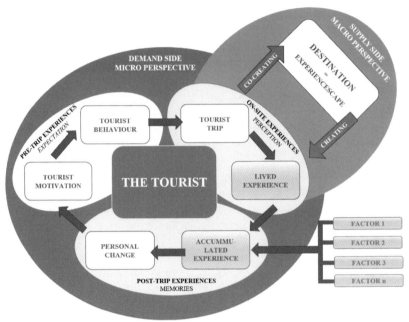

4 Conclusion and Future Research

The chapter demonstrates the significance and relevance of the concept of experiences in terms of experience creation and consumption, partaking and reminiscing experiences, as well as the objective and subjective meanings of experiences. In summary, the major gaps identified are the dominance of objective approaches and the focus on experience creation, the pre-assumption of past experiences and measurement through pre-defined and countable factors, and the neglect of objective-subjective approaches. Based on the review of existing literature and major contributions to the field, seven assumptions about tourist experiences have been identified and are illustrated in Figure 5.

Figure 5: Assumptions about Tourist Experiences that Require Research

I.	The individual past tourist experience is an **accumulation of several independent factors.**
II.	The individual past tourist experience has an **influence on travel behaviour and destination choice.**
III.	'Experienced' tourists can have **different levels of experiences**, which determine future travel behaviour and destination choice.
IV.	The levels are defined by **different accumulation sets.**
V.	Different accumulation sets can result in **different or similar** behaviour and destination choice.
VI.	The increased level of individual tourist experiences influences the **destination's success and strategic destination management.**
VII.	The destination's success depends on the **understanding** of the individual's level of experience.

Research is required to fill knowledge gaps and to test those concepts that are taken for granted, yet remain under-studied. A holistic understanding of the processes behind experience accumulation and of the drivers that influence these processes will encourage a better knowledge base in relation to today's tourists. Research is not only required in order to explain tourists' past behaviour, but also to predict future travel intentions and behaviours as well as destination choice.

Acknowledgement

The authors would like to thank Trish Brothers (Auckland University of Technology) for copy-editing this chapter.

References

Aho, S. K. (2001). Towards a general theory of touristic experiences: Modelling experience process in tourism. *Tourism Review, 56*(3/4), 33–37.

Andersson, T. (2007). The tourist in the experience economy. *Scandinavian Journal of Hospitality and Tourism, 7*(1), 46–58. doi: 10.1080/15022250701224035.

Andersson, D. E., & Andersson, A. E. (2013). The economic value of experience goods. In J. Sundbo & F. Sørensen (Eds.), *Handbook on the experience economy* (pp. 85–98). Cheltenham, UK: Edward Elgar Publishing.

Björk, P. (2014). Tourist experience value: Tourist experience and life satisfaction. In N. K. Prebensen, J. S. Chen, & M. Uysal (Eds.), *Creating experience value in tourism* (pp. 22–32). Oxfordshire, UK: CABI.

Bosangit, C., Hibbert, S., & McCabe, S. (2015). 'If I was going to die I should at least be having fun': Travel blogs, meaning and tourist experience. *Annals of Tourism Research, 55*, 1–14. doi: 10.1016/j.annals.2015.08.001.

Boswijk, A. (2013). The power of the economy of experiences: New ways of value creation. In J. Sundbo & F. Sørensen (Eds.), *Handbook on the experience economy* (pp. 171–177). Cheltenham, UK: Edward Elgar Publishing.

Cambridge Online Dictionary. (2017). Experience (in the English Dictionary). Retrieved from http://dictionary.cambridge.org/dictionary/english/experience.

Chen, J. S., Prebensen, N. K., & Uysal, M. (2014). Dynamic drivers of tourist experiences. In N. K. Prebensen, J. S. Chen, & M. Uysal (Eds.), *Creating experience value in tourism* (pp. 11–21). Oxfordshire, UK: CABI.

Cohen, S. (2010). Searching for escape, authenticity, and identity: Experiences of 'Lifestyle Travellers'. In M. Morgan, P. Lugosi, & J. R. B. Ritchie (Eds.), *The tourism and leisure experience: Consumer and managerial perspectives* (pp. 27–42). Bristol, UK: Channel View Publications.

Csikszentmihalyi, M. (1988). The flow experience and its significance for human psychology. In M. Csikszentmihalyi & I. S. Csikszentmihalyi (Eds.), *Optimal experience: Psychological studies of flow in consciousness* (pp. 15–35). Cambridge, UK: Cambridge University Press.

Cutler, S. Q., & Carmichael, B. A. (2010). The dimensions of the tourist experience. In M. Morgan, P. Lugosi, & J. R. B. Ritchie (Eds.), *The tourism leisure experience: Consumer and managerial perspectives* (pp. 3–26). Bristol, UK: Channel View Publications.

Desforges, L. (2000). Traveling the world: Identity and travel biography. *Annals of Tourism Research, 27*(4), 926–945.

Ek, R., Larsen, J., Hornskov, S. B., & Mansfeldt, O. K. (2008). A dynamic framework of tourist experiences: Space-time and performances in the experience economy. *Scandinavian Journal of Hospitality and Tourism, 8*(2), 122–140.

Fischer, E. (2009). *Das kompetenzorientierte Management der touristischen Destination: Identifikation und Entwicklung kooperativer Kernkompetenzen*. Wiesbaden, Germany: Gabler.

Fox, K. (2008). Rethinking experience: What do we mean by this word 'Experience'? *Journal of Experiential Education, 31*(1), 36–54.

Jantzen, C. (2013). Experiencing and experiences: A psychological framework. In J. Sundbo & F. Sørensen (Eds.), *Handbook on the experience economy* (pp. 146–169). Cheltenham, UK: Edward Elgar Publishing.

Jensen, Ø., Lindberg, F., & Østergaard, P. (2015). How can consumer research contribute to increased understanding of tourist experiences? A conceptual review. *Scandinavian Journal of Hospitality and Tourism, 15,* 9–27. doi: 10.1080/15022250.2015.1065591.

Larsen, S. (2007). Aspects of a psychology of the tourist experience. *Scandinavian Journal of Hospitality and Tourism, 7*(1), 7–18. doi: 10.1080/15022250701226014.

LaSalle, D., & Britton, T. (2003). *Priceless: Turning ordinary products into extraordinary experiences.* Boston, MA: Harvard Business School Press.

Lehto, X. Y., O'Leary, J. T., & Morrison, A. M. (2004). The effect of prior experience on vacation behavior. *Annals of Tourism Research, 31,* 801–818. doi: 10.1016/j.annals.2004.02.006.

Li, Y. (2000). Geographical consciousness and tourism experience. *Annals of Tourism Research, 27,* 863–883. doi: 10.1016/S0160-7383(99)00112-7.

Mazursky, D. (1989). Past experience and future tourism decisions. *Annals of Tourism Research, 16,* 333–344.

Merriam-Webster Online Dictionary. (2016). Experience. Retrieved from https://www.merriam-webster.com/dictionary/experience.

Mossberg, L. (2007). A marketing approach to the tourist experience. *Scandinavian Journal of Hospitality and Tourism, 7*(1), 59–74.

Noy, C. (2004). This trip really changed me: Backpackers' narratives of self-change. *Annals of Tourism Research, 31*(1), 78–102.

Noy, C. (2008). The poetics of tourist experience: An autoethnography of a family trip to Eilat. *Journal of Tourism and Cultural Change, 5*(3), 141. doi: 10.2167/jtcc085.0.

O'Dell, T. (2007). Tourist experiences and academic junctures. *Scandinavian Journal of Hospitality and Tourism, 7*(1), 34–45.

Oxford Dictionary. (2017). Experience. Retrieved from https://en.oxforddictionaries.com/definition/experience.

Pearce, P. L., & Kang, M.-H. (2009). The effects of prior and recent experience on continuing interest in tourist settings. *Annals of Tourism Research, 36,* 172–190. doi: 10.1016/j.annals.2009.01.005.

Pearce, P. L., & Lee, U.-I. (2005). Developing the travel career approach to tourist motivation. *Journal of Travel Research, 43,* 226–237.

Pearce, P. L., & Moscardo, G. (1985). Travellers' career levels and authenticity. *Australian Journal of Psychology, 37*(2), 157–174.

Peters, M., Weiermair, K., & Katawandee, P. (2006). Strategic brand management of tourism destinations: Creating emotions and meaningful intangibles. In T. Keller & T. Bieger (Eds.), *Marketing efficiency in tourism: Coping with volatile demand* (pp. 65–80). Berlin: Erich Schmidt Verlag.

Pine, B. J., & Gilmore, J. H. (1999). *The experience economy: Work is theatre & every business a stage*. Boston, MA: Harvard Business School Press.

Pine, B. J., & Gilmore, J. H. (2011). *The experience economy* (updated ed.). Boston, MA: Harvard Business Press.

Prebensen, N. K., Chen, J. S., & Uysal, M. (2014). Co-creation of tourist experience: Scope, definition and structure. In N. K. Prebensen, J. S. Chen, & M. Uysal (Eds.), *Creating experience value in tourism* (pp. 1–10). Oxfordshire, UK: CABI.

Quan, S., & Wang, N. (2004). Towards a structural model of the tourist experience: An illustration from food experiences in tourism. *Tourism Management, 25*(3), 297–305.

Ritchie, J. R. B., & Crouch, G. I. (2003). *The competitive destination: A sustainable tourism perspective*. Oxon, UK: CABI.

Ryan, C. (1997). The chase of a dream, the end of a play. In C. Ryan (Ed.), *The tourist experience: A new introduction* (pp. 1–24). London, UK: Cassell.

Ryan, C. (2002). 'The time of our lives' or time for our lives: An examination of time in holidaying. In C. Ryan (Ed.), *The tourist experience* (pp. 201–212). London, UK: Continuum.

Selstad, L. (2007). The social anthropology of the tourist experience: Exploring the 'Middle Role'. *Scandinavian Journal of Hospitality and Tourism, 7*(1), 19–33.

Smed, K. M. (2012). Identity in tourist motivation and the dynamics of meaning. In R. Sharpley & P. R. Stone (Eds.), *Contemporary tourist experiences: Concepts and consequences* (pp. 130–146). New York, NY: Routledge.

Snepenger, D., Snepenger, M., Dalbey, M., & Wessol, A. (2007). Meanings and consumption characteristics of places at a tourism destination. *Journal of Travel Research, 45*(3), 310–321. doi: 10.1177/0047287506295909.

Stephenson, N., & Papadopoulos, D. (2006). *Analysing everyday experience: Social research and political change*. New York, NY: Palgrave Macmillan.

The American Heritage Dictionary of the English Language. (2017). Experience. Retrieved from https://ahdictionary.com/word/search.html?q=experience.

Tung, V. W. S., & Ritchie, J. R. B. (2011). Exploring the essence of memorable tourism experiences. *Annals of Tourism Research, 38*(4), 1367. doi: 10.1016/j.annals.2011.03.009.

Uriely, N. (2005). The tourist experience: Conceptual developments. *Annals of Tourism Research, 32*(1), 199–216.

Urry, J., & Larsen, J. (2011). *The tourist gaze 3.0*. London, UK: SAGE.

Volo, S. (2009). Conceptualizing experience: A tourist based approach. *Journal of Hospitality Marketing & Management, 18*(2), 111–126. doi: 10.1080/19368620802590134.

Wirtz, D., Kruger, J., Scollon, C. N., & Diener, E. (2003). What to do on spring break? *Psychological Science, 14*(5), 520–524. doi: 10.1111/1467-9280.03455.

About the Authors

Dr. María Isabel Ramos Abascal holds a Tourism PhD degree from the Universidad Antonio de Nebrija (Madrid) and tourism DEA from the same university titled 'Theoretical construct of gastronomy as cultural tourism product in Mexico'. She also has a Masters in Touristic Enterprises Management from Anahuac University (Mexico) and here she also studied a Masters in Research, a Degree in Public Relations and a diploma in Cuisines and food culture in Mexico; social practices, meanings and ritual contexts, by the National School of Anthropology and History. Maria is a member of the Mexican Cuisine Permanent Seminar at the Anthropology National Coordination Office (Mexico), member of the Conservatorio de la Cultura Gastronómica Mexicana, expert in tourism by the United Nations World Tourism Organization (UNWTO) and she participated in the course of Tourism Education Quality Excellence at the University of Perugia and several courses at Le Cordon Bleu and the Disney Institute including the Cultural Program at Epcot. She has written several articles, book chapters and is the spokesperson of the Group restaurateur Alsea and Culinary Curator at the TV Show: En Ruta 'T', Tortas, tacos y tamales. She has spoken at international forums and is a Professor at Anahuac University in the Faculty of tourism and gastronomy.

Dr. Alisha Ali is a Principal Lecturer and Hospitality Subject Group Leader at Sheffield Hallam University, UK. Her research interests are sustainable development, technology applications and impacts for hospitality and tourism, hospitality operations, innovation in hospitality and tourism, destination management and online research methods. Alisha has worked both locally, regionally and internationally in the hospitality and tourism field and has a background in consultancy working with government offices, destination management organisations (DMOs) and hospitality businesses. She is the Regional Editor – Europe - Journal of Hospitality and Tourism Technology (JHTT) and guest edited a special issue of the Journal of Information Technology & Tourism on ICT for sustainable tourism.

Ellen Böhling is current Managing Partner at Inspektour International GmbH, Germany, a globally operating group of experts who have specialised in destination brand research as well as the analysis of trends in tourism and travel behaviours. Prior Ellen has worked independently as a consultant in Argentina for several years as well as a research assistant, project leader and lecturer at the West Coast University of Applied Sciences in Heide, Germany. She is active in the fields of market research, further education and consulting in tourism since 2004 with special interests in tourism and destination management, destination branding, strategic marketing and sales management.

Prof. Dr. Bernd Eisenstein is a Professor for International Tourism Management at the West Coast University of Applied Sciences in Heide, Germany. Since 2006 he has also been the director of the Institute for Management and Tourism (IMT) at the West Coast University of Applied Sciences. He has completed his business degree and geography degree at Trier University where he subsequently completed his doctorate, supervised by Prof Christoph Becker. Bernd had lecturing positions at Trier University and the University of Applied Sciences Worms (Germany), and has conducted and coordinated numerous consultancy and research projects, in particular in the fields of destination management, tourism demand and strategic tourism management.

Sarbjit S. Gill is a Bachelor of Tourism Management (Hons) graduate from Thompson Rivers University, and currently a Tourism Marketing Consultant for the Adventure Travel Trade Association. He manages organization's six social media platforms and co-manages company's consumer brand. He has previously worked with the destination development firm Solimar International in Washington, DC, and co-owned and operated a small-business: Undies for Humanity. His future aspirations entail of a graduate program in Tourism Development or Tourism Economy fields, and he wishes to pursue socio-economic research that makes a difference.

Eva Holmberg, Lic Econ, is a Senior Lecturer in tourism and methods HAAGA-HELIA University of Applied Sciences. She teaches students at both bachelor and master in courses such as brand management, responsible tourism and destination management. Her research interests are mainly related to destination management, branding and responsible tourism development and inquiry learning.

Prof. Dr. Eric Horster (MA and Doctor rerum politicarum) studied applied cultural sciences at the University of Lüneburg. After completing his doctorate, he became the director of the B.A. and M.A. courses in International Tourism Management (ITM) and the Online Master's Study Programme in Tourism Management as well as Professor of International Tourism Management at the West Coast University of Applied Science. This also explains his collaboration in the project 'Open Universities in Schleswig-Holstein: Learning in the Net, Advancement on Site' (LINAVO). He has conducted research in the fields of digital market research and digital monitoring in tourism at the Institute for Management and Tourism (IMT).

John S. Hull is an Associate Professor of Tourism Management at Thompson Rivers University in British Columbia, Canada. He is also a Visiting Professor at the Harz University of Applied Sciences, Germany, an instructor at the Castello Sonnino Educational Centre in Tuscany, Italy and a member of the New Zealand Tourism Research Institute (NZTRI). His research addresses the sustainability of tourism in peripheral regions focusing on creative tourism, culinary tourism, geotourism, Arctic tourism, mountain tourism, indigenous tourism and wellness tourism.

Kaija Lindroth (MA, eMBA) is Degree Programme Director of two international Bachelor programmes at HAAGA-HELIA Porvoo Unit: International Sales and Marketing, and Tourism. She is responsible for the internationalisation of HAAGA-HELIA Porvoo Campus degree programmes, and passionate about developing professional networks for Porvoo Campus needs both towards the industry and the academia. Her research interests include network studies among small tourism entrepreneurs, social impacts of tourism and events, as well as tourist behaviour. She has been actively involved in the community of tourism researchers both in Finland (Finnish Society for Tourism Researchers: board member) and internationally (TTRA European Chapter: board member and President).

Dr. Michael Lück is a Professor in the School of Hospitality and Tourism, and Associate Director for the Coastal and Marine Tourism research programme at the New Zealand Tourism Research Institute, both at Auckland University of Technology, New Zealand. He is founding co-chair of the International Coastal & Marine Tourism Society (ICMTS). Michael has more than 10 years work experience in the tourism industry and his research interests include (marine) wildlife tourism, the cruise industry, ecotourism, interpretation and education on wildlife tours, the impacts of tourism, and aviation. He has published in a number of international journals, is founding editor-in-chief of the academic journal *Tourism in Marine Environments*, Associate Editor of the *Journal of Ecotourism* and *Human Dimensions of Wildlife*, and editorial board member of *Marine Policy* and *Frontiers*. Michael has edited or co-edited ten volumes on ecotourism, marine and polar tourism, events and low cost airlines, as well as the *Encyclopedia of Tourism and Recreation in Marine Environments* (CABI), and co-authored the introductory text *Tourism* (CABI).

Ismael Castillo Ortiz (MBA and PhD in Organizations Direction, México) is chairman at Ladiuva Consultora hospitality and restaurant consulting company. Prior to his entrepreneurship activities, he worked in strategic planning, research, innovation and business strategies for culinary professionals and hospitality top brands in America. He has over 20 years of experience in international and multi-cultural business environment. He also won a Turquoise Foundation Scholarship in Monaco Montecarlo.

Tomas Pernecky is Associate Professor in the Faculty of Culture and Society at the Auckland University of Technology, New Zealand. His wide-ranging research interests extend to the fields of tourism and events studies, which he employs as contexts for examining a variety of philosophical, conceptual, theoretical and methodological issues. His teaching has been officially recognised by receiving the 2014 Vice Chancellor's Award for Excellence in Teaching, and the subsequent nomination by AUT for the 2015 Tertiary Teaching Excellence Award (TTEA). He has edited three books on a range of events-related topics, and published a monograph titled *Epistemology and Metaphysics for Qualitative Research*.

Dr. Brooke Porter is a specialist in the human dimensions of the fisheries and the marine environment. Her current work explores tourism as a development and conservation strategy in lesser-developed regions. She has worked in various capacities with non-governmental organisations (NGOs), international aid agencies and educational institutions. Dr. Porter worked in Maui, Hawai'i for 9 years serving as Conservation Director for Pacific Whale Foundation. She has worked on fisheries development projects in Eritrea with the United Nations. Dr. Porter has also worked in the industry as a naturalist aboard whale watching tours in both Hawai'i and New Zealand. She currently serves as a Scientific Adviser to The Coral Triangle Conservancy, a NGO that focuses on reef protection and restoration in the Philippines.

Jill Poulston is an Associate Professor and leads the hospitality postgraduate programmes at Auckland University of Technology (AUT) and is an Associate Director of the New Zealand Tourism Research Institute. Before becoming an academic, she worked in senior hotel management for over 15 years, and is interested in ethical issues, thinking and hospitality workplace problems, as well as related topics such as organic food, sustainability, sexual harassment and diversity. Jill is on the Editorial Advisory Boards of Hospitality & Society, International Journal of Contemporary Hospitality Management and the Journal of Culture, Tourism, and Hospitality Research, and reviews regularly for these and other journals and conferences. Jill teaches Leadership and Ethics in Hospitality to postgraduate students, and supervises and examines masters and doctoral research on her topics of interest.

Lars Rettig, MA is Head of Public Relations and Consulting, Project 'Open Universities in Schleswig-Holstein: Learning in the Net, Advancement on Site' (LINAVO), West Coast University of Applied Science. Since 2012 he has been running the interdisciplinary team Public Relations and Consulting within the research and development project LINAVO.[1] Furthermore, he developed the online Masters' degree programme in Tourism Management at the West Coast University of Applied Science. Prior to that, he worked as a market researcher for the North Rhine Westphalia State Association for Tourism. He studied applied sciences with the subjects of Tourism Management, Business Administration and Music at the University of Lüneburg with two semesters abroad in Spain and Peru. His interest in research lies at the interface between (cultural) tourism, digitalisation and the further education of tourism stakeholders.

Jarmo Ritalahti is a Principal Lecturer of Tourism at HAAGA-HELIA University of Applied Sciences. His main research interests in tourism focuses on intermediation and business tourism and pedagogical development and pedagogy in higher education. He was responsible of the new pedagogical approach and curricula development at HAAGA-HELIA's Porvoo Campus project in 2007–2014. Principal lecturer, Jarmo Ritalahti is also engaged in regional tourism research and development projects.

Dr. Heike Schänzel is a Senior Lecturer and programme leader postgraduate at Auckland University of Technology in New Zealand. Her research interests include: tourist behaviour and social experiences; families and children in tourism; femininities and paternal masculinities in tourism research; innovative and qualitative research methodologies and critical theory development in tourism. She is passionate about better understanding family fun (along with the avoidance of conflict) and the facilitation of sociality and meaningful experiences within the context of leisure, tourism and hospitality.

Sabrina Seeler holds a Master's Degree in International Tourism Management from the West Coast University of Applied Sciences in Heide, Germany. She is a

---

1   LINAVO is an acronym for the research and development project 'Open Universities in Schleswig-Holstein: Learning in the Net, Advancement on Site'. FKZ 16OH12030.

current PhD student at the Auckland University of Technology (AUT), New Zealand, researching the accumulation processes of experiences in tourism. Sabrina is also a casual lecturer in the School of Hospitality and Tourism at AUT. Prior to her PhD studies, she has worked as a research assistant and project leader at the Institute for Management and Tourism at the West Coast University of Applied Sciences in Heide, Germany, with a focus on primary market research. Her research interests are: strategic destination management, destination branding, consumer behaviour in tourism and tourist experiences.

F. Anne Terwiel (PDP, GDBA, MBA) is a Senior Lecturer in the Tourism Management Department at Thompson Rivers University and lectures at Hochschule Narz in Germany and Universitat Autonoma de Barcelona in Spain. Anne teaches in the areas of global tourism, tourism business operations, business and resort management and sports event management. Anne's current research and publication stream involve volunteer satisfaction and volunteer and physical legacies as a result of sports mega-events and the Olympic and Paralympic Games; snow sports resort safety; and resort guest and employee satisfaction. Anne has presented at international conferences in Argentina, Austria, China, Korea, Norway, Russia and the USA on such diverse topics as Olympic volunteer management, sports safety equipment and resort marketing. Anne sits on the Scientific Committee of the International Society for Skiing Safety, the National Education Committee of the Canadian Ski Instructors Alliance (CSIA). She is on the Board of Directors of the Sun Peaks Health Association and the Kamloops Sports Council. She is a master trainer for Destination British Columbia and an evaluator for the Canadian Tourism Human Resource Council. Anne is a CSIA Level 4 instructor and master trainer, and a Canadian Ski Coaches Federation (CSCF) Level 2 ski coach and course official, and has volunteered at regional, provincial, national and international alpine ski races, including the Olympic Games.

Mona Vaahtera is a graduate of HAAGA-HELIA University of Applied Sciences Porvoo campus. Her bachelor thesis conducted in 2015 was study related to the eagerness of Finnish travelers to travel to Greek archipelago during the refugee crisis.

Schriftenreihe des Instituts für Management und Tourismus (IMT)

Herausgegeben von der Fachhochschule Westküste

Die Bände 1-6 sind im Martin Meidenbauer Verlag erschienen und können über den Verlag Peter Lang, Internationaler Verlag der Wissenschaften, bezogen werden: www.peterlang.com.

Ab Band 7 erscheint diese Reihe im Verlag Peter Lang, Internationaler Verlag der Wissenschaften, Frankfurt am Main.

Band 7 Anja Wollesen: Die Balanced Scorecard als Instrument der strategischen Steuerung und Qualitätsentwicklung von Museen. Ein Methodentest, unter besonderer Berücksichtigung der Anforderungen an zeitgemäße Freizeit- und Tourismuseinrichtungen. 2012.

Band 8 Wolfgang Georg Arlt (Ed.): COTRI Yearbook 2012. 2012.

Band 9 Michael Lück / Jan Velvin / Bernd Eisenstein (eds.): The Social Side of Tourism: The Interface between Tourism, Society, and the Environment. Answers to Global Questions from the International Competence Network of Tourism Research and Education (ICNT). 2015.

Band 10 Bernd Eisenstein / Christian Eilzer / Manfred Dörr (Hrsg.): Kooperation im Destinationsmanagement: Erfolgsfaktoren, Hemmschwellen, Beispiele. Ergebnisse der 1. Deidesheimer Gespräche zur Tourismuswissenschaft. 2015.

Band 11 Michael Lück / Jarmo Ritalahti / Alexander Scherer (eds.): International Perspectives on Destination Management and Tourist Experiences. Insights from the International Competence Network of Tourism Research and Education (ICNT). 2016.

Band 12 Lars Rettig: Digitalisierung der Bildung. Warum und wie lernen wir ein Leben lang? Forschungsergebnisse zur Online-Weiterbildung im Tourismus. Bedeutung – Erwartung – Nutzung. 2017.

Band 13 Bernd Eisenstein / Christian Eilzer / Manfred Dörr (Hrsg.): Demografischer Wandel und Barrierefreiheit im Tourismus: Einsichten und Entwicklungen. Ergebnisse der 2. Deidesheimer Gespräche zur Tourismuswissenschaft. 2017.

Band 14 Alisha Ali / John S. Hull (eds.): Multi-Stakeholder Perspectives of the Tourism Experience. Responses from the International Competence Network of Tourism Research and Education (ICNT). 2018.

www.peterlang.com